The Call of Jesus

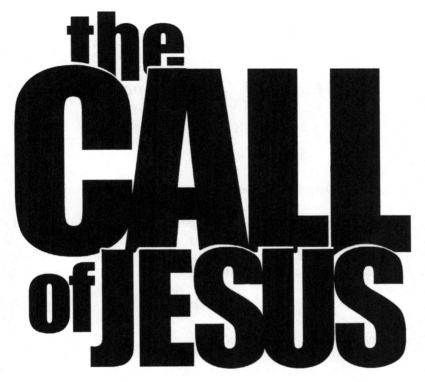

the CALL of JESUS

finding the person of peace

TORBEN SØNDERGAARD

THE CALL OF JESUS

finding the person of peace

By Torben Søndergaard

Paperback: ISBN: 978-1-952484-00-1

ePub (iPad, Nook): ISBN: 978-1-952484-01-8

Mobi (Kindle): ISBN: 978-1-952484-02-5

PUBLISHED BY THE LAST REFORMATION

PUBLISHED IN THE UNITED STATES OF AMERICA

This book may be purchased in paperback from TheLastReformation.com, TheLaurusCompany.com, Amazon.com, and other retailers around the world. Electronic versions are also avcailable from their respective stores. Available in Spring Arbor for retailers.

ACKNOWLEDGEMENTS

A big thanks to Marcia Neuhold
for helping with this book. You have been
a big blessing, together with Sandra, Nancy, Kayleigh,
and many others out there who have helped
in making this book a reality.

Let's pray that it will now be a big blessing for others
and that it will be used by God to bring the body
back to what He has called us to.

TABLE OF CONTENTS

ACKNOWLEDGEMENTS 5

INTRODUCTION 9

CHAPTER 1:   *Christ, Mission, And The Church* 15

CHAPTER 2:   *The Twelve And The Seventy* 23

CHAPTER 3:   *Being The Good Ground* 31

CHAPTER 4:   *Two And Two* 41

CHAPTER 5:   *The Leading Of The Holy Spirit* 49

CHAPTER 6:   *The Harvest Is Plentiful* 59

CHAPTER 7:   *Believe That The Harvest Is Ready* 67

CHAPTER 8:   *Send Out Workers* 77

CHAPTER 9:   *As Lambs Among Wolves* 87

CHAPTER 10: *Carry No Money*. 99

CHAPTER 11: *Do Not Greet Anyone On The Road*. 113

CHAPTER 12: *Person Of Peace*. 123

CHAPTER 13: *Eat And Drink Whatever They Provide*. 133

CHAPTER 14: *Do Not Move From House To House* 143

CHAPTER 15: *Wipe Off The Dust* 155

CHAPTER 16: *Heal The Sick And Preach The Gospel* 165

CHAPTER 17: *The Kingdom Of God Is Near You* 179

CHAPTER 18: *The Book Of The Apostles* 191

CHAPTER 19: *The Whole Story* 201

CHAPTER 20: *Jesus, Our Savior* 211

CHAPTER 21: *Luke 10 Testimonies* 223

CHAPTER 22: *Finding The Person Of Peace* 237

CHAPTER 23: *We All Need Family* 251

CHAPTER 24: *How To Grow Up* 267

CHAPTER 25: *Dear Pastors And Leaders* 283

CHAPTER 26: *Let The New Life Begin* 295

ABOUT THE AUTHOR 315

INTRODUCTION

I t is a great honor for me to present this book to all of you finally. Over the last twenty years, I have had the privilege of traveling to many different countries all over the world, where I have been teaching and training thousands of believers to live a life as a disciple of Jesus Christ. Where I have been allowed, I have taught them about bearing fruit, being led by the Holy Spirit, seeing people getting healed, and sharing the Gospel. Many times, I have seen Christians sitting in churches for twenty or thirty years without leading a single person to Jesus Christ. After attending the discipleship training weekend, their lives change drastically. They begin leading people to Christ at every opportunity, and they experience the life we read about in the book of Acts.

These discipleship training weekends are so fruitful that I often hear from pastors and others that this is the best form of discipleship they have ever seen. Using the patterns of Luke 10 and the Book of Acts during our discipleship training weekends, commonly called "kickstarts," we focus primarily on what it looks like to follow Jesus as a disciple. It is my opinion that this is the way we need to live today. The book of Acts is the only book in the entire Bible that gives us a complete glimpse of how the early disciples went out and led people to Christ.

The book of Acts is similar to a diary where we can see how the first disciples walked around while being led by the Holy Spirit. We can see how they lived a life full of signs, wonders, and miracles, a life where people around them came to faith, repented after hearing the gospel, and were baptized in water and with the Holy Spirit. The book of Acts shows that repentance, baptism in water, and baptism with the Holy Spirit all happened on the same day. This practice is very different from today because many people now divide up repentance, baptism in water, and baptism with the Holy Spirit. In the book of Acts, we also see how the gospel spread all over. It is an exciting book that gives us something to compare our lives to because we believe Jesus is the same yesterday, today, and forever. And if Jesus is the same yesterday, today, and forever, then the Holy Spirit is also the same yesterday, today, and forever. Therefore, what the first disciples experienced in the book of Acts is something we can experience today.

During these kickstart weekends, we teach from the book of Acts, but we also focus a lot on Luke chapter 10 where we read how Jesus sent out the seventy disciples, and how He gave them specific instructions about what He wanted them to do.

The words Jesus spoke in Luke 10 were not only for those who lived during that time, but also for us who are living today.

After teaching from Luke 10, I have often had people tell me that is something very concrete and that they can apply the teaching to their everyday lives. Many people have asked me excitedly if this teaching in Luke 10 is something I have written about in my books, or if it is something I wanted to write about in the future. I know this book is one that many people have been excited about for a long time.

In the summer of 2005, my wife and I received a powerful

prophetic word. God said He wanted to take us through a desert, a time when we were going to learn how to rely entirely on Him and not on people. God wanted to take us through a time when He would form us and teach us a lot. I can say that He has done this because, for the next four or five years after we received that prophecy, we went through a very difficult period of time. Everything seemed like it was going wrong. We moved three times, and there were rumors told about my family and me. We lost many friends. My wife, Lene, became ill and was in a sickbed for quite some time. Then I was fired from my job. I could no longer pay our bills, and everything looked hopeless. Although I had that prophetic word to strengthen me during this desert period, it was still really hard for us. It was so hard for me that, at one time, I wanted to die. Now, looking back, I can see that it was during this desert period that we found God in a new way. It was during this challenging time that I discovered He is faithful and that we can trust Him. It was while we were out in this desert that He set us free from our traditions and revealed the way of living as a disciple of Jesus. It became a new beginning for us.

Today, we are so thankful that God allowed us to go through that desert period because we now see so much fruit that has come out of it. It was a period where we needed to start all over, and God needed to open our eyes to help us see what Jesus was calling us to. We needed to go through this time so God could help us lay down our vision for our life and receive His. That desert period became a new beginning for us, and we see that it has also become a new beginning for many other people around the world who have received this simple teaching God revealed to us during that time. We are now seeing a movement spreading all around the world. We are seeing hundreds of thousands of people getting healed and set free, and we are seeing tens of thousands of people coming to faith in Jesus. God revealed things to my family and me that He is showing to many people around the world. God is taking His people back to the simple life we read about in His Word, the life they lived in the book of Acts. It is the life of a true disciple and follower of Jesus Christ. This life carries signs and wonders. It is a life led by the Holy Spirit, where people are coming to faith daily, and getting baptized with water and with the Holy Spirit. It is a life where you not only learn about Jesus but also live it out in obedience to Him daily. What we are witnessing now is remarkable, but this is just the beginning, and it is going to change the world.

This book and my previous books were born out of that desert experience when God showed us so much. I wrote in my first book, **Christian, Disciple, or Slave**, what a true disciple of Jesus looks like and what it is like to walk with Him and live as His disciple daily. In my last book, **The Last Reformation**, I wrote about the church and the best way we can make disciples as Jesus called us to do. That book also includes our personal story, how we got out of the church system, and how we came into this amazing life with God. In this book that you are now reading, **The Call of Jesus**, we are going to look at the mission Jesus gave us. The focus is not on how you become disciples of Jesus or what the church is. The focus here is on how to live out this life. This book will look at what Jesus wants us to do and how we go out and do it. Most of what you will learn here will be new for many people, although it is very uncomplicated.

> **Sometimes, we do not see the simple thing**
> **right in front of us, but simple people**
> **understood Jesus, and a higher**
> **theological education is not needed**
> **to understand what He wants us to do.**

Yes, sometimes we can be blind to something simple right in front of us. It is like the saying, *"You can't see the forest for the trees."* If someone cannot see the forest because of all the trees, this means they are so focused on the small things that the big picture is blurred. Sometimes, when people are focused solely on the details of the mission, they forget the ultimate purpose for which they were sent. But when the vision becomes clear, you wonder why you never saw it before. You wonder how you could have been doing what you were doing all your life, without seeing the simple and clear thing Jesus has called us to do.

This new revelation will alter the vision of many and give insight into the mission Christ gave us. For others, it will be a confirmation of what the Holy Spirit has been speaking to your hearts for years. I believe this book, *The Call of Jesus*, will create a greater faith and a greater desire to live out the life to which Jesus has called us. This book will also give you practical tools you can use to see even more fruit in your life. My prayer is that, through this book, God will open your eyes, that we will all see what Jesus has called us to, and that we will truly understand that God wants to use every one of us to bear fruit in our daily lives.

God bless you with this book, and may it speak to you and set you free.

—Torben Søndergaard
A disciple of Jesus Christ

1

CHRIST, MISSION, AND THE CHURCH

We always need to start with Jesus and His Word. Jesus is our foundation, and His words are not dependent on time and place. What He said in Israel 2000 years ago is something we can build on today, no matter where we live.

In some church denominations, people talk a lot about the vision of the church and about the calling of each person. I personally came from a church that talked a lot about that; therefore, when I later worked on planting churches in different cities, I spent a lot of time with my friends talking about what our calling was as a church and what it was God wanted us to do. We were praying and seeking God and trying to find out what our calling and mission were as a church in that specific city. At that time, I believed it was so important to know our exact calling as a church because Proverbs 29:18 states, *"Where there is no vision, the people perish."* A church vision can be different from church to church.

It could sound like this: "We want to be a family-focused church where the whole family likes to meet. We believe in healthy congre-

gations, assemblies, and ministries that are expressing the good news
of God's kingdom that transforms lives and communities worldwide.
Or like this: "Our dream is to be a faithful, growing church that
demonstrates true community, deep Christian spirituality, and a
passion for justice."

Many years ago, I believed it was so important to find our vision
as a church and our calling as individual people. Yes, I thought without
this, we could not obey God's call for our life. However, I have since
found out that you do not need to spend time finding a special vision
for your church or yourself.

Maybe what I am saying here about finding a vision for your church
or finding out what God's call is for your life is very new for you. Or
maybe you know exactly what I am talking about. The question is,
should we spend a lot of time and energy seeking God to find what our
specific calling is? What I mean by a "specific calling" is that some
people believe they are supposed to be a youth leader, or a pastor, or
that they are supposed to be a worship leader and make a CD one day.
And some churches think their call is to be a family church while others
are more focused on being a Bible-believing church.

Overall, it does not sound wrong to focus on finding the vision of
individual churches and the calling of each individual Christian.
However, where do we actually find this in the Bible? We do not find
any place in the Bible where people spent a lot of time and energy
seeking God to find out what their personal and unique callings were.
In fact, the focus was not on finding a personal, specific calling at all.
Instead, the focus was on Jesus and how to obey Him in what He has
already commanded us to do.

**In the Bible,
we see the focus was on Jesus, His Word,
and how to obey Him.**

I truly did believe, at one time in my life, that you could not have a
church if that church did not have a clear vision. I also believed that
every member in the church needed to know what their specific calling

was. This could actually be a problem because this "calling" could be very different from what Jesus is saying in His Word. For example, someone may believe they have a calling as a worship leader. Another may believe they have a calling to be a businessman. This could be a problem because while they are so focused on these "callings," they are not focusing much on what Jesus is actually saying to us in His Word about simply being His disciples.

Thankfully, through a desert period that my wife and I experienced, God opened our eyes and revealed that we had a wrong understanding about "callings." Today, I no longer believe in seeking specific callings. I now see God doing more things than ever before. He is changing the lives of thousands of people all over the world. Today, our calling is simple. It is Jesus and His Word. Yes, my wife and I are very different and do not do things the same way, but our calling is the same—to serve Jesus and obey His Word with everything we have in us. Yes, we all have dreams and goals in life. Those dreams and goals can be different from person to person, but we need to understand that our main focus is to be a disciple of Jesus. We need to realize the most important goal in life is to be obedient to what Jesus has told us to do. Jesus is not only our Savior. He is our vision, our calling, and our goal in life. Today, I do not need to seek God a lot to find out what His will is for my life because it is already written down in the Bible. I know, for some of you, this realization about callings may not have a lot of meaning because you are used to coming from a church denomination where they did not focus much on finding your calling or vision. However, many of you will understand exactly what I am talking about.

I want to say that it is time for us to stop and really take time to think about what we are doing. When we said yes to Jesus, we said no to ourselves. We find no callings in the Bible about being the best football player or about being a television star. I am not saying these things are wrong, but our focus should be to obey Jesus, to reach people with the Gospel, and to make disciples.

Matthew 7:24-27 states:

Therefore everyone who hears these words of Mine and puts them into practice is like a wise man who built his house on the rock. The

rain came down, the streams rose, and the winds blew and beat
against that house, yet it did not fall, because it had its foundation
on the rock. But everyone who hears these words of Mine and does
not put them into practice is like a foolish man who built his house
on sand. The rain came down, the streams rose, and the winds blew
and beat against that house, and it fell with a great crash."

From this verse, we read that those who are building on the rock
are not people who are only hearing the Word of God, but those who
are also obeying it. Matthew 7:24-27 makes it clear that it is not enough
to "hear," like many do Sunday after Sunday. We also need to "obey."
Yes, we need to live it out.

You do not need to spend a lot of time
seeking God to find a special calling
for your life and for your church.
You just need to receive what Jesus has said
in His Word, and start living it out.

There is an amazing freedom here if you can understand it, a
freedom to really receive Jesus' call for your life and to understand that
what He is saying is not only for His disciples at that time, but also for
those of us who live today.

There are three big subjects in the Bible that people speak about
today: ecclesiology, missiology, and Christology. Ecclesiology, missiology, and Christology include teaching about the church, teaching
about mission, and teaching about Christ. My question is this: *which*
of these three subjects should come first in our lives? If we look at the
church today, we find it often places its focus around the teaching of
the church. The next teaching the church focuses on is the mission,
and then lastly, it focuses on the teaching of Jesus.

I admit that some years ago, I too was focused so much on teaching
about the church that I forgot the most important teaching of all—

Jesus. Of course, I did not stand up on the church platform and say that I forgot Jesus. I did not even realize at the time that I had forgotten Him because everything I was doing was because of Him. I built the churches because of Him, and I did the mission because of Him, but I realize now that my focus was wrong.

If we are honest, I believe a lot of us have forgotten the most important thing. We have forgotten to spend time with Jesus, and we have forgotten to focus on what He is saying in His Word. It is all about Jesus, about what He is saying in His Word, and about how He wants us to do His mission. From this focus on Jesus first, and how He wants us to do His mission second, the teaching of the church would arise third.

What if, instead of starting with church first, mission second, and Christ third, we started with Christology first? What if we looked at Jesus first, and then later ended up with church? What would that look like? If we started all over and really took the time to look at Jesus, His Word, and what He has said to us, everything would look completely different because we would not be led by our church vision, our church building, our church culture, our hierarchy, or our economy.

If we started all over with what is most important—Jesus—many of the things that steal our time, focus, energy, and money (which are all needed to run a church) would no longer be necessary. We would realize that many of the things we do for Him today are actually stealing our time and distracting us from what He has actually commanded us to do.

Today, much of what we think makes up a "real" church and much of what we do today to "serve Christ" is actually stealing from us our first love for Him that we once had. The fire we had for Christ in the beginning is being stolen from us because we are focusing so much on the church instead of focusing on Him and how we can obey Him.

We sometimes forget that Jesus has not called us to build big, beautiful churches with lots of members. I am not saying it is a bad thing to have a place to meet and gather with others, but I am saying this should never be the end goal. Jesus has called us to make disciples, where we baptize them, and teach them to do all He has commanded us. This is our life's goal, and it is so clearly written in the Bible, right in front of us. We can sit in our big, beautiful churches with a lot of

> **We, as Christians, are often so busy
> with all our church activities
> that we forget the most important thing:
> to listen to Jesus and do what He says.**

activities and still not fulfill the goal Jesus has given to us. It is time to stop doing what we have been doing and go back to what Jesus is calling us to do. The goal must always center on being a disciple of Jesus, and then He will take us and build His church. This is what Jesus is saying in Matthew 16:18. He will build His church with us, and our job is to make disciples. Jesus is the One who will build the church. This church that Jesus is building is being built with living stones. The church is, and will always be, formed of believers coming together to serve Jesus. As a follower of Jesus, you desire to see people hear the Gospel and become born again, to see them become disciples of Jesus Christ just like you did.

This is the calling Jesus gives us in Matthew 28:19-20, which states:

Go therefore and make disciples of all the nations, baptizing them ... teaching them to observe all things that I have commanded you; and lo, I am with you always, even to the end of the age. (NKJV)

This desire to see people born again and becoming disciples is in the heart of every person who is truly born again and on fire for Jesus. The desire to see this is often the reason many Christians have spent so much time and money in their churches. It is because they want to fulfill this goal. I believe many of us could use our time and money in a very different way than how we are using it now. I do not say this as a critic because I have been there myself. I do say this as a desperate shout to everyone to stop doing what you are doing and look at the call Jesus gave us. I do believe we can continue doing church and mission the way we currently are and succeed in some way, but I also believe there is a better way, and that is doing it the way Jesus called us to.

Jesus says in Matthew 11:28-30:

Come to Me, all you who labor and are heavy laden, and I will give you rest. Take My yoke upon you and learn from Me, for I am gentle and lowly in heart, and you will find rest for your souls. For My yoke is easy and My burden is light. (NKJV)

Jesus is saying His yoke and burden are light, and if we do what is right, we shall not be tired. If this is true, then why do we see so many church leaders getting tired and falling away from their faith? Why do we see so many church members becoming tired and not only leaving the church, but also their faith? I believe there can be many reasons for this. However, I am convinced that one of the reasons is because we do so many things that Jesus has not actually called us to do. Jesus never said we should do church the way we do it today. He never said we should have meetings with the same program, worship, and speech Sunday after Sunday. He never said we should try to get people to come into our church so we can tell them about Jesus.

We often forget that before Jesus gave His disciples the great commission in Matthew 28:16-20, He spent over three years with them, and in that period, He had been teaching them what He wanted them to do. Jesus taught them what the mission was about, so when He gave them the great commission, they knew exactly how He wanted them to go out and do it. This is the reason they did not go out and build big, beautiful churches and set up Sunday meetings where people could come hear the Word of God, like people often do today. All this can be good as long as it does not remove the focus from what Jesus really wants us to do. But the truth is that today, 2000 years after Christ was on earth, we are spending our time, our energy, and our money to get our churches to succeed. We spend our time, energy, and money to get people to come to our church meetings. However, we do not do what Jesus told us to do. Maybe this is the reason we see so little fruit and why we see so many people losing their faith and their first love for God. We, as Jesus' disciples, have been fishing the whole night without catching anything, as Jesus' disciples did in John 21:3-6. Now it is time we do what He says, that we act on His Word. It is as simple as casting the net on the other side. Let's not focus so much on the church first, mission second, and Christ third. Let's start with Christ first and then let Him reveal the mission to us, then let the church unfold the way Jesus has planned.

2

THE TWELVE AND
THE SEVENTY

**The call Jesus gave was not only to the twelve or the
seventy disciples we read about in the gospels. It
was also to you and me - who are living today.
When we start to obey Jesus' Word, we will bear the
same fruit, and experience the same amazing life
these disciples did.**

Try to imagine the last moments that Jesus spent with His
disciples before He was taken up into Heaven to sit at the
right hand of the Father. The disciples had been walking with
Jesus daily for the last three years. They had seen, heard, and experienced so many amazing things in those years. They had also
experienced how God raised Jesus from the grave, how He conquered
death as He had foretold. Then, in the last forty days, Jesus had
presented Himself to them again and again, talking to them about the
Kingdom of God. But now the time had come for Him to leave. Try to
imagine how great a moment this truly was. Before Jesus went up into
Heaven, He spoke His last words to them. I believe these last words He
spoke to His disciples would have been important for Jesus and

especially important for His disciples. This is not to say that the other things Jesus said to His disciples over the previous three years were not important, but somehow these last words were particularly special. I believe these were words He really wanted them to remember.

We read some of the last words Jesus spoke to His disciples at the end of the gospels of Matthew and Mark.

Matthew 28:18-20 states:

And Jesus came and spoke to them, saying, "All authority has been given to Me in heaven and on earth. Go therefore and make disciples of all the nations, baptizing them in the name of the Father and of the Son and of the Holy Spirit, teaching them to observe all things that I have commanded you; and lo, I am with you always, even to the end of the age." Amen.

Mark 16:15-19 states:

And He said to them, "Go into all the world and preach the gospel to every creature. He who believes and is baptized will be saved; but he who does not believe will be condemned. And these signs will follow those who believe: In My name they will cast out demons; they will speak with new tongues; they will take up serpents; and if they drink anything deadly, it will by no means hurt them; they will lay hands on the sick, and they will recover."

These last words spoken by Jesus to His disciples, I believe, were words of great value to Him, words that were close to His heart. Jesus wanted His disciples to continue the work He had started, and He desired for this to spread into all nations. He wanted His disciples to continue His work in all the nations by making disciples and teaching everyone to obey what He had commanded. When we later read what Jesus commanded His disciples, whether it was to the twelve or the seventy, we have to understand that what He commanded them to do was not only for those who lived during that time. No, it was also for His church going forward, including all of us who are alive today.

Jesus gave clear commandments to the twelve disciples in Luke chapter 9 and Matthew chapter 10, and to the seventy in Luke chapter 10.

**The Word Jesus spoke to His disciples
is also for us who live today.
Yes, much has changed over the
last two thousand years, but
Jesus' Word is forever the same.**

There is a difference between the twelve and the seventy. Matthew 10: 5-7 states:

These twelve Jesus sent out and commanded them, saying: "Do not go into the way of the Gentiles, and do not enter a city of the Samaritans. But go rather to the lost sheep of the house of Israel. And as you go, preach, saying, 'The kingdom of heaven is at hand.' ..."

Jesus instructs them (the twelve) to spread the Gospel only to the Israelites because the Gospel needed to first be spread to the Jews before the Gentiles.

The twelve disciples Jesus chose are actually symbolic for the twelve tribes of Israel. The seventy disciples are symbolic of the Gentiles because the number seventy was representative of the seventy nations of the world. Clearly, there is something very symbolic happening in Luke 9-10 and Matthew 10. The idea of the Jews receiving the Gospel before the Gentiles is also shown through Jesus helping a Canaanite woman in Matthew 15:24 where Jesus stated, *"I was not sent except to the lost sheep of the house of Israel."* Paul also, in Romans 1:16, continues the idea that the Gospel is first for the Jews and then for the Gentiles by stating, *"For I am not ashamed of the gospel of Christ, for it is the power of God to salvation for everyone who believes, for the Jew first and also for the Greek."* Here, when it says for "the Greek," it is important to understand that Greek is actually another word for the Gentiles, or non-Jews.

As you can see, there is a very clear picture of Jesus first sending out the twelve disciples to reach all of the Israelites with the Gospel. Then, later, we see Jesus sending out the seventy to reach all the foreign nations with the Gospel. Some Bible translations have translated the "seventy disciples" into the "seventy-two disciples." However, as we can see, there is a good explanation as to why it should be seventy. The Danish Bible, called *The New Testament in Everyday Danish (NLT)* says, "Some Scriptures talk about seventy-two disciples, but the real number is seventy because this is the symbolic number for all foreign nations. In Genesis chapter 10, we see the seventy nations of the world. The sending out of the twelve apostles and later the seventy was symbolic because Jesus' message would first be preached to the Jews and then to all other nations." So, as we can see, Jesus started with the twelve disciples to reach the Jews, and then the seventy disciples to reach the Gentiles. The last words Jesus gave them all were to keep following Him, to obey what He has commanded them to do, and to teach others to do the same. Since Jesus is forever the same, His Word will never change. Therefore, we who live today need to obey His Word because His Word is for everyone, whether we are Jew or Gentile.

Now we are going to read what Jesus said in Luke 10:1-12, when He sent out the seventy:

> *After these things the Lord appointed seventy others also, and sent them two by two before His face into every city and place where He Himself was about to go. Then He said to them, "The harvest truly is great, but the laborers are few; therefore pray the Lord of the harvest to send out laborers into His harvest. Go your way; behold, I send you out as lambs among wolves. Carry neither money bag, knapsack, nor sandals; and greet no one along the road. But whatever house you enter, first say, 'Peace to this house.' And if a son of peace is there, your peace will rest on it; if not, it will return to you. And remain in the same house, eating and drinking such things as they give, for the laborer is worthy of his wages. Do not go from house to house. Whatever city you enter, and they receive you, eat such things as are set before you. And heal the sick there, and say to them, 'The kingdom of God has come near to you.' But whatever city you enter, and they do not receive you, go out into its streets and say, 'The very dust of your city which clings to us we wipe off against you. Nevertheless know this, that the kingdom of God has come near you.' But I say to you that it will be more tolerable in that Day for Sodom than for that city.*

In this book, I will go through these verses one by one, and show that these words are also for today. Jesus' Word has never changed, and it never will change. We might not live in Israel, and many things in our culture and technology are very different today, but this does not change the importance of what Jesus has commanded us to do. Before we take a closer look at Jesus' words in Luke 10, we are going to look at what happened when the seventy disciples returned to Him after going out and doing what He had commanded.

We read in Luke 10:17:

Then the seventy returned with joy, saying, "Lord, even the demons are subject to us in Your name."

What we need to realize here, is that these seventy disciples came home rejoicing! This is what should be happening when we serve God. When we step out in faith on Jesus' Word and see His Spirit working through us, it should bring forth great joy! We should not be able to contain our excitement! I have seen this excitement in many people when they take their first step out, pray for someone for the first time, share the Gospel with someone for the first time, baptize someone in water for the first time, or baptize someone with the Holy Spirit for the first time. They cannot hide their excitement! They are so full of joy because they realize God wants to use them to spread His Kingdom! This same joy and excitement is what the first disciples experienced!

John 4:34 states:

Jesus said to them, "My food is to do the will of Him who sent Me, and to finish His work."

This is the same as what you can experience today when you step out in faith and do His will. When you obey Jesus' commands and reach out to other people, you too will experience a spiritual fullness where you truly feel that doing the will of God is your food. You will feel satisfied in a way that reading books and listening to teaching can not do.

Later, in John 6:35, it is written:

*And Jesus said to them, "I am the bread of life. He who comes to Me
shall never hunger, and he who believes in Me shall never thirst.*

I do not know what you think about when you read this verse. Jesus is
saying we should come to Him, and when we do, we should never hunger
or thirst. This is truly what we experience when we start to step out in faith
upon His Word. We will feel full, not hungry or thirsty, and we will feel
excited. This does not mean that we will not want more of Jesus or that we
will not want to experience greater things in Him, but it does mean we will
not be busy trying to travel around the world seeking, just because we feel
something is missing. We will not feel the need to jump on a plane and fly
to a conference just because we feel something is missing.

You can start to obey Jesus wherever you are, and when you do,
you will feel filled up in a way you have never felt before. You will
experience an amazing peace and realize you do not need anything
else. All you need is to continue obeying and continue growing.

An amazing revelation in Luke 10 is that this is for everyone. Jesus
did not only give these commands to pastors or to people with a special
status or special callings and talents. The commands Jesus made in
Luke 10 are for both the young and the old in Christ. You do not have
to wait to get started obeying Jesus in what He is saying here. Many
Christians are sitting in church today feeling frustrated. They are
frustrated because they are waiting. They are waiting for something.
They are waiting for their turn to be used by God. They are waiting for
the pastor to notice them and give them an opportunity to be used by
God. But I am telling you that you do not need to wait anymore. Jesus
has already given you His calling and commandment for your life, and
it is so clearly written in front of you.

One of the most powerful things I have experienced while teaching
at a "kickstart," as we call it, is to witness people realizing they do not
have to wait anymore for God to use them. They realize that what Jesus
is saying in Luke 10 is actually for them, and it is for right now. We
need to understand that we can serve God every day, wherever we are.
We do not need a special platform to serve God because our platform
is everywhere. It is out there among people in their houses, on the
streets, or in the shops.

**If you understand the vision
Jesus has given us and start to live it out,
you will experience that the frustration and
feelings of being unsatisfied will disappear.
You will feel full, happy, and satisfied.
To obey Jesus is so much more than studying,
attending meetings, and attending
Christian activities.**

When you understand the vision Jesus has given us in Luke 10 and start to live it out, you will experience a new and exciting life, a life where God will use you to bear fruit. When we put our church tradition aside and stop thinking about church first, mission second, and Jesus third, and focus instead on Jesus and what He says first, everything else falls into place. If we truly did this, the church would be so different. We would no longer see Christians sitting in church year after year feeling frustrated and losing their first love for Christ.

When you look at Jesus' Word and start to live it out, God will use you in a new way. You will truly experience the life we read about in the book of Acts, a life that is impossible to live out using only two hours a week in a church. When we start to obey Jesus and do His mission the way He said to do it, He will take us and put us together as living stones, not only inside the church building on Sundays but also outside of it 24/7.

Yes, Jesus will build His church. The church He wants to build looks so different from the church many people experience today. I have been involved in planting three different churches in different cities, and it is only now that I have started to understand what church is really about. Church is not about the meetings, programs, or the fancy buildings we go to Sunday after Sunday. The church Jesus desires consists of a family where we love each other and obey Jesus together. Yes, this can occur in a church building or in another place, but the "church" is not a building. It is the people.

Let's look at the Word Jesus gave us because here we find the perfect platform where we can be used by Him, no matter where or who we are. In **Matthew 28:18-20**, we read Jesus' last words to His disciples:

And Jesus came and spoke to them, saying, "All authority has been given to Me in heaven and on earth. Go therefore and make disciples of all the nations, baptizing them in the name of the Father and of the Son and of the Holy Spirit, teaching them to observe all things that I have commanded you; and lo, I am with you always, even to the end of the age." (NKJV)

Amen! It is time we start obeying what Jesus has commanded us. Therefore, in this book, we will look at Jesus' words in Luke 10, verse by verse, and examine together how we are to obey them in the world in which we are living now.

3

BEING THE GOOD GROUND

**Jesus' call to follow Him is for everyone,
but the sad truth is, not many are willing to
take up their cross and pay the price to follow Him.
To follow Jesus is a calling where you need to be
willing to pay a high price. This is something we do
not often like to even talk about, let alone do,
but those who are willing to pay the price
will find Jesus and experience eternal life.**

---

uke 10 starts with these words, *"After these things the Lord appointed seventy others also, and sent them two by two before His face into every city and place where He Himself was about to go."* When chapter 10 starts with "after these things," or "after this," we need to remember that the Bible, like every letter, was originally written without chapters and verses. Those chapters and verses were added hundreds of years later. This often causes us to misunderstand what the Word is actually saying because of the way the Bible has been divided. To understand what Jesus is saying in Luke 10:1, when He starts with "after these things," or "after this," we need to go back to the former chapter and read what is written there. We will do this now.

Looking back, Luke 9:57-62 states:

Now it happened as they journeyed on the road, that someone said to Him, "Lord, I will follow You wherever You go." And Jesus said to him, "Foxes have holes and birds of the air have nests, but the Son of Man has nowhere to lay His head." Then He said to another, "Follow Me." But he said, "Lord, let me first go and bury my father." Jesus said to him, "Let the dead bury their own dead, but you go and preach the kingdom of God." And another also said, "Lord, I will follow You, but let me first go and bid them farewell who are at my house." But Jesus said to him, "No one, having put his hand to the plow, and looking back, is fit for the kingdom of God."

And now Luke 10:1 states:

After these things the Lord appointed seventy others also, and sent them two by two before His face into every city and place where He Himself was about to go.

It is important for us to get these words from the former chapter to understand that there is a cost to following Jesus. Being a disciple of Jesus really means we need to lay down our own dreams and our own ambitions. We must be willing to put our hand to the plow without looking back. When we do that, we will experience a life with Jesus that is better than anything we could imagine.

We see again and again that when Jesus walked here on earth and called people to follow Him, the call was always the same, but the response people gave Him was different from person to person. Matthew, a tax collector, abandoned his responsibility of collecting taxes upon hearing Jesus calling. He willingly left everything behind to follow Jesus, and Jesus used him mightily (Matthew 9:9-13). We also see another man who got the same calling as Matthew—the rich, young ruler we read about in Matthew 19. He also got the call to follow Jesus, but his response was different from Matthew's. He was not willing to pay the price and ended up going away sad (Matthew 19:16-26). We see again and again that the calling was the same, but the response was different. Some were willing to pay the price, while others were holding back.

Jesus makes it even more clear in Mark 4 when He talks about the parable of the sower. In this parable, a farmer is going out to sow his seed. This serves as a picture of us sowing the Word of God. The seed (the Word of God) lands on four different types of grounds, producing four different reactions. These grounds serve as a picture of different kinds of people or different kinds of reactions that people have when they hear the Word of God. Today, we are not only the ones sowing the seed, but each of us is also one of these four types of ground.

**We must decide if we will be the good ground,
one who obeys Jesus no matter what.
If we do this, we will see a lot of fruit,
and He will be honored throughout our life.**

The first ground we read about speaks about the seed that "… fell by the wayside; and the birds of the air came and devoured it" (Mark 4:4). These are the people who hear the Word of God, but as soon as they hear it, Satan comes and steals what was sown in their hearts. These are the people we meet who are not interested in opening up and receiving the Word of God. When we meet these people, it is important that we shake the dust off our feet and move on, which is something I will discuss a little later.

Some people are the second type of ground. Mark 4 explains the second ground by stating the seed fell on "… *stony ground, where it did not have much earth; and immediately it sprang up because it had no depth of earth. But when the sun was up it was scorched, and because it had no root it withered away.*" These are the people who hear the Word of God and receive it with gladness, but they have no root in themselves and let the Word wither and die. This occurs when people receive the Word of God but persecution sets in, and these people fall away because the Word never went deep enough into their hearts. They had never been truly willing to pay the price for Jesus.

Persecution is often something we do not speak about, but is actually a big part of following Jesus. Jesus talked more about persecution than anything else, and He made it very clear that persecution and resistance were not things He alone would experience, but that His disciples would also experience.

2 Timothy 3:12 makes this clear, stating:

Yes, and all who desire to live godly in Christ Jesus will suffer persecution.

I want to say that it is not always that these people fall away in the sense that they stop attending church. Many people continue to go to church while their hearts have fallen away from their first love of God. The Bible makes it very clear that everyone who is living a godly life in Jesus will experience persecution. When they start to live out this life and obey Jesus, they will become a threat to Satan; therefore, Satan will send persecution. This persecution is often a surprise for many people, especially in the western world. People in the western world often think persecution only happens in other parts of the world because this is where they see people being thrown in jail or beaten for their faith. But persecution is not always physical. In fact, persecution has many faces, and it still hurts even if it is not physical. If we take a look at Jesus' life, people called Him many things and spread many rumors about Him. We even read in Matthew 12:24 that the Pharisees accused Jesus of being of Beelzebub (lord of the demons). The Bible states that if they called Jesus these awful things, they will also call us, His disciples, these awful things, too.

We see this clearly in Matthew 10:24-25, which states:

"A disciple is not above his teacher, nor a servant above his master. It is enough for a disciple that he be like his teacher, and a servant like his master. If they have called the master of the house Beelzebub, how much more will they call those of his household!

The truth is, many Christians are sleeping in their churches. They do not live as disciples of Jesus. Therefore, they do not experience this true persecution that Jesus faced. When Christians are sleeping, Satan stays away and lets them continue sleeping. He does not want them to wake up and realize they need to obey Jesus' Word. However, when you wake up and start to obey Jesus' Word and live as His disciples, Satan will come and give you persecution because you have now become a threat to him and his kingdom. You will often be surprised where the persecution comes from. A lot of the persecution we will experience as believers will not come from outside in the world from people who do not know God. Instead, it will come from people in the churches who are sleeping, themselves. Persecution, many times, comes from the people who are close to us, and that can really hurt. Jesus experienced persecution from the religious people, and sometimes from His own family.

When persecution sets in, many people choose the easy solution. Yes, there is an easy solution to persecution, and it is called compromise. You do not have to do much to get the persecution to stop or decrease. All you have to do is compromise. To compromise is to stop being so radical in your words and your deeds. It is to live like the other sleeping Christians around you. If you do this, the persecution will surely stop. But if you compromise, you are the second type of ground that Jesus talks about in Mark 4, and you will not bear good fruit. Maybe what I am saying sounds harsh, but it is often what we see. If you do not want to be this second ground, which does not bear good fruit, you need to decide you will never compromise, no matter how hard the persecution may get.

There is a third ground we read about in Mark 4:7 that states:

And some seed fell among thorns; and the thorns grew up and choked it, and it yielded no crop.

This third ground represents the people who let the worries of this world, the deceitfulness of riches, and the longing for other things quench the Word so it does not bear fruit. These are the people who hear the Word of God and receive it in their heart. For a while, things actually go well. But after some time, their daily worries and daily life duties come in and take up their time so that they do not bear fruit. When I read about the third ground, I think about the many people who want to serve God, but suddenly do not have time to serve Him because they are distracted. They are distracted by their house, car, garden, and hobbies. There are many things in this world to worry about so that these distractions and worries often take up their time, and they have no time left to obey God. Although they may want to follow Jesus, they have made a life (especially in the western world) where they do not have the time because of all the responsibilities that come with a house, car, garden, etc. Because of all the responsibilities in their life, they often have only a few hours left on Sunday to serve God by going to a church service. When Jesus talks about this in Mark chapter 4, He calls it the "deceitfulness of riches." Riches are so deceitful that many people do not see it before it is too late. We often think we would be happier if we got a bigger house or car, or had a better job, but because we are seeking the "better" things of this world, we do not have any time or energy left to serve Jesus. We want to serve Jesus, but what about the kids? What about what others are thinking if we go this way or do this or that? Yes, there is so much to worry about that we end up doing nothing. If so, we are truly the third ground, and we will not bear a lot of fruit.

Thankfully, there are also people who are the fourth ground, the good ground. These are the people who do not compromise or give up when they experience persecution. Persecution, for these people who are the fourth ground, causes them to seek Jesus even more, and God actually uses the persecution to prune them so they will bear even more fruit.

This is shown in John 15:2 which states:

Every branch in Me that does not bear fruit He takes away; and every branch that bears fruit He prunes, that it may bear more fruit.

The people who are the fourth ground are not deceived by the riches of the world or by worries or by anything this world can offer. They prioritize Jesus above everything else and would rather live a simple life in order to have more time and energy to focus on God. These are the people who bear a lot of fruit—thirty, sixty, one hundred fold. The Bible talks about two types of fruit.

There is the fruit of the Spirit, as shown in Galatians 5:22-23:

But the fruit of the Spirit is love, joy, peace, longsuffering, kindness, goodness, faithfulness, gentleness, self-control. Against such there is no law.

Although the fruit of the Spirit is an important part of being a disciple of Jesus, when I talk here about bearing fruit on the fourth ground, I am focusing on the fruit that is produced when you go out and obey Jesus' calling. Jesus speaks about this kind of fruit in Matthew 4:19 which states, *"Follow Me, and I will make you fishers of men."* John 15:16 also speaks about this fruit, stating, *"You did not choose Me, but I chose you and appointed you that you should go and bear fruit, and that your fruit should remain, that whatever you ask the Father in My name He may give you."* It is clear that Jesus wants all of us to go out into this world as fishers of men and bear a lot of good fruit.

**The price Jesus paid on the cross is not only for you
and me. It is also for the whole world.
It is for those who do not yet believe;
therefore, we need to go out and let our light shine,
so the world can see and believe.**

When I think about the four different grounds Jesus speaks about in Mark 4, I see many people in the churches who are ground number two or three. People who are ground two are very quick to compromise what the Bible says for the sake of peace. People who are ground three let the deceitfulness of riches and the worries of the world steal their time, so they do not do what they are called to do.

My family and I have gone through periods in our life where we were one of these grounds, but, thankfully, God started to work in us and show us we were not living as true disciples of Jesus. When we started to taste this new life, we started to see that for many years we were blinded by the fear of persecution and the deceitfulness of riches, and that we needed to change many things in our lives so we could become the good ground that bears a lot of fruit. At one time we had bought a house and had been spending a lot of money renovating it. We spent a lot of time and money fixing up our house and creating a life surrounded by material things. During this time we did not see a lot of fruit, but when we got a taste of what it is like to be a true disciple of Christ, we were hungry for more. Eventually, God led us to get rid of everything—our house and our car. We started to live a much simpler life so we could prioritize our time and energy and focus more on seeking and obeying God. We decided to move into a small apartment where we suddenly had peace and the time to serve God. We did not need to work as much as before because we did not have a mortgage payment or car payment. We were free to spend our time serving God. We experienced persecution at other times that and almost made us start compromising, but we decided we would not become ground number two. This kept us going. We did not compromise, and later we saw a lot of fruit come out of this.

I hope the parable in Mark 4 will speak to you and challenge you to ask yourself which ground you are on. Are you the good ground that bears a lot of fruit? When we are talking about the different kinds of ground, we need to understand that we can decide which ground we want to be. Jesus' calling is for everyone, but how we respond to this calling is up to us.

Sometimes I feel frustrated when people think we got to where we are today without paying a price. This is not true. We paid a big price to get here, and it is still costing us today. My family and I experience a lot of persecution, and people can be very cruel to us. We have not always been able to give our kids what other parents could give their kids because of the simple way we were living, and our kids have grown up hearing bad things about who we were and how we lived. Although it has not been easy, we have seen, and continue to see a lot of fruit, and this is what it is all about. God is faithful, and He is truth.

What should you do with your life to become good ground and bear a lot of fruit? I do not know. You need to talk with God about it. Use this amazing parable and ask yourself where you are. We can all have desert periods in our life where we do not see as much fruit as in other times. However, these desert periods are important. There are periods in our lives when things need to change, and we need to do something radical for Jesus. As we start to look at the call of Jesus in Luke chapter 10, verse by verse, it is up to you to choose how you want to respond to it. It is up to you if you want to be good ground, where you receive the Word of God, act on it, pay the price, and see a lot of fruit.

4

TWO AND TWO

It is amazing when you go out
into the harvest with someone, but remember
you are never alone because today each of us
has the Holy Spirit in us, and Jesus has
promised to go with us.

We will now start to go through Jesus' words in Luke chapter 10. We will look at what Jesus did, what He said to His disciples, and how we obey this today. The first verse we read in Luke 10 is this, *"After these things the Lord appointed seventy others also, and sent them two by two before His face into every city and place where He Himself was about to go.."*

We read here that Jesus started by sending them out two by two. When Jesus did this, He knew what He was doing. I think it is so important to realize that Jesus sent them out this way because there are many benefits to going two by two. Deuteronomy 32:30 states, *"How could one chase a thousand, and two put ten thousand to flight ..."* Clearly, there is power in being two. Before we look at the benefits of going out two by two, we need to understand that it is not a law to have two every time we go out. The reason I am starting this chapter by saying this is because I have met many believers who want to go out and obey the Call of Jesus, but they feel so alone. When people feel alone and read these words about Jesus sending people out two by two, it makes it even more difficult for them to go out and obey Jesus because they start to think it is wrong to go out alone, and therefore they do nothing.

These verses, however, do not say it is absolutely necessary to go out two by two. This is important to understand because we see very clearly in Acts 8 that Philip was sent out alone; however, Philip was not actually alone because God was there. The Holy Spirit was in Philip, and God used Philip mightily, even when it looked like he was alone. When you think about it, you and I, like Philip, are never alone because today we have something the first disciples in Luke 10 did not have— the Holy Spirit. When we read Luke 10, we need to remember that it took place before they were baptized with the Holy Spirit. Luke 10 was before the cross and before Jesus died and was resurrected. Therefore, He had not yet sent the Holy Spirit here on earth like He has now. Yes, Jesus sent the disciples out and gave them the power to heal the sick and cast out demons. But that authority was only given to the seventy disciples at that time. Now, however, this same power and authority has been given to all of us through the Holy Spirit. It is clear that in Acts 8, when Philip was led out to the desert where he found the eunuch, he was not actually alone because he had the Holy Spirit in him, and Jesus, by the Holy Spirit, was walking with him. Many of us have had strong experiences obeying God's Word *alone*, being led by the Holy Spirit, but I do see many benefits to going out two by two.

One big advantage when it comes to discipleship is that by going out two by two, we can learn from one another. When we talk about discipleship, we need to understand that it should not only occur on a platform in a church. Discipleship also needs to happen in everyday life. It is something we can live out, together, and although there are some things you can teach from a platform in a church, there are many things you will never be able to teach or show from that platform. In order to learn these practical applications that can not be taught or shown from a platform in a church, you will need to leave the church and go out into real life in order to learn it and live it out. Although the church can teach some things, there is a difference between teaching it and actually showing how to live it out in the real world.

Real discipleship is shown through our example. This means we show how people can obey God, and we show how God can work through us. Showing by example how we live as a disciple of Jesus is a much stronger testimony for making disciples than just teaching about it. Many in the churches today do not know how to obey Jesus in the real world because no one has ever taken the time to accurately show them how to do it. Today, there is a big gap between what we hear in the church (teaching) and how we live it out in real life (obeying). People today are struggling with how to apply, in the real world on Monday, what they have been taught in church on Sunday.

But let us look at Jesus. How did Jesus start doing it? Matthew 4:19 states:

Then He said to them, "Follow Me, and I will make you fishers of men."

When Jesus said this, what was the reaction of the people? They actually followed Jesus. Jesus did not set up a Bible study with people once a week to do a teaching about how to live the life of a disciple. Instead, He showed them. They followed Him out into the real world where He taught them how to live out the life by being an example for them.

> **Real discipleship cannot be done inside the four walls of the church. We need to learn to walk together and live life together, like Jesus did with His disciples. This is where the real discipleship begins.**

I believe life with God is really about discipleship, and not so much about receiving a special anointing or gifting where you suddenly know everything. This also applies when it comes to receiving boldness. When I tell people that as disciples of Jesus, we are to obey everything Jesus commands us, including casting out demons, healing the sick, and leading people to Christ, it can be difficult for them to imagine that they have the ability to do this, since many of them have been sitting in church for so long without doing anything. They often think it is too big of a task for them, and they think they do not have enough boldness to do it. However, we need to understand that we have everything we need to obey Jesus through the Holy Spirit. Yes, maybe you need boldness to do this, but this boldness will come by doing it little by little.

I have met many people who are actually more bold than I am, maybe not in leading people to Christ, healing the sick, or casting out demons, but they are so much more bold in other areas of their lives than I am. Let's look at the example of washing clothes and cooking food. I am sure most of you are much more bold than I am when it comes to washing clothes and cooking food. These are things I do not really know a lot about because I got married very young, so I actually never properly learned how to cook food or wash clothes. Therefore, washing clothes or cooking food would be a big task for me, and a difficult task for me to overcome. It would probably take the whole day for me to wash just one set of clothes, and I would probably be exhausted afterward. However, when *you* wash clothes, it is so different. You just do it with no problem. You are so bold when it comes to washing clothes. Why do you have so much boldness washing clothes and cooking food, and I do not? Is it because you have a special anointing for washing clothes that comes over you every time you wash clothes? And is it difficult for me because I do not have this special anointing for washing clothes? Is this how it works, or is it much more simple than this?

The truth is, you are much more bold than I am in this area because you have more experience in this area than I do. Boldness is something that comes through experience. It is not a special gift or anointing. Today, I do not have any difficulty standing up and speaking or praying in front of thousands of people, but I can still remember the first time I had to pray out loud. I was at a prayer meeting with six people from the church. I remember how nervous I was as my turn to pray approached. When it was my turn to pray, I prayed only a few words, and it was so hard for me to do. It was so hard for me to overcome the fear I had of praying out loud. After I prayed, I remember I could have changed my t-shirt because it was so wet from my sweat. That was how nervous I was. I remember the first time I had to stand in front of a small group of people and speak to them. I was so nervous. I also remember how nervous I was the first time I cast out a demon, the first time I healed the sick, the first time I baptized someone in the Holy Spirit, and so on. Yes, there is always a first time, and the first time is always difficult because you are so nervous. You think you can not do it because you have never done it before, and therefore you lack the boldness. But the truth is, after you have done it a few times, it becomes easier and easier. You become more and more bold. In the end, you do not even think about it anymore. You just do it. It becomes natural like washing clothes or cooking food. Boldness really comes through experience, and you can get this experience for yourself.

When we talk about going out and obeying Jesus, you can do this alone, but, of course, it is always easier if you do it with someone else alongside you. It is much easier if you have someone beside you who can help and support you. If you do this with somebody who is more experienced than you, the experienced person can really help you gain the boldness you need, and it will become much easier for you. This is what is so beautiful about discipleship. It is not something we can do alone. We really need each other. It is all about learning from each other to do things better. Maybe you first start following another person who is more experienced than you, and you are able to see how this person does it. Eventually, it becomes your turn to do the same as you have seen them do. Now it is you doing it, but the other person with more experience is still there if you need help. This helps create boldness, so it is much easier for you to get started. This is exactly what the Bible is talking about when it comes to discipleship. When you start an apprenticeship, you are following your master to learn through the example the master gives you. Although you start as an apprentice, the goal is for you to become like your master. Our goal in discipleship is to become like our Master.

I remember years ago, when I started an apprenticeship as a baker, a disciple of a baker. This is what discipleship is. Discipleship is like an apprenticeship. On the first day I started, I could not bake anything. But the whole reason I was there was to follow my master and learn by his example. By following my master's example, I was supposed to become more and more like him. It was really not easy in the beginning. I made many mistakes and often thought I would never learn it. However, I kept going, and my master was there beside me, teaching me and showing me what to do. Having him beside me gave me a sense of security and helped me a lot. In the end, I learned, and it became much easier. I ended up becoming like my master. This is what it is to learn through the power of example, the way Jesus did things. This is where the word "discipleship" comes from. The New Testament (NLT) explains in a footnote, "In that time and culture, teaching often happened through following a master, and people learned through the power of example. A disciple was like an apprentice rather than like a student, and that was why the apprentice and others called Jesus 'master.' "

> **We can all learn to do the things**
> **Jesus called us to do. We can all learn to**
> **preach the Gospel, heal the sick, cast out demons,**
> **baptize people in water and in the Holy Spirit.**
> **All of these things can become natural for us,**
> **but people need to start to learn it by**
> **doing it again and again.**
> **This is how you get boldness.**

If we understand discipleship like this, it is possible to help a very shy person become very bold and to step out to obey Jesus in just a short time. I have seen this again and again. I see this often when people go out on the streets to be kickstarted. When I use the term "kickstarted," I am referring to when someone takes a person out on the streets for the very first time to share the Gospel and pray for healing for a stranger. It is so interesting when someone is kickstarted because within a short period of time, maybe half an hour or an hour, the person who has never prayed for healing for a stranger before, or stopped a stranger to talk about Jesus, quickly becomes bold and starts to do it with everyone. And it is all because someone took the time to kickstart this person.

I have seen thousands of lives getting changed through being kickstarted and discipled. By taking someone out and spending only an hour with them, and by teaching and showing them how to obey Jesus' commands by the power of example, it will change not only that person's life, but the lives of many other people around them. This is because when someone is first kickstarted and taught how to step out and share Jesus and to heal the sick in the name of Jesus, they learn to adapt this into their everyday life and to live it out wherever they are. This form of discipleship is something we just started doing a few years ago, and we are now seeing hundreds of thousands of people being healed, and thousands of people coming to faith and being baptized as a result of this. It is so effective because it is not only about learning how to share Jesus and heal the sick, it is about discipleship and actually becoming like Jesus. It is about teaching people, by the power of example, how to live out this life together. This kind of discipleship is something you do not experience if you do it alone, so this is why many people prefer to go out on the streets with another person.

Another great thing about going out two by two is that when you are out with another person and you meet someone who is willing to talk with you, one person can talk while the other person prays silently for the conversation and listens to the Holy Spirit for direction. Perhaps the Holy Spirit will speak to you and tell you to add something to the conversation. When people go out two by two, you are able to support each other, and you will be much more effective in reaching people with the Gospel because of the support and protection you can offer one another.

First Peter 5:8 states, *"Be sober, be vigilant; because your adversary the devil walks about like a roaring lion, seeking whom he may devour."*

Satan is smart, and he is waiting to trap us. This is another good reason to walk together with other people. Personally, I never travel alone because after doing a kickstart weekend, I am often very tired, and because I am so tired, I am also very weak and vulnerable. It is therefore good to have people with me to protect me and help me.

Overall, there are many good things we can say when it comes to Jesus sending the disciples out two by two, but if you are in a place where there are no people around you who want to do this with you, do not let this be a hindrance to you. We are never really alone. We are never alone because God is with us, and we have the Holy Spirit inside of us.

5

THE LEADING OF
THE HOLY SPIRIT

**The Holy Spirit wants to be as big a part
of our everyday lives as He was in the
lives of the first disciples.
He wants to guide us, work through us,
and make it so that there are no differences
between our lives and the lives of the first disciples
we read about in the book of Acts.**

In the last chapter, we looked at how Jesus sent out His disciples two by two. He did not send them out to all the cities around. He only sent them to the cities He was going to visit. What this means is something we are now going to look at.

After these things the Lord appointed seventy others also, and sent them two by two before His face into every city and place where He Himself was about to go. (Luke 10:1)

We read here that Jesus sent them out to those places He later wanted to visit. Today, Jesus does not walk here on earth, and He is not physically in Israel as He was at that time. Now, He is sitting in Heaven at God's right hand, but this does not mean He has totally left us alone. No, Jesus has sent someone else in His place, and that, of course, is the Holy Spirit. Now, it is the Holy Spirit, the Spirit of Christ, who is "walking" here on earth. We can also say it like this: we are now the body of Christ, filled up with His Spirit. And just like Jesus wanted to go visit specific places then, I am convinced that, today, the Holy Spirit also wants us to go to certain places to meet the people there.

All the way through the book of Acts, we read how the Holy Spirit worked through the first disciples. He was a big part of their life, as it was He who was leading them. In the book of Acts, we read things like, "For it seemed good to the Holy Spirit, and to us" (Acts 15:28), "So, being sent out by the Holy Spirit" (Acts 13:4), and "they were forbidden by the Holy Spirit" (Acts 16:6). We see this even more clearly if we look at the disciple Philip in Acts 8:26-40.

One day in Philip's life, he experienced an angel of the Lord speaking to him, telling him where to go. When he arrived where the angel said he should go, he saw a chariot, and then the Holy Spirit spoke to him saying that he should run over to the chariot and speak with the man there. When he obeyed and went there, he met the "person of peace" (I will come back to this later). The man there was ready, seeking God. Philip then shared the Gospel with the eunuch, and he repented. As soon as the eunuch saw water, he was immediately baptized. Just after the baptism, Philip experienced something amazing. The Holy Spirit suddenly took him away to another place. It is really amazing when we read how God worked in Philip's life. God was a part of the early church, just like He wants to be a part of your life and my life today.

What we read in the book of Acts with Philip and the other disciples is really amazing. But you need to understand that this is something we also can experience today because the Holy Spirit is the same today. Yes, this is the normal Christian life the early disciples were living, and this is the life God wants every one of us to live. A really big part of following Jesus is listening to the guidance of the Holy Spirit, to walk by the Spirit. Jesus is our example, and He showed us what it meant to be led by the Spirit. This is our goal, to walk like Him. There is nothing that excites me more than being led by the Holy Spirit. There is nothing like really walking in those things that God has already prepared for us to walk in. When you have tasted this life of being led by the Holy Spirit and have seen what the Holy Spirit can do, you want more.

I am so thankful to have been allowed to experience so many amazing things when it comes to being led by the Holy Spirit. I have experienced more than many other people, but I say this with the greatest humility. When I look around and compare my life with what other people have seen, I often have many more testimonies. It is not my intention to brag because I know this is all about HIM. I am saying this to make a point. I am saying this because I want to illustrate something. The reason I am saying I have been allowed to experience more when it comes to being led by the Holy Spirit is for a few different reasons.

I am convinced that one of the reasons I have been allowed to experience these things is because of praying and fasting. Praying and fasting is so important. This is a big part of our Christian walk, especially when it comes to learning to listen to the Holy Spirit. We all have ears, but, sadly, not everyone has learned to use them to listen to the Holy Spirit. I admit that this is not always easy, but I do know fasting is very important. When you fast, you deny your flesh what it wants, and it becomes weak. At the same time, you sharpen your spirit by giving your spirit a lot more focus. Because you are focusing on God, it is easier to hear the Holy Spirit. Through fasting and praying, you can learn to listen to the Spirit and to identify the voice of the Spirit.

Being led by the Holy Spirit is for everyone, but we can only learn to be led by the Spirit if we are willing to listen and obey what we feel the Spirit is saying to us.

As important as praying and fasting are, obedience is, too. We need to obey what God is saying, both when it comes to what He is saying directly to us and also when it comes to what He has already said in His Word. I see many Christians who really believe in prayer. However, prayer in itself is not enough. They are praying, fasting, and seeking God but are not doing anything. It is because they are waiting for God to move them. Unless God speaks very clearly and directly to them, or unless God is the One actually moving them (whatever that even means), they will not do anything. I sometimes call these people 'overly-spiritual' because they focus too much on hearing the voice of God and on the guidance of the Holy Spirit. They often do not experience anything because they are waiting for God to make the move. On the other hand, I have also met people who are very active and do a lot all the time, but they forget their personal life with God. They forget it is not only about doing but that we also need to have a relationship with God. We need to be praying and fasting. These people are doing a lot, but they are often walking in their own strength. These people do not experience many testimonies of what it is like to be led by the Holy Spirit.

I believe the secret to being led by the Holy Spirit is somewhere between those two groups of people. Yes, it is important to pray and listen to the Holy Spirit, but we need to understand that this is not enough when it comes to experiencing a life led by the Holy Spirit. It is good that we obey and act, but this is also not enough in itself. I believe the reason I personally have been allowed to experience so much is because I do both things. I am seeking and listening to God, but I do not stop and wait for Him to tell me to move. God has already told me what I need to do, I do not need anything more to start doing it. When I read what He is saying in His Word, I just need to obey it, no matter what I feel. I do not need to wait for Him to speak to me in a deeper way. I do not need to wait until He says "go" before I go because He already said "go" two thousand years ago. He is still commanding us to go today. I go because He said to, but while I am going, I am listening, and I am being led by the Spirit.

I am convinced that it is the people who have this simple balance who will experience much when it comes to being led by the Holy Spirit. Yes, it is important to pray and fast and through praying and fasting to focus on getting a strong relationship with God. But you should not wait for Him to speak to you in a direct way, or wait for Him to come with the Holy Spirit in a special way before going out on His Word. No, we go because Jesus has already said to go. We do it because He has already said it in His Word. What God said in His Word at that time is as true and relevant as if Jesus was standing in front of us saying it today.

So what are we waiting for? Yes, we know, of course, that there is a place in the Bible where Jesus did not say go, but, instead, He said to wait. He said this at one time to His disciples because they had not yet received the baptism of the Holy Spirit. I would say the same to you today. Have you received the Holy Spirit? If not, then wait. Do not go out before you have the Holy Spirit. You do not have to wait ten days to receive the Holy Spirit like the apostles did at the time Jesus told them to wait. At that time, they needed to wait because the Holy Spirit had not yet been sent to earth because Jesus had not yet gone to the Father. But now, the Holy Spirit is here. Therefore, you can receive Him today. It is important to find people who have the Holy Spirit who can pray for you to receive the Holy Spirit. When you receive the Holy Spirit, you too can go out on His Word because Jesus said, "Go."

I believe it is important that we have the attitude of doing whatever Jesus said to do, no matter if we feel like it or not or if we experience God speaking directly to us or not. It is important that when you go out on His Word, you are praying, listening, and asking the Holy Spirit if there is anything He wants to say to you today. This is when things start to happen. For example, if you look at a car, you can sit behind the wheel and turn the wheel as much as you want, but no matter how much you turn the wheel, nothing will happen when the car is not moving. Because the car is not moving, it actually is more difficult to turn the wheel, but when the car starts to move, it is both easier to turn the wheel and also to move the car where you want it to go. This is the same with God and with being led by the Holy Spirit. We can sit in our church and pray to God, and wait for the Holy Spirit to lead us. We can pray and fast, but nothing will happen because we are doing nothing. But when we start to obey and go out on the Word of God by faith, while having a strong life with God of praying and fasting, we will then experience that it is so much easier to be led by the Holy Spirit. I believe this is what Philip experienced in Acts chapter 8 as we already talked about. Philip was a man who was filled with the Spirit, but when persecution set in, he and many others were spread throughout Samaria. It was not that the Lord spoke to Philip to go to Samaria. No, it was because of difficult circumstances and persecution that he ended up going out to Samaria. While he was out there, he started preaching the Word and doing what God had called him to do. And it was out there, while he was working for the Kingdom, that the Holy Spirit spoke to him and led him into new things. It did not start with God speaking directly to Philip, but it started with Philip going out on the Word of God. As a result, God started to lead.

I have so many testimonies that show this is often how it works. I have an example that reminds me of Philip in this eighth chapter of Acts. Some years ago, I was in the city, walking, praying, and testifying to people I met about Jesus. It was a day when I did not feel anything, and I did not experience God speaking to me. But while I was out serving God, I suddenly experienced the Holy Spirit starting to lead me. I was on my way home when I felt I heard God say, "Stop! Turn around, and go back." I stopped in the middle of the street and thought, "What now?" Although there was a little doubt, I knew this was God speaking to me. So I stopped and turned around. Behind me, I saw a man standing with his back toward me. I thought to myself, "God, is this him that You want me to go and talk to?" I did not want to approach him from behind, so I walked in a big circle around him. When I came to the other side of the man, I was standing in front of the window of a shop. I turned my head to see the front view of the man, but to my surprise, the man was gone. This was not what I expected. I became confused because I thought God had said, "Stop! Turn around, and go back." Now I was standing in front of a shop window, feeling confused, and looking for the man I thought God wanted me to go to, but he was gone. I looked again at my surroundings and realized I was standing in front of a barber shop, which looked very weird because, as many of you know, it has been many years since I have been in a barber shop, since I do not have much hair. While I was standing there, my first thought was that maybe I did not actually hear God's voice, and those were just my own thoughts. Then something crazy happened. Right there in front of that shop, somebody tapped me on my shoulder and said, "Sorry, but you are blocking the door, and I need to go in there." When I turned around, I saw a young man who was waiting for me to move so he could go into the barber shop. When I saw him, I became very excited right away because I knew it was God who had spoken to me and that this was the person He wanted me to meet. I knew this because in front of me stood a young man with one arm in a sling under his jacket. So I said to him, "Excuse me, can I ask you something? I am a Christian, and I believe in God. What about you?" He was really surprised I had asked him that question, and he answered very excitedly. He said it was funny I would ask that because three weeks ago his grandmother had died. She had a Bible laying at her home, and he had gotten her Bible. For the last three weeks, he had been reading the Bible every day but did not feel he was really understanding what he was reading. So that morning he had prayed to God and asked God if He is real to send someone to him to show him that He is real. So I said to him, "Right now, God is going to show you He is real." I then asked him what was wrong with his arm, and he told me he had an accident and had internal bleeding in his whole arm. So I put my hand on his arm and prayed, and in one second, he was completely healed and could move his arm without any pain. He was in shock. Afterward, we had a longer conversation about God, and that day was a new beginning for him.

This is just one of many amazing examples of how the Holy Spirit can lead us. But again, God did not speak to me while I was sitting at home, waiting for a special calling or a special word from Him. No, He spoke to me when I was out there doing His will, just like we read in the Bible. I love stories like this because it reminds me of Philip and the eunuch in Acts 8. Jesus is truly the same, yesterday, today, and forever. Yes, of course, God can speak to us while we are at home, and I also have many examples of that. But I have so many more examples that look like this, that God speaks and guides us when we are out doing His will.

We are living in another time than that of the early disciples in the book of Acts. Today, we have cars, planes, internet, and other things they did not have, but the Spirit is the same, and we can therefore experience the same things they experienced when it comes to being led by the Holy Spirit.

Another story of being led by the Holy Spirit is from Cape Town, South Africa. This story really shows how the Holy Spirit is able to lead. One day, some years ago, my wife Lene told me she had been praying to God for an open door to go away on a mission trip. In the same moment she told me she had been praying for this, I got an email with an invitation to Cape Town in South Africa. We did not know the people who invited us, but we knew it was God who was behind this, so we took a plane and flew down there. While I was sitting in the plane, I felt like God spoke to me and said He wanted to take me to a special area in Cape Town where there was a lot of crime and a lot of poor people. When we arrived in Cape Town after a long flight, we met our host family, and I told them God had just been speaking to me in the plane telling me I needed to go to that area of Cape Town. When they heard this, they said it was not possible because it was a very dangerous area and a place you just did not go to unless you knew someone, especially if you were White. But what happened was amazing. The next day, we went out on the streets to kickstart some friends to share the Gospel and pray for sick people, and there out on the streets, we met an older woman with a cane. She told us she had been walking with her cane for seven months because she had destroyed her hips after being in a taxi where there was a fight. She had needed to jump out of the car while it was still moving. I had my friend who was being kickstarted pray for her. After my friend prayed for that woman, she was completely healed. Both of them ran around with excitement over what had just happened, and they started to dance. I was standing there with her cane in my hand. This is what I love about South Africa—the excitement is so easy to see. They are not afraid to show their joy when God does something.

After they danced around, she told me she had an orphanage at home and that some of the kids in her orphanage were very sick. She asked if we could come and pray for them in her house. Where do you think she lived? Yes, exactly! She lived in the middle of the area to which I felt God wanted me to go. It became even more amazing because she then started telling me she knew it was God behind this because just before she was ready to leave in a taxi to drive home that day, she had felt a voice telling her to get out of the taxi and go 500 meters "this way" and take a bus instead. It did not make any sense to her, but she did it anyway. Now, she knew it was God who had spoken to her because if she had not gotten out of that taxi and taken the bus, she never would have met us.

The next day, we were supposed to meet at the local police station close to her home because that was the most secure place to meet. When we arrived there, we were supposed to call her, and she was going to come to meet us there. But when we arrived and parked outside the police station, my friend shouted, "Oh, no! How could I do that? How could I forget my telephone at home?" He suddenly realized he had forgotten his phone and knew it would take too long to drive home and back to the police station again, so we knew that was not an option. He did not have her number to call to meet her. So, here we were, sitting outside the police station in the car without any way to contact the woman we had met the day before on the street. Then I got the idea that we should go into the police station and ask if anyone knew the woman because I had recorded her healing on my phone. I thought maybe if I showed people in the police station the video, someone might recognize her. We went into the police station and showed the people there the video, but no one knew her. Suddenly, the woman we were looking for came into the police station. We were totally shocked and asked why she came down to the police station when she was supposed to wait until we called her. She told us she had just felt God wanted her to come down there right away. She was also very surprised to see us there. In that same moment, as the three of us were standing together in the police station, the police chief came out of his office and told us all to come with him to his office. When we went into his office, he told us he had been seeking God the whole morning because there was so much crime. He had awakened early to pray to God and told God they needed somebody to help them. He told God that the only way they could be helped was through Jesus. And then he told me I was sent here by God to help them and asked me to pray for everyone in the police station and everyone in the jail. So that day we had a prayer meeting in the police station, together with the police, and we later started a fellowship in the woman's house. Yes, this was really an unforgettable day for all of us. What I really love is all the details you see in this story and how the Holy Spirit is able to lead and put it all together.

I hope this will help you to see that the Holy Spirit is the same always and that He is still able to lead us. If we had not gone down to the city that day, and had that woman not heard that she should get out of the taxi, had my friend not forgotten his telephone, and so on, all of this would not have happened. But, with God, nothing is impossible. And again, it started when we set out to do it. That day we went to the street. I did not experience God saying, "The Lord is saying today that you will go down and meet a woman." No, I just went down because God has been saying to go for centuries and because there was a girl who wanted to get kickstarted. And so we went. While we were there, we were listening, and we were open to the Holy Spirit. I can tell many stories like this about how the Holy Spirit leads us when we obey Him. A life of praying and fasting is important, but it has to go together with a life of obedience to the Word that God has already said, and to what He is saying to us now. When we do that, amazing things will happen. This is a life God has for all of us. There is truly nothing like being led by the Holy Spirit.

When Jesus was here on earth, He was led to different places. These were the places He sent His disciples out to. We are Jesus' body here on earth. He still wants to go to those who are seeking Him, but now it is you and me who need to move. When we are moving, it is much easier for God to turn the wheel as we looked at before. We all need to have a life in relationship with God. We need to walk with Him in prayer and fasting. When we are seeking God and going out on His words, we are listening to the direction He, by His Holy Spirit, is leading us. When we do this, we will end up having amazing testimonies like we read in the book of Acts. Jesus is the same yesterday, today, and forever, and now we are His body working here on earth. He is here, and we are His body, full of His Spirit, continuing the work Jesus started.

6

THE HARVEST IS PLENTIFUL

The harvest is not only great,
but it is also ready. Our enemy has tried to
blind us by saying there are still three months
to the harvest, but this is a lie. Look up and
see that the harvest is ready today. When you
realize this and start to live it out,
everything will change.

Now, we are going to look at something very important, an area our enemy, Satan, has been very busy spreading lies about. He has gotten the church to believe the harvest is not yet ready. In Luke chapter 10, verse 2 (NIV), Jesus says:

He told them, "The harvest is plentiful, but the workers are few. Ask the Lord of the harvest, therefore, to send out workers into his harvest field.

The first words of Jesus here in Luke 10:2, are "The harvest is plentiful." Although many people have heard this many times, there are actually only a few people who understand what Jesus is saying here. Let me ask you, what do you think when you hear the words, "The harvest is plentiful?"

When I heard these words many years ago, I thought it was a negative thing that the harvest was plentiful. I saw it as something negative because it meant there was a lot of work to do. At that time, I had no idea how we could reach all these people. Now, I understand that the harvest being plentiful is by no means something negative. It is a very positive thing! It is actually a really amazing thing! What is negative is the next thing Jesus says in Luke 10:2, that *"the workers are few."*

First, let us look at what the first part of Luke 10:2 says, *"The harvest is plentiful ..."* (NIV). Before I continue, I want to explain what Jesus is talking about here in Luke 10:2 when He uses the words "the harvest." In this case, the harvest is a picture of those people out in the world who are ready to receive Jesus. We can also call them "the wheat." These are the good wheat who need to be harvested and taken into the barn. But, as you will see later, there is not just wheat in the fields. There are also weeds out there, or tares, which grow side by side with the wheat. The tares have been planted by the enemy (see Matthew 13:24-30). The wheat are those people who are ready to receive Jesus, and the weeds are those who will not receive Jesus. From the latter group, we move on away from them. More about this later.

In the same way Jesus uses a picture of the wheat and weeds, He also uses a picture of the sheep and the wolves (see Matthew 10:16). The sheep represent those of us who belong to Him, the good Shepherd, and the wolves represent our enemy, those who are against the Kingdom of God, the Gospel, and therefore against us. I will use these pictures many times throughout this book, so it is important that everyone understands them before I continue.

First, you need to understand the good news Jesus is giving here. The good news is that the harvest is plentiful. Try to imagine a farmer standing and looking over his fields during harvest time, seeing that this year the harvest is really great. What do you think the farmer feels while looking out over his great harvest? Do you think he feels discouraged because of how much work he will have to do? Of course not! It is good news for a farmer when the harvest is great. A farmer would never be sad he has a great harvest, because this is what he has been working toward for the whole year. The farmer would be excited and full of joy, ready to go out and collect his harvest, even when it means he has more work to do than usual.

Jesus, in John 4:35-38, says something important about this great, plentiful harvest:

> Do you not say, 'There are still four months and then comes the harvest'? Behold, I say to you, lift up your eyes and look at the fields, for they are already white for harvest! And he who reaps receives wages, and gathers fruit for eternal life, that both he who sows and he who reaps may rejoice together. For in this the saying is true: 'One sows and another reaps.' I sent you to reap that for which you have not labored; others have labored, and you have entered into their labors."

Here, Jesus is saying that the harvest is not only great, but it is also ready. It is one thing to have a plentiful harvest that is not ready. You could look over it with joy, but you would still need to wait until it is ready. The harvest we are standing in front of, though, is both plentiful, and ready for harvest! It is so amazing when you actually think about it! Try to imagine that we are standing in front of a great harvest that is ready and waiting for us. If you take the time and really listen to Jesus' Word, it is truly amazing what He is saying. This means the people in America, or Europe, or wherever you live are ready for harvest! There is a great and plentiful harvest just waiting for us!

But as I said before, our enemy, Satan, has been busy blinding the church with his lies. There are only a few who actually see this, who understand it, and who go out to bring the harvest in. I have traveled to many different countries. Almost everywhere I go, I experience the same things. I always meet Christians who have a wrong view of the harvest. I have heard so many people tell me they think it is amazing what God is doing in other places in the world. They always tell me that no one is open to the Gospel in their own city or wherever they are. They often tell me people in their own country are too religious, or materialistic, or something else, and that they do not want God. They say things are so different in their own country. Yes, most

Christians I have met have a totally different view of the harvest than what Jesus says about it.

Every time I visit a country, I hear people come up with many excuses as to why things are not happening in their city. They usually put the blame on the harvest. People really believe that the reason nothing is happening, or that very little is happening in their cities, is because of the harvest. I have never met any Christian who tells the truth by stating, "The reason there aren't more people who are saved in our city is not the harvest's fault because Jesus says the harvest is great and it is ready. The reason there aren't more people saved is because of us. We are lazy, and we do too little to reach people." No, I have never heard people say anything like this to me, but it is more biblical and more in line with what Jesus is saying. When you look at the Word of God, Jesus makes it very clear that the harvest is not the problem and that the harvest is never going to be the problem. The problem is the workers. The people "out there" are not the problem. The problem is you. It is us. It is the church.

The reason people in many places are not getting saved is because of the church. The problem is to be found with the workers, not out in the harvest. But the good news is that we can do something about that.

When I visit a country and tell people what God has been doing in other countries, I often hear people say, "Wow, that is amazing!" But then they continue to tell me how difficult it is in their city or their country, how the harvest there just is not ready, and how they therefore can not see the same thing there. They come up with many excuses as to why things do not happen in their area. But could the reason things do not happen in your city or country be because of you? Have you ever considered that the reason things do not happen where you are is because of how you are living? Have you ever thought that the reason things are happening in other countries is because of the way these people are living? Could it be that our wrong understanding of the harvest is one of the reasons we see so little happen?

I know we need faith from our side if we want to see people saved. Yes, it does demand faith from our side to see people saved. I will explain what I mean by that. We know God is the One who leads people to Christ, but I know from my own experience and from the experience of many others that what we do and how we look at the harvest is so important when it comes to seeing people saved. During the first six years I was a Christian, I did not see one person come to Christ. I did not see anyone get born again or get baptized in water or get baptized with the Holy Spirit through me. But then something happened. No, nothing changed out in the harvest, but something changed inside of me. I started to get the faith that this was possible. Do you know what happened when I got that faith, when my eyes were opened? When I started to get the faith that it was possible, I started to see people get saved, and the more I experienced, the more my faith grew and the more my eyes were opened. Now it is a natural part of my everyday life to see people saved and born again.

Today, seeing people being saved and born again in many places, I realize my faith and how I look at the harvest matters. It was not the harvest around me that suddenly got ready and changed. No, it was me who suddenly got the faith and understood that the harvest was ready. Because of this, I changed what I did and how I lived. When I changed what I did and how I lived, I started to see things I did not see before. When I started to believe the harvest was ready as Jesus says, that faith changed my whole attitude toward the harvest out there, and it also changed the way I shared the Gospel with people. Suddenly, I spoke with people and shared the Gospel with them with the expectation that those people would listen, repent, and get born again.

It was because of my own lack of faith during the first six years that I did not see anyone saved. I did not expect it. My fear, blindness, and unbelief stopped me from doing what God wanted me to do and seeing what He wanted me to see. But now, I believe what Jesus is saying, and my faith has cast away that fear, so it does not stop me anymore. Now, I share the Gospel with people, not just hoping that one day in the future they might repent and be born again. Now I share the Gospel expecting them to listen, repent, and be born again. This influences not only how I share the Gospel but also how people listen and receive it. Now I see people all over responding to the Gospel.

Yes, this can all sound a little confusing, but in practice it is actually very simple. Our faith controls our works, our deeds, and our actions. Our faith influences our actions, and it is our actions that make things happen around us. Do you have faith that people will be healed when you lay hands on them? If you do, then that faith will cause you to lay hands on the people you meet, and it will result in them being healed. It is very simple. Do you not have faith that they will be healed? Then that lack of faith will influence what you do. It will probably cause you to not lay hands on people and pray. Why? Because you do not have the faith for it, and because you do not have the faith to do it, you will therefore not see anyone healed. If you do have the faith, you will act according to your faith, and you will see amazing results. It is the same way when it comes to people being saved. If you do not expect them to be saved, you will not share the Gospel with them. When you do have faith to share the Gospel, expecting people to be saved, this is what you will experience. This will make you share the Gospel in a way people will receive it and get saved.

If you are blind when it comes to the harvest and do not have faith that people in your city are open to the Gospel, that blindness and lack of faith will likely cause you to not really try to reach the people at all. We need to open our eyes to what Jesus is saying, and start believing it.

Let us open our eyes and see what Jesus is saying. When we see that the harvest is ready, like He says, and start to live like the harvest is ready, everything will change. It will not only change our lives but also the lives of many others.

In the Gospel of John, we read something special when it comes to the harvest. In John 4, we read that Jesus and His disciples were traveling and that they wanted to travel to Galilee. However, in John 4:4, we read that Jesus needed to travel through Samaria. Why did Jesus need to travel through Samaria? This is interesting because, at that time, Jews did not want to travel through Samaria. Jews would rather walk a longer way around Samaria to get somewhere than to travel straight through it. I am convinced, though, that Jesus needed to go through Samaria because He wanted to show us something very important when it comes to the harvest. We read that Jesus came to a town in Samaria called Sychar where He met a woman at a well. At this time, Jesus told His disciples to go and buy food because He wanted to be alone with this woman at the well. Jesus talked and prophesied over this woman and her life, and she realized He was the Messiah. When

Jesus' disciples returned, in John 4:27-42 (NIV), we read:

> *Just then His disciples returned and were surprised to find Him talking with a woman. But no one asked, "What do you want?" or "Why are you talking with her?" Then, leaving her water jar, the woman went back to the town and said to the people, "Come, see a man who told me everything I ever did. Could this be the Messiah?" They came out of the town and made their way toward Him. Meanwhile His disciples urged Him, "Rabbi, eat something." But He said to them, "I have food to eat that you know nothing about." Then His disciples said to each other, "Could someone have brought Him food?" "My food," said Jesus, "is to do the will of Him who sent Me and to finish His work. do not you have a saying, 'it is still four months until harvest'? I tell you, open your eyes and look at the fields! They are ripe for harvest. Even now the one who reaps draws a wage and harvests a crop for eternal life, so that the sower and the reaper may be glad together. Thus the saying 'One sows and another reaps' is true. I sent you to reap what you have not worked for. Others have done the hard work, and you have reaped the benefits of their labor." Many of the Samaritans from that town believed in Him because of the woman's testimony, "He told me everything I ever did." So when the Samaritans came to Him, they urged Him to stay with them, and He stayed two days. And because of His words many more became believers. They said to the woman, "We no longer believe just because of what you said; now we have heard for ourselves, and we know that this Man really is the Savior of the world."*

What is it that Jesus is trying to teach us here? What does He want to show us when it comes to the harvest? He wants to show us that how we see the harvest is important. At that time, people looked at the Samaritans as people unworthy to spend time with. The Jews believed Samaritans were not open to receiving anything they came with. But Jesus saw something else. He saw past the rumors, the unbelief, the fear, and all the outward things. Jesus saw the harvest, and He saw the longing they had for God.

Although Jesus' disciples had very little faith that the harvest was ready in Samaria, Jesus had great faith that the harvest was ready. His lesson to His disciples, and to us today, is that we should open our eyes to see that the harvest is big and ready. To say that people in your city, or people in your country, are not open to the Gospel is actually going directly against Jesus' Word. If Jesus came to earth today and went to your city and walked around in His physical body, He would show us something. Yes, right away, He would give us a lesson, just like the lesson He gave His disciples in Samaria. He would rebuke us and show us how wrong we are in our view of the harvest. The truth is, many people today look at their city or country the same way Jesus' disciples looked at the people of Samaria. But the problem at that time was not the people in Samaria. The disciples themselves were the problem, along with their wrong view of the harvest. It is the same today. The problem today is not the harvest. The problem is how we look at the harvest. We do not need to change the harvest because, according to Jesus, the harvest does not need to be changed. We need to change our own view of the harvest. Then our actions will change, and this will change the fruit we see.

Please listen to the words of Jesus and open your eyes to see that the harvest is ready. Do not say that it takes three months for the harvest to be ready because today is the day of salvation (2 Corinthians 2:6). The harvest is not and will never be the problem. The problem is the workers. The problem is us, but we can do something about it.

We will continue looking at this in the next chapter because it is so important. I pray you will take the time to listen to Jesus' words when it comes to the harvest. I pray you will believe them and that it will change you in such a way that it changes your actions toward the people around you, which will also change the fruits you see. Yes, we start with listening, and then we believe, and then our faith makes us act on what we believe. This is what makes us see and experience fruit.

7

Believe That
The Harvest Is Ready

**May God open our eyes
so we can start to see the harvest
the same way Jesus saw it.
This is the key if we want to see people saved.
If people believe there are three months for
the harvest to be ready, we will never see people
come to faith like we see in the Bible.**

When I speak about the harvest and teach that the harvest is plentiful and ready, I have seen all over the world how people's faith has started to grow. Yes, I have seen many people who have discovered this truth of the harvest being plentiful and ready, and I have seen them start to live it out. When you really start to understand that the harvest is ready, as Jesus did, things really start to happen. This is why our enemy Satan tries so hard to get us to believe the harvest is not plentiful and ready. I have heard many testimonies of Christians who have sat in a church building for many years and never seen one soul saved. When these people suddenly have their eyes opened and start to see what the Bible says about the harvest, it becomes a natural thing for them to see people come to faith. It is important to know that our view of the harvest will form how we share the Gospel, which also forms what fruits we are seeing.

Some years ago, my family and I drove from Denmark to Poland. At the meetings there, I told the people what God was doing all over the world and how we were seeing people getting healed on the streets, repenting to God, getting baptized in water, and receiving the Holy Spirit. But, almost everywhere I told these testimonies, I heard the Christians say the same thing. "Oh, it is so amazing what God is doing in those countries, but this is Poland. Poland is so Catholic and religious that you cannot just go out on the streets to pray for sick people and see them get healed. It is very seldom we actually see people getting saved here." Yes, everybody was very excited about what I was telling them, but as excited as they were, everyone came with an excuse saying Poland is different because it is so Catholic or too religious. What I was actually hearing was their unbelief because what the heart is full of is what the mouth speaks. This is what Luke 6:45 says. So, by listening to their words, I saw their unbelief and lack of faith when it came to seeing people being healed, repenting, being baptized in water, and receiving the Holy Spirit.

These people I met in Poland, sadly, were doing what many people around the world are doing today. They were building their faith on their experience. We should always build our faith on what the Word of God says and never on our experience. We can never let our experience decide if the Word of God is true or not. No, the Word of God is true no matter what we believe and no matter what we have experienced so far. If we start believing what the Word is saying, we will also, in the end, see that our experience will match it. This was the problem I was facing in Poland. People were building their faith on their experience. I was hearing their unbelief and experiencing how difficult it was for them to understand that these things could actually happen there in Poland, too.

Yes, most people in Poland really believed that the things my family and I saw in different places were happening because the harvest was ready in those places, but they reasoned, however, that these things did not happen in Poland because the harvest was *not* ready there. We experienced this in every place we visited in Poland. But, one day, something amazing happened. I was at a McDonald's with some young people from the church. I was sitting with these young people, and I asked two of the girls if they wanted to experience God. Of course, they said, "Yes." So I told the girls they needed to do what I told them to do for the next fifteen minutes, and if they did this, they would experience God. They looked at me curiously, but they agreed. I then stood up and said to them, "Come, follow me." We ran outside. There, I stopped people and asked if they were sick. Eventually, I found someone who was sick, so I asked one of the girls from the church to put her hand on this person and pray a short prayer for healing. She did this, and to her big surprise, that person got healed. We continued and found another person who was sick, so the other girl from the church placed her hand on this sick person, and this person was also healed. After fifteen minutes, we went back to the McDonald's. Both girls had just prayed for one person each and both had been healed. These two girls were so excited and told the other young people from the church how God had healed sick people through them. Later that evening, more people went out from the church, and more people got healed and heard the Gospel.

The next day at the church meeting in Poland, a young woman came to me and told me she was one of the people who had gotten healed at McDonald's the day before. She told me she had come to the church that day with four other people from her family. She shared with me that she had been seeking God for a long time because she knew there had to be more to life than what she knew. After this woman got healed outside of McDonald's and heard the Gospel, she had gone home and given everything over to God. She had met God and was now so happy and excited! That day in the church, I took her up in front for everyone to see, and she told her testimony as evidence that the harvest is ready also in Poland. While she was in front of everyone, I placed my hands on her and prayed for her. When I prayed for her, she was baptized with the Holy Spirit and started to speak in tongues in front of everyone. This was really an eye-opener for the whole church because what happened to this woman was something they normally did not see happen to anyone. They started to understand more and more what Jesus was saying about the harvest being plentiful and ready. They started to realize that the harvest was not the problem but that we are the problem. They were the problem. These people at the church in Poland started to understand that when we start to live how Jesus has told us to, we will also see that what He is saying about the harvest is true, no matter where we are.

**If the harvest were the problem, then we would
need to wait for God to fix the harvest.
But, we know it is not the harvest that is
the problem, so what are we waiting for?
It is time to reap the harvest.**

It is time we stop saying that people in our city or country are not open to the Gospel. We should also not say that there is still three months for the harvest to be ready because in saying the harvest is not ready now, we are going against what Jesus says about the harvest. The harvest is ready now. Now is the time to reap.

I know of a missions organization in Norway that also went on a trip to Poland some time ago. The leader of this organization had heard about a city in Poland where a priest had said that in this city, it was impossible to see the Kingdom of God break through. The leader in the church there had people tell him that nothing had ever happened in that city and nothing ever would. There were many rumors among the Christians when it came to this particular city in Poland. We could say that the way the Christians looked at this city in Poland was similar to the way the first disciples looked at Samaria. But, despite what the leader of the missions organization in Norway heard, he did something very interesting.

On the way to Poland, he told the team they were going to a city where people were really open to the Gospel. He said this to the team to help them expect God to do great things in that city. Some people might say this leader was lying to the team because he told them the opposite of what the Christians in Poland were saying. However, he was not just simply focusing on the rumors about that city. Instead, he spoke what was true according to the Word of God. And what happened? The team from Norway believed what the leader had said about the city, and this caused them to arrive in the city with big expectations of what God was going to do there. This caused the team to preach the Gospel in faith while believing and expecting people would respond to it and get saved and healed. Do you know what happened in that city? Yes, the team found that people there were open to the Gospel. They actually experienced what they believed, and many people got healed, and many came to Christ. The team saw so many things that many people in Poland were shocked. They couldn't believe what they had seen with their own eyes. Yes, how could this city, like Samaria, receive the Gospel like that? I hope you are starting to understand how important it is that we have the right view of the harvest. The way we see the harvest influences our actions, which, again, influences the fruit we see.

I have helped people again and again to believe Jesus' words when it comes to the harvest and when it comes to what God wants to do through His followers. This is what I often teach at the kickstart weekends we have all over the world, but I do not only teach about these things with words. I also teach these things in practical ways because I believe the strongest teaching is when people experience it themselves. Jesus was not in Galilee when He was teaching about the harvest in Samaria. No, He took His disciples with Him to Samaria so they could see and believe what He was saying. This is often what we do at the kickstarts. We take people out on the streets after a short teaching and then we show them how things work. We have done this, place after place, country after country, and we have seen many Christians having their eyes opened. When the Christians who come to these kickstarts experience the first person getting healed through them, their faith starts to grow, and they start to develop a passion for seeing more people healed and coming to Christ. When a Christian gets the faith and understanding that the harvest is ready and that people can get saved through them, they will not stop. No, this desire to see people come to Christ becomes a part of their life, which causes them to see people come to faith often.

One of the places I visited in Poland was a very small church. I remember the priest at that church, Michael, did not have any faith when it came to his church or his city. Michael really did not believe anything special could or would happen with him or the church congregation. If I was to judge what came out of his mouth, I would say that he had very little faith. I would say this because most of what he said was negative and full of unbelief. He had been a priest at that church for many years and had not seen one single person come to faith, healed, or baptized with the Holy Spirit. Michael said it was impossible for the people in his church to reach anyone in their city because people in his city were so closed off to God, or they were too religious. But, despite his negative view of what God could do through the people in his church, we had a good talk that afternoon. That same evening, we had a meeting with his church and, to his big surprise, he saw many of the things happen that he thought were impossible. This became an eye-opener for him. He had really needed this eye-opener. At the end of the meeting, I had him pray for a member of his church who was not baptized with the Holy Spirit yet. When he prayed, the Holy Spirit came and the person shouted out in a new tongue. This person, who had just been baptized with the Holy Spirit and received a new tongue, along with Michael, had never, until that moment, seen this happen before.

Yes, this really became a true eye-opener. Since that evening at the church, Michael and his congregation have seen many people saved, healed, and baptized with the Holy Spirit. One year later, I received a message from Michael. In his message he said, "Hi, Torben. I would like to share something with you. This year, eight people in our church have been baptized with the Holy Spirit, and they are all speaking in tongues now. When you came to us, you showed us something very important, and this started something inside of me that has just grown and grown. God is good, and we now expect even more things to happen. God Bless you. —Michael." This was so amazing, and I really hope this is what happens when people read this book. I hope this book will create change, faith, and expectation within you, so that you will start to bear fruit wherever you are.

What actually happened with Michael from Poland? Why did he

start to experience so much? What happened was that he suddenly got the faith that it was possible, and that faith changed his actions and how he did things. Michael started to speak to other people in a new way. In faith, he started to expect things to happen, and he experienced that these things truly did start to happen.

It was not because the harvest around him suddenly changed that day I came to visit. No, the harvest has always been the same. As Jesus says, the harvest has always been ready. It is the workers, in this case Michael, who changed. Michael started to believe Jesus' words, which caused him to start doing things as Jesus said in the Bible. He started to believe God would work through him. Because of this, Michael saw things he had never seen before.

> **Is there an area in your life where you need
> a breakthrough in regards to seeing people repent,
> be healed, or baptized with the Holy Spirit?
> Then do not hold back. Go after it!
> You will experience a breakthrough, and this
> will become a normal life for you.**

I have many examples like the story with Michael. I will also tell a story from Denmark, so you will know this is not just about Poland. This is also about Denmark (where we lived at the time) and any other country because the harvest is truly ready no matter where we are. If you are from a country other than Poland or Denmark, I could also come up with examples from your own country of what God has done there because it is the same all over the world.

Some years ago, I got in contact with a man my age who was living in southern Denmark. He really wanted to see people saved and experience the things we read about in the book of Acts. Some years before, he had gone on a YWAM missions trip to Mexico. In Mexico, he saw a non-Christian come to faith. This was the first time he had ever seen someone come to faith, and it created a longing in him to see the same thing in Denmark where he lived. So, when he came home to Denmark, he started sharing the Gospel with people, but nothing happened. He went out on the streets but did not experience anyone getting healed or coming to Christ. In the end, he came to the conclusion that he had experienced nothing in Denmark because the harvest was different in Denmark than in Mexico. Yes, he believed that Mexico was a country open to the Gospel and Denmark was a country closed to the Gospel. He believed the reason for Denmark not being open to the Gospel was because Denmark was very materialistic.

Some years later, I got in contact with him. He got baptized on his own faith and experienced a deliverance and freedom from sin. Shortly after he was baptized, I took him out on the street and kickstarted him. That day, out on the streets, for the first time ever, he prayed for somebody who got healed through him. This did something inside of him, and he developed the faith that the sick would get healed when he prayed for them. This caused him to start praying for more people, and because of this, many people started getting healed. Yes, every week, he saw people getting healed through his prayers. A short time later, he saw the first person get saved. When he saw this first person get saved in Denmark, something changed inside of him. To make a long story short, it changed something inside of him so much that during the next two years, he and his wife led a total of twenty people to faith who were all from non-Christian backgrounds. These twenty people got saved, baptized in water, and baptized with the Holy Spirit. Was it that the harvest suddenly changed in Denmark, or was there another reason he started to see people getting saved like this? The answer is, actually, that he had his eyes opened. He now saw that the harvest was ready, which changed how he did things, which also changed the results of what he did. Yes, he got the faith that what Jesus says in His Word is true. When we get this faith, it changes everything.

When a Christian is awakened and starts to live the life God has called them to, they will see that the harvest is truly ready, as Jesus says it is, and this is what I call a revival. The problem is not the harvest. No, the problem is the workers, but we can do something about that. Think about what would happen if the whole body of Christ had their eyes opened so they could start living life the way Jesus is calling us to live it. If this happened, the world would be changed in just a few years.

So, believe what Jesus is saying. The harvest in your city is plentiful and ready, waiting for you. We are not talking about it being ready in three months or three years. It is ready today. The harvest is not the problem and will never be the problem. It is time to open your eyes and see this. Take Jesus' words and meditate on them. Pray that God will open your eyes to this truth. When you start believing what Jesus is saying here, you will act on it and end up experiencing it. Then you will also be able to testify together with us and many others that the harvest is truly ready and plentiful, just like Jesus says it is. Wow, what amazing news!

76

8

SEND OUT WORKERS

**Instead of praying to God for a revival,
we should pray for God to send out workers
into the harvest. This is a more biblical prayer
and it is a prayer God will answer.**

After Jesus said that the harvest is great, as we have looked at in the last two chapters, He continued to talk about where the problem lies. As we have seen, the problem is not with the harvest but with the lack of workers.

In Luke 10:2, we read:

He told them, "The harvest is plentiful, but the workers are few. Ask the Lord of the harvest, therefore, to send out workers into his harvest field."

The harvest is plentiful, and the workers are few. But here, Jesus gives a solution to the problem when He continues, *"Ask the Lord of the harvest, therefore, to send out workers into his harvest field."* Yes, the harvest is truly big and ready, but the workers are few; therefore, we need to pray to God for Him to send out more workers into the harvest.

There are several interesting things about what Jesus is saying here in Luke 10:2. The first interesting thing is that the Bible translates one of Jesus' words, "to send." But, the Greek word *ekballo* could also mean "to drive out." This word *ekballo* is the same word used when referring to driving out a demon. One of the first places in the Bible you see this word *ekballo* used is in Matthew 10 where Jesus commands us to drive out demons.

Matthew 10:7-8 states:

As you go, proclaim this message: "The kingdom of heaven has come near." Heal the sick, raise the dead, cleanse those who have leprosy, drive out (ekballo) *demons. Freely you have received; freely give.*

In Matthew 10:7-8, "drive out demons" is the same word *ekballo* that we find in Luke 10:2. What we are praying is that God will "drive out" workers into His harvest. We often need to be driven out before we actually go out into the harvest. It is almost like what we see when a demon is driven out of a person. That demon does not want to go out of the person; therefore there is a battle that takes place. We need to admit this is often how it is for Christians when it comes to going out into the harvest. Yes, it is not always so easy for Christians to go out, and it is not often that Christians want to go out into the harvest. They often think, "Why go out into the harvest when we have it so good? It is so cozy here inside the church!" Therefore, the words "drive out" are actually a better picture of what we need to pray for.

This is not a new problem that the workers do not want to go out into the harvest. We see this same problem also existed in the beginning of the book of Acts, where we read Jesus commanded His apostles and His first disciples to go out into the whole world to spread the Gospel. We read the apostles and first disciples actually stayed in Jerusalem for some time before they were driven out into the harvest, away from Jerusalem, due to the great persecution they received. Jesus had already commanded them to go out into the harvest, but what we see here is that it was actually the persecution that drove Philip out into Samaria where there was a great revival. This was the place where many people thought the harvest was not ready. This was also the place where Jesus, sometime before, had demonstrated that the harvest was in fact big and ready there. Through two thousand years of history, we have seen many times how persecution and other circumstances have been used by God to get the people to go out into the harvest.

Another interesting word to look at here in Luke 10:2 is the word "pray" or "ask." Jesus states, *"The harvest truly is great, but the laborers are few; therefore pray the Lord of the harvest to send out laborers into His harvest."* Here, we see we are commanded to ask/pray, but there is actually a word that explains more what asking and praying is. It is the word "beg." The reason we do not often use the word "beg" is because it sounds negative, and it is not a word we normally use in this setting. But, if we read Luke 10:2 again, using these words, it actually becomes even stronger. It would then say, "Beg the Lord of the harvest to drive out workers into His harvest." These are some really strong words Jesus is using here. Jesus is saying to us today that we should beg, pray, and cry out to God to drive out workers to the harvest. How many of us are actually doing what Jesus is commanding us to do here? I know many people often pray the Lord's Prayer and many even pray it daily. But, why not also pray this prayer that Jesus is saying here in Luke 10:2? Jesus has not only commanded us to pray the Lord's Prayer, but also this prayer.

**Let's pray daily
for God to drive the workers into His harvest.
If we do this, we will see great results, not only
in the harvest, but also in our own lives.**

This prayer we read about in Luke 10:2 is a big part of being a disciple of Jesus. We are all called to pray this prayer, and I do not mean we should pray it in a fast, habitual, or ritualistic way. We need to pray it in a way that shows it really means something to us. We should pray it from our heart, knowing this prayer is something that is also after God's heart. And, because we know this, we can pray in faith and confidence that God hears us, as the Bible says He does.

1 John 5:14-15 states:

This is the confidence we have in approaching God: that if we ask anything according to His will, He hears us. And if we know that He hears us—whatever we ask—we know that we have what we asked of Him.

Some years ago, I heard about a "virus" that was spreading all over the world. This virus was called the "Luke 10:2b" virus. This "virus" started back in 2002 when two young people started to pray out of Luke 10:2. But, in order to remember to pray this prayer, these two young people set their watch to beep every day at 10:02 in the morning and 10:02 in the evening. When the clock would beep, they were reminded of these words in Luke 10:2 so that they would pray to God to send out workers to the harvest. We can see that God has answered their prayers because we now see many people all over the world going out into the harvest, and we see more and more people praying this same prayer.

I have heard many testimonies about how God has answered this prayer and how He is really sending, or "driving," out workers into the harvest. Twenty years ago, when I started to evangelize on the streets in Denmark, it was almost unheard of to evangelize on the streets, and many churches actually looked down on me for doing that. According to many churches, evangelizing on the streets was not something we should do because sinners should have to come to the church if they want to get saved. The churches believed we should not have to go to them. Churches did not always say it directly like that, but it was how the people interpreted it; therefore, it was not popular to go out on the streets and stop people you did not know to ask if you could pray for them. Thankfully, though, the attitude of the churches in Denmark has really started to change in the last four or five years.

Things have actually changed so much that a few years ago, there was a headline on the front page of a Christian newspaper in Denmark about how much things were changing. On December 29th, 2014, on the front page of the paper was written,

"2014 Was The Year Where Believing Christians Really Started To Go Out On The Streets. If This Continues, Then The Church Will Really Be On The Streets In 2015."

Yes, this was the headline of the newspaper! The headline was about a church in Copenhagen that started to go out every week on the streets to pray for people.

The newspaper stated: "Church street is just one of many independent initiatives where normal, believing Christians are going out on the streets and are asking random people if they can pray for them. One of the first people to do this was Torben Søndergaard. Many people have followed in his example, and there are many Christians doing this who are not in personal contact with Torben Søndergaard."

This is really amazing. God has really answered our prayers because we prayed in faith and according to His Word. I also pray many more of you will be infected with this Luke 10:2b virus and also start to pray to God, to drive out more workers into the big and ready harvest.

Something amazing happens when people pray this prayer from Luke 10:2. It actually changes the person who is praying it. Prayer touches us and creates something inside of us. Take the Lord's Prayer, for example, where Jesus says we should pray, "Our Father in heaven, hallowed be Your name ..." Have you ever thought about why we should pray and declare God's name to be hallowed/holy? Would our prayers or lack of saying special words in our prayers change God and His nature from being holy to unholy? No, God is holy no matter what people may think of Him. But when we pray this, we actually remind ourselves that God is holy.

Prayer is also important for us because it transforms *us*. When you start to pray out of Luke 10:2, you will start to experience how this prayer will actually create something within you. After praying this prayer for just a short time, you will understand that it is truly on God's heart to see people saved. We see this in Luke 15:4-7, when Jesus talks about leaving the ninety-nine sheep to find the one sheep that was lost. In John 4, we see the importance of Jesus finding the one lost sheep by looking at the story of the woman at the well. He traveled the whole way to Samaria to find this woman. We also see this again when the Holy Spirit led Philip out into the desert to find the eunuch. God saw the eunuch's desire to find Him, so the Holy Spirit led Philip all the way out into the desert for this one man. God's desire is that everyone comes to repentance and comes to know Him.

This Luke 10:2 prayer will create that same desire in you to see the lost found. After a short time of praying this prayer, you will start to experience that it is not enough just to pray. You will understand you also need to do something to reach the lost. When you start to be desperate to see people saved, you will be willing to use your time, money, and whatever you have, to reach the people around you. This prayer is so important. I really hope you will all start to pray it. Yes, this prayer will not only drive other workers out into the harvest it will also drive you out.

I would like to share a testimony with you about how God answers our prayers, and how He actually uses us to answer other people's prayers. I hope this testimony will help you when it comes to hearing the voice of God.

Some years ago I was out walking in a forest. While I was walking in the forest, I saw forest workers sitting on a bench eating their lunch. I continued walking and praying to God, when I suddenly felt like God said, "Stop! Go there and talk to them about Me." My first thought was that it was just my own thoughts I heard, especially because I did not want to go over and interrupt them. I knew that if I did this, I would feel embarrassed. I knew they would all look at me and wonder why I am interrupting them in the middle of their lunch break. But, the more I thought about it, the more I started to think maybe it really was the voice of God I had heard and not just my own thoughts. So, I came to the conclusion that the only way I could find out if it was my thoughts or God speaking to me was for me to go over and talk to these workers.

When I walked over to them, they all looked at me like, "What is this guy doing here?" I nervously asked them if I could borrow five minutes of their time, and then I started to tell them about how God saved me. After five minutes of talking to them, I thanked them and walked away awkwardly. It all seemed so embarrassing because they were all sitting there looking at me, and none of them said one word.

When I walked away I thought, "Okay, maybe it was just my own thoughts and not God who was speaking to me." One week later something amazing happened that convinced me it really was God who spoke to me that day. Yes, one week later a girl came to me, grabbed my hand, and started to thank me. I was very surprised and asked her what she was thanking me for. She then began to tell me that her brother was once a Christian but had been falling away for some time. She told me the whole family had been praying for God to send someone to talk to him so he would come back to God and that I was an answer to their prayers. When he was working in the forest that day, I had come to him with words that spoke directly to him, and he had now come back to God. She was so thankful for what I had done and how God had sent me to answer her family's prayers.

What can we learn from a story like this? We can learn that God is standing on His Word. Every prayer according to His Word is a prayer we know He hears. This girl and her family had been praying according to the Word of God, for God to send out workers into the harvest, and out to her brother. God did this by sending me. I know this is just one example, but I know there are thousands of testimonies just like this.

> **God does not only want us to pray**
> **to the Lord of the harvest to send out workers,**
> **He also wants to send us out into the harvest and**
> **to use us to answer other people's prayers.**
> **When you hear that still, small voice telling you**
> **to go and talk to somebody, do it.**
> **It could be an answer to another person's prayer.**
> **It could be God sending you to them.**

Out of this story, we can also learn that when God speaks, He does not always speak in a clear way so that we know it is Him speaking. Often, God speaks to us through a little thought or little idea we get. Personally, I have experienced God speaking to me many times, but I have never heard Him speak to me with an audible voice I could actually hear. After I experienced God speaking to me through a small thought like in this story, I started to realize that sometimes those small thoughts are actually God speaking to us, so I started to act on it. In time, it has become easier for me to discern when it is God who is speaking or when it is just my own thoughts.

Do you want to see people saved? Do you want to obey Jesus? Then start to pray according to God's Word. Pray that God will drive out workers to His harvest. I know many who have been praying for a revival for many years, and this is good. But it is a problem if they expect God to do it all in one day, or if they only call people to come to the church building to give their lives to God. I do not see this in the Bible. I do not see this is the way God is going to do it. To pray for a revival as if it is totally up to God to do it is not a biblical prayer. Are you aware that we can pray wrong? If we pray for things that are not biblical, we will not see any results.

James 4:3 talks about this by stating:

When you ask, you do not receive, because you ask with wrong motives, that you may spend what you get on your pleasures.

Matthew 6:7 states:

And when you pray, do not keep on babbling like pagans, for they think they will be heard because of their many words.

In this verse, Jesus is saying that we are not heard by our many words.

Many years ago, I remember I met someone new to the faith who came to me very excited and said, "I got an idea! Who is the one in the world creating all the problems? It is Satan! So I got the idea to bring all the Christians all over the world together to pray for Satan to get saved! And if Satan got saved then we would not have any problems anymore." When I heard this new believer say this, I could not stop smiling. Of course, we know this is not a good idea because this is not a prayer according to the will of God. Satan will never get saved no matter how many people pray for him to repent. So we can agree it would be a waste of time to gather all the Christians all over the world to pray for Satan to get saved.

We need to understand that in this same way, many people will not have their prayers answered because they are not praying things according to the Word of God. We can pray and pray for the whole world to suddenly, in one moment, believe in Jesus, but this is not going to happen because it is not a biblical prayer. Instead of praying many unbiblical prayers, if we start to pray according to the Word of God and pray for God to send out workers into the harvest, He will answer this, and we will see fruit like we have never seen before.

Romans 10:13-16 states:

For, "Everyone who calls on the name of the Lord will be saved." How, then, can they call on the one they have not believed in? And how can they believe in the one of whom they have not heard? And how can they hear without someone preaching to them? And how can anyone preach unless they are sent? As it is written: (in Isaiah 52:7), "How beautiful are the feet of those who bring good news!" But not all the Israelites accepted the good news. For Isaiah (53:1) says, "Lord, who has believed our message?"

So, let us all start to pray/beg for the Lord to drive out workers into His harvest. Let us also pray that the Luke 10:2b virus will spread to all Christians, so that we can see a prayer movement that will make a big impact on the world, and so we can see millions of disciples going out into the harvest. It is actually very simple. It is right here in front of us in God's Word. The harvest is ready, and we need to pray for workers and go out ourselves! If we just start to do these simple things, we will see the revival for which people have been longing for years! Let us start today, and let us share these simple truths with others we know!

I will start here by praying, "God, I pray that those who read this book will be able to receive this simple truth we find in Your Word. I pray they will see that the harvest is truly ready and waiting on them. I pray they will make a decision to seek You and that they will pray You will send more workers out to the harvest. I also pray You will send them. Put a longing in their hearts to go out to the harvest. Send them out to the lost people out there. God, send them out into the harvest like never before. God, we ask You, in Jesus' name, to send workers out into Your harvest. In Jesus' name, we pray. AMEN."

9

AS LAMBS AMONG WOLVES

When we walk out on Jesus' Word, we know that He is with us. This is a promise He has given to us, and we know we can count on this promise even when we feel scared or insecure.

We have now seen that the harvest is not the problem. It is actually ready and waiting on us. We now know we need to pray to God to send more workers and that we ourselves need to go. We need to take a step of faith, knowing that the harvest is ready. In this chapter, we are going to look at the next words Jesus said. These words, for many, can seem very scary and intimidating, but it is not as bad as it looks. Let's look at what Jesus is saying and what He promises when it comes to taking this first step.

After Jesus says that the harvest is ready and the workers are few and that we should pray the Lord of the harvest to send out workers, He says in Luke 10:3:

Go your ways: behold, I send you forth as lambs among wolves. (KJV)

We will start by looking at these first three simple words, *"Go your ways."* These words tell us we need to go. Yes, we need to go out into the harvest because the harvest will not come to us. It is our job to go out into the harvest. For example, try to imagine a man who is a farmer. Now imagine this farmer looking out over his harvest. He sees the harvest is great and ripe. It is time to collect the harvest, but instead of going out into the harvest to start collecting it, the farmer, instead, stands at the barn door and starts shouting to the fields for the harvest to come in. Imagine the farmer standing there in front of his barn doors shouting, "Come in, harvest, come in! The barn is ready!"

If you saw a farmer standing in front of his barn doors shouting at his harvest to come in, you would think he was crazy. You would think there was something very wrong with him because we know it is not possible to collect the harvest by standing and shouting at it to come in. Imagine the farmer did this for some time and saw nothing was happening. He saw the harvest was not coming into the barn, so he started shouting even louder, and still nothing happened. The harvest did not move. The farmer then started to question if there was something wrong with the harvest, since it was not listening to him and was not coming into the barn. Yes, he started to think the harvest was not yet ripe, since it was not coming in. Then he started to think the harvest was not coming into the barn because the barn was dark and dirty. So right away he started to clean up the barn and put in a nice carpet and warm lights so the barn would be clean and cozy. After the farmer was finished, he stood in front of the barn doors and shouted at the harvest to come into the barn. The farmer shouted, "Come in, harvest! Come in! The barn is now clean and cozy! You can come in now! I even put up warm lights! Come into the barn!"

But to the farmer's big surprise, the harvest still did not move. Again, he questioned what was wrong with the harvest because it was not coming into the barn. So the farmer then decided to play nice, soft music, thinking the right atmosphere would bring in the harvest. He set up some speakers to play, and again he stood in front of the barn door and shouted at the harvest to come in. But, still, the harvest did not come into the barn. The farmer became really disappointed and again questioned what was wrong with the harvest. He believed the harvest was ready, but he saw that the harvest was not moving, so he became angry. He became so angry that he started to curse the harvest. He shouted how bad the harvest was and how the harvest was not ready since it was not coming into the barn. The farmer shouted that this was the worst harvest he has ever seen and that the harvest would not come in, no matter what he did. The farmer started to curse the harvest with everything in him, but still nothing happened.

Of course, this situation would never happen in real life. We will never see a farmer behaving like this because no farmer thinks like this. If he did, he would not survive very long as a farmer. We know this does not happen in real life because every farmer or every person knows the harvest is not created to walk into the barn by itself. The harvest is exactly where it is supposed to be and will never move from there on its own. It is the farmer's job to go out, collect it, and bring it into the barn.

> **Few people start going to church on their own.**
> **We must go out where they are and bring them in.**
> **When we do this, we will experience that the**
> **harvest is great, and it is ripe, as Jesus said.**

Are we not doing exactly what that farmer did in our churches? We use a lot of time, money, and resources to make our churches (barns) look nice and cozy with beautiful carpets and lights. We even play music to set the right atmosphere. We do all of this with the belief that if the church is nice and cozy and the sermon is just right, then people will start to come into the church by themselves and get saved.

Some years ago, my friend called many churches in Denmark in order to research how many people were baptized in the last year in those churches and what the churches were doing to evangelize. It did not come as a big surprise when his research showed that there was a big connection between how much a church evangelized and how many new believers came into that church.

Some time ago, I met a person whom I respect very much.

His name is Brother Yun, also known as "The Heavenly Man." This man was one of the key people who were part of a great revival in China, which saw ten thousand house churches start between the years of 1980 to 1990. I love this man's books and testimony because it is so close to the life we read about in the book of Acts. His testimony, like the disciples' lives in the book of Acts, was not only a supernatural life with miracles, but also a life with persecution where people need to give up everything to follow Christ. When I read his book, *The Heavenly Man*, I experienced God speaking to me and telling me that I would meet Brother Yun face to face one day and have the opportunity to tell him what a big blessing he has been in my life. Shortly after God spoke to me about this, I met him. God opened the door. "The Heavenly Man" came to Denmark, and I had the opportunity to sit down and eat breakfast with him. We sat together with some priests and leaders in our city. As we were all sitting there, I asked Brother Yun and his translator what the difference was between the Christians in China and the Christians in the Western part of the world. They answered right away, "There are two things that are very different. The first is that the Christians in China are all evangelists and cannot stop telling people about God and about the things they have seen and experienced. The second thing is that in China, the Christians are not afraid to pay a high price to follow Jesus." They told me that 80% of the church in China are true disciples who are ready to pay a high price to follow Jesus, and only 2% of the church in the Western world are true disciples of Jesus who are willing to pay this high price.

Wow, what a strong answer. Yes, I can truly see these are two main reasons why the Christians in China experience all they do and see revival, and why the Christians in the Western world experience as little as they do and do not see revival. How often we deceive ourselves by thinking the reason people in China experience God in such a strong way is because the harvest is ripe and plentiful there and that God is doing something amazing there, unlike what we see in the West. We think they are seeing so much more there simply because of God and because the harvest is ready compared to the Western World.

The truth is that the Christians in China experience God doing what He does in such a strong way because they are actually evangelizing, sharing the Gospel with people in their everyday lives. These people in China cannot stop telling people about Jesus, and they are not afraid to pay a high price to follow Him. They go out on Jesus' words, and they experience a great harvest. Yes, they experience people coming to faith in a way we in the West do not because they are living differently than we do. The truth is that if we in the Western world would not be afraid to go out on Jesus' words and pay a high price to follow Him, we would experience the same things they do. I am also convinced that if the Christians in China would live like most of the Christians in the West, they would experience the same things the Christians here in the West do, which is not very much. And if the Christians in the West lived like the Christians in China live, I am convinced that we in the West would also experience the same as the people do in China, which are many amazing things.

If we in the West wake up and start to live like we should, we would also see many people coming to faith, and we would see a movement arise that would change our countries.

The difference between the "Christians" in the West and the "Christians" in China is not a result of the harvest or that God just wants to do something special there and not here. No! God wants people to come to faith in Him the same everywhere! But, the reason they see what they do, and we do not, has to do with how we as Christians are living, and nothing else. Again, we find the problem and the solution are with us, not with the harvest out there. We need to start living the life Jesus has commanded us to live and stop living this comfortable life in our nice churches while we wait for the harvest to come to us by itself. I know this is provoking, but this is the truth. We need the truth if we want to see a change. It is time to wake up and start obeying Jesus and really live for Him! Let's stop deceiving ourselves like we have done for so many years by giving the harvest the blame for everything.

Let's continue and see what Jesus is actually saying to us in Luke 10. Jesus says, *"Go your ways;"* but then continues with, *"behold, I send you forth as lambs among wolves"* (Luke 10:3 KJV). I believe many people have read this text without thinking about what Jesus is actually saying here. Jesus is the Good Shepherd, and He is saying something in Luke 10:3 that would get every shepherd fired right away. The shepherd's job is to keep the sheep safe and away from the wolves. But here in Luke 10:3, Jesus is doing the opposite. Instead of keeping the lambs as far away from the wolves as possible, Jesus takes the lamb and sends it out directly to the wolves.

How responsible is that, if you really think about it? Try to imagine Jesus, the Good Shepherd, standing there holding a little lamb in His arms. Maybe you have seen a picture like this before, with Jesus standing with a sweet little lamb in His arms. Now imagine Jesus petting the little lamb. The lamb is cozy and happy. All of a sudden, Jesus sees the wolf. The wolves are standing out in the field, smelling the lamb's tasty scent in the air. The wolves start to drool when they see the little lamb, as they are starving for fresh meat. Then Jesus does the unthinkable. He takes this sweet little innocent lamb, sets it down on the grass, and asks the lamb if it can see the hungry wolves waiting in the field. Then Jesus gives the lamb a push from behind and says, "Go, little lamb! Go! Out with you! I am sending you out as lambs among wolves!" Wow! Why would Jesus do that? What good shepherd in his right mind would take a sweet little innocent lamb and send it out to a pack of hungry wolves?

Try to take some time to really think about what is happening here. What self-defense does a lamb have against a wolf? Lambs are not fast, and they do not camouflage well, as their soft, white wool against the green grass makes them easy to spot. Lambs do not have a big growl to scare off other animals. Their little "baa" would not scare away any animal. A lamb is actually one of the most defenseless animals.

There is really not much about a lamb that would help it survive in the wild. This may be why Jesus uses the picture of a lamb with its shepherd because the only thing that would keep this lamb alive is its shepherd. Lambs are not dangerous or fast, and they are not able to camouflage, climb trees, or dig holes in which to hide. But, lambs do have something other animals do not have, and that is a shepherd to watch over them. Without a shepherd, a lamb would not survive for long in the wild. Since lambs are clearly such helpless animals, why would Jesus send us out as lambs among wolves? Well, there is a simple answer to this question. Jesus does *not* send out the lambs among the wolves while standing back to watch. No, He sends out the lambs, and He actually goes with them. This is an important aspect of being sent that we need to understand. Jesus does not send us out while He stands back to watch. No, He sends us out, and He goes with us.

In Matthew 28:19-20, we read:

Therefore go and make disciples of all nations, baptizing them in the name of the Father and of the Son and of the Holy Spirit, and teaching them to obey everything I have commanded you ...

But Jesus did not stop there. He continued by saying:

And surely I am with you always, to the very end of the age.

In Mark 16:20, we read:

Then the disciples went out and preached everywhere, and the Lord worked with them and confirmed his word by the signs that accompanied it.

Wow, what we read here is amazing! Do you long to see more of Jesus in your life? Then do not hold back. Go out on Jesus' words. If you do this, you will experience that Jesus is with you like you have never experienced before. When we go out, Jesus is truly by our side. We should not be afraid of the wolves out there. Yes, they can seem scary. They can cause us to fear and make us think, "I can't do this. I can't go up to this person. I can't talk with them. No, I can't step out like this. If I do it, what will happen?" We come up with so many excuses why we can not take the steps we need to take.

There is also a good reason Jesus warns us about the "wolves," or enemies and demons, out there who will try to cause us to fear. They are there to scare us, and they are doing a good job. But, if we do not go out, we will not see that Jesus is with us. If we do go, we will see that He is there. We do not see these "wolves" as physical wolves that want to eat us, but we do view the devil and many people who are against the Gospel as scary and dangerous. It is important to know that opposition and resistance to the Gospel are all part of serving God.

These things are part of being a disciple of Christ.

In Matthew 10, when Jesus sends out His twelve disciples, He actually says more about what it means when He sends us out as lambs. This is shown when, in Matthew 10:16, He states, *"I am sending you out like sheep among wolves. Therefore be as shrewd as snakes and as innocent as doves."* Jesus then continues, in Matthew 10:17-39:

> *Be on your guard; you will be handed over to the local councils and be flogged in the synagogues. On My account you will be brought before governors and kings as witnesses to them and to the Gentiles. But when they arrest you, do not worry about what to say or how to say it. At that time you will be given what to say, for it will not be you speaking, but the Spirit of your Father speaking through you.*

> *Brother will betray brother to death, and a father his child; children will rebel against their parents and have them put to death. You will be hated by everyone because of Me, but the one who stands firm to the end will be saved. When you are persecuted in one place, flee to another. Truly I tell you, you will not finish going through the towns of Israel before the Son of Man comes.*

> *The student is not above the teacher, nor a servant above his master. It is enough for students to be like their teachers, and servants like their masters. If the head of the house has been called Beelzebul, how much more the members of his household!*

> *So do not be afraid of them, for there is nothing concealed that will not be disclosed, or hidden that will not be made known. What I tell you in the dark, speak in the daylight; what is whispered in your ear, proclaim from the roofs. Do not be afraid of those who kill the body but cannot kill the soul. Rather, be afraid of the One who can destroy both soul and body in hell. Are not two sparrows sold for a penny? Yet not one of them will fall to the ground outside your Father's care. And even the very hairs of your head are all numbered. So do not be afraid; you are worth more than many sparrows.*

> *Whoever acknowledges Me before others, I will also acknowledge before My Father in heaven. But whoever disowns Me before others, I will disown before My Father in heaven.*

Do not suppose that I have come to bring peace to the earth. I did not come to bring peace, but a sword. For I have come to turn a man against his father, a daughter against her mother, a daughter-in-law against her mother-in-law—a man's enemies will be the members of his own household.

Anyone who loves their father or mother more than Me is not worthy of Me; anyone who loves their son or daughter more than Me is not worthy of Me. Whoever does not take up their cross and follow Me is not worthy of Me. Whoever finds their life will lose it, and whoever loses their life for My sake will find it.

These verses show us what is waiting for us out there. Yes, you can be a Christian and sit comfortably in the church your whole life and never experience anything like we have just read in Matthew 10:17-39. But, I guarantee you, as soon as you become a true disciple of Christ and start to go out into the harvest and start obeying Jesus' words, you will experience those things mentioned. Maybe you will not experience them exactly the way Jesus describes here, but you will experience situations that will look very similar.

I know many people who have been sitting in church for many years who have not experienced persecution. As soon as they start to go out on Jesus' words, they experience that Jesus is with them. They start to see fruit in their lives. But, together with this amazing new fruit, they also start to experience persecution. Persecution comes as a surprise to many people because it comes from unexpected sources. People think persecution only happens in third-world countries or Muslim countries, but I guarantee you that persecution is everywhere. Maybe we will not experience persecution exactly like we read here in the book of Matthew, where people were being flogged in the synagogue, but maybe this persecution will come from the religious churches. And maybe we will not experience physical persecution where people beat or kill us like we read in the book of Matthew, but people might persecute us with their words.

We might see people starting to hate us or spreading false rumors about us. They might also include our friends and our family. But, we need to understand that even if our friends and family start to hate us, God is still in control of everything, and we have nothing to fear. So, do not be afraid to step out on the Word of God. Do not be afraid to go out as lambs among wolves because you will see that Jesus is truly with you. Yes, you will experience persecution, but you will also see that God is in control. You will experience that Jesus is truly alive. Your life will become an exciting and supernatural life like we read about in the book of Acts. But, you will never experience this life if you are not willing to take the first step out there as lambs among wolves. God is with you, and He will bless you even through the persecution.

Mark 10:29-30 states:

> *"Truly I tell you," Jesus replied, "no one who has left home or brothers or sisters or mother or father or children or fields for me and the gospel will fail to receive a hundred times as much in this present age: homes, brothers, sisters, mothers, children and fields—along with persecutions—and in the age to come eternal life."*

So, do not be afraid! Take the first step, and you will see that Jesus is with you! Jesus' Word to you and me is, "Go!" We should go out as lambs among wolves. He did not say, "Stay here because there are wolves out there." No, He said, "Go!" Yes, there are wolves out there, and they will never disappear. They are there to put fear in you, and that is just how it is. Remember this the next time you are going to take a step and go to someone or open your mouth to speak about Jesus with people you know or do not know.

You might feel the fear is coming. You might feel like a little lamb and just want to say, "Baa," while your legs are shaking like a little newborn lamb trying to take its first small steps. But then remember Jesus' words, and instead of saying, "Baa," say, "AMEN," knowing that Jesus is going with you! Then, boldly take that first step in faith!

I do not know what your wolves are that are trying to stop you from obeying Jesus, but I do know that if you "Go," you will see that Jesus is with you as He promised. Go, and keep going, and it will become easier for you each time. Open your mouth and keep doing that. Tell people about Jesus, and He is with you! Jesus never promised us that it would be easy, and He has not promised us that He will remove the wolves.

He has promised us that He is with us when we go and that everyone who confesses Him in front of people, He will confess in front of His Father Who is in Heaven.

> *Do not be afraid of those who kill the body but cannot kill the soul. Rather, be afraid of the One who can destroy both soul and body in hell. Are not two sparrows sold for a penny? Yet not one of them will fall to the ground outside your Father's care. And even the very hairs of your head are all numbered. So do not be afraid; you are worth more than many sparrows. Whoever acknowledges Me before others, I will also acknowledge before My Father in heaven. But whoever disowns Me before others, I will disown before My Father in heaven.*
> (Matthew 10:28-30)

10

CARRY NO MONEY

**If we are ever going to see a breakthrough
in the Western world, we need to destroy
the biggest god—Mammon—the god of money.
We need to stop being dependent on money
and riches and learn, instead, to be dependent
on God and His Holy Spirit.**

The next thing Jesus says in Luke 10 is very important for us to understand, especially those of us who are living in the materialistic Western world where Mammon (money) is the biggest god of them all.

We read in Luke 10:4:

Do not take a purse or bag or sandals; and do not greet anyone on the road.

As I have said before, when Jesus sent His disciples out into the harvest, He gave them very specific instructions about what they should do, and in this case also, about what they should not take with them. He even said they should not greet anyone on the road, something we will look at more in the next chapter.

Almost everything in our lives today and in our churches in the Western world is centered around money. We are controlled by what we have and what we lack. It is also money that, for many, is the main factor when it comes to missions, church life, etc. If the money is there, we will do it, and if it is not, then we do not. But, in the Kingdom of God, money is not the problem, and money should never control what we can or cannot do. It is really important for us to learn to be dependent on God instead of on our money or lack of money. We often think we would really see a breakthrough if we had a lot of money and that then we could do many things for God, as if our growth or our obedience stands or falls with money. We think that if we have money, we can do many things for God, but if we do not have money, there is not much we can do. This is *not* how it should be. We should not be dependent or controlled by money and what we have. Instead, we need to understand that God has all the silver and gold in this world. Everything belongs to Him, and with Him, we lack nothing. What is clear in the Bible is that the lack of money is not the problem. The lack of workers is the problem.

Jesus told us many times that we are not of this world and that we should not seek the things of this world like the heathens do. Instead, we who are born again and who are disciples of Christ should seek the Kingdom of God and do His will first. We will see that the rest will indeed be added to us when we seek the Kingdom of God and do His will first.

We all need to decide who we want to serve because we cannot serve both God and Mammon. The one we serve, the one we depend on, is the one who controls us. No, money in itself is not evil. It is the love of money, as Paul said, that is the root of all evil (1 Timothy 6:10). We should never be controlled by money, and as Jesus says very clearly, we cannot serve both God and Mammon.

Matthew 6:24 states:

No one can serve two masters. Either you will hate the one and love the other, or you will be devoted to the one and despise the other. You cannot serve both God and money.

After Jesus says this, He continues with Matthew 6:25-32:

Therefore I tell you, do not worry about your life, what you will eat or drink; or about your body, what you will wear. Is not life more than food, and the body more than clothes? Look at the birds of the air; they do not sow or reap or store away in barns, and yet your heavenly Father feeds them. Are you not much more valuable than they? Can any one of you by worrying add a single hour to your life? And why do you worry about clothes? See how the flowers of the field grow. They do not labor or spin. Yet I tell you that not even Solomon in all his splendor was dressed like one of these. If that is how God clothes the grass of the field, which is here today and tomorrow is thrown into the fire, will He not much more clothe you—you of little faith? So do not worry, saying, "What shall we eat?" or "What shall we drink?" or "What shall we wear?" For the pagans run after all these things, and your heavenly Father knows that you need them.

Although the heathens are seeking after all this, we should not be seeking after these things. It should be very different for us, as we should not be living like the people of this world. We should not be controlled by fear or the worries of this world. We should not be controlled by Mammon, the god of this world. No, our focus should be on doing God's will and serving Him. We should be listening and doing what He says without first seeing if we have enough money to do it. If it is truly God who has spoken, He will also take care of everything and give us what we need.

Matthew 6:33 states:

But seek first His kingdom and His righteousness, and all these things will be given to you as well.

If we look a little closer at the people living in the Western world and everything they have, then compare it to the people living in the third world who do not have the same money, the same buildings, and the same resources, it becomes clear that growth can easily happen without relying on money. A good economy does not necessarily mean there will be a breakthrough in the Kingdom of God. Actually, a good economy can sometimes hurt the possibility of having a breakthrough in the Kingdom of God because when we have money, we can easily become dependent on our money instead of being dependent on God. We can even become distracted from doing His will. With money it is also easy to do many things God is not in. We do these things because we have the money, instead of seeking Him and only doing what He is calling us to do.

The truth is, in many other countries where they have almost nothing, they learn in a very different way to trust God as their Provider and to really discern between the will of God and their own desires. On the other hand, in the Western world, we can do so much without God because we have all the resources to do what we want, and we do not need to be concerned about what God wants us to do. I once heard a quote saying that if God removed His Holy Spirit from the earth, 90% of all activities in the churches would continue like nothing happened. This is a scary thought, but I truly believe it is not completely wrong.

Do you really want to see true growth and see the Spirit of God work like in the book of Acts? Then we really need to learn to be dependent on God and not on what we have or do not have. We need to learn to listen and only do what God wants us to do. Again, this is often much easier when we do not have the money, and therefore are truly dependent on Him to come through. If this is from God, then He will provide. If not … Yes, if not, then we cannot do it, and we then find out what God is saying to us.

The truth is, although some people spend a lot of money, time, and energy organizing big conferences in order to see the Spirit of God work and change people's lives, God does not need these big conferences to change people's lives. Of course, God can change people's lives in big conferences, but big conferences, nice churches, and all of our money in itself will not change one person's life if God is not working with His Spirit.

We cannot buy real growth in the Kingdom of God. This only comes by seeking God and doing His will. Money can gather people, but only the Holy Spirit can lead to true repentance. Not only should we trust God when it comes to our finances, but we should also trust God when it comes to our ministry and our everyday life, like we read in the Bible. We need to live a life that is close to God, and where God is part of our decisions. This life of dependency on God is for everyone, not only for the people living in third-world countries. It is often very difficult for people in the Western World to come into that place where they really learn to trust God in everything. We often think we are so rich because of our fine cars and our big houses, but actually, we in the West are the ones who are truly poor. We are poor in spirit, and this is one of the reasons we do not see the Kingdom of God grow in the West like we see in the third-world.

In third-world countries, because of their poverty, they needed to learn to trust God. This has caused their faith to become so much stronger. This is often the reason they see breakthroughs there that we do not see here in the West. Our "riches" in the West have caused many of us to become distracted, so we do not have time to work for God in the harvest because we need to work a lot to pay the bank. Let's be honest, we need to pay the bank for our house, car, and other things because most of what we have is not actually ours. Most of what we have belongs to the bank, and we need to pay what we owe to the bank, so we need to work a lot, which means we do not have much time to do what is really important in life. The truth is, we do not feel more happy by owning more things. It is actually often the opposite. The more you have, the more likely you are to worry about it. "What if something happens to it?" or "How am I going to pay off what I have?" It is very easy to become a slave to what you have.

If we are going to see a breakthrough in the Western World, we really need to stop living like the heathens do. We need to stop following Mammon. We cannot serve Mammon. As I said earlier, Mammon has destroyed our faith and our trust that God will provide for our needs. Mammon has also stolen our focus and our time away from God, so that we really do not have time to do what is important. I often talk about this when I am out doing a kickstart weekend. I sometimes say that the harvest is great, but the workers just do not have time because they need to work so much to pay the bank for everything they think they need to have. When I say that many today do not have time to serve God, that is actually not the whole truth.

The problem is not that people do not have time because we all have

Let's just say it like it really is. The harvest is great, but the workers have chosen to prioritize their houses, gardens, and fancy cars instead of prioritizing the Kingdom of God.

the same amount of time. We all have twenty-four hours per day. The difference is in how people prioritize their time. Some people prioritize their time in order to get all the material things they want in life. They prioritize their time to get a big house and a fancy car. These people need to work a lot to maintain their lifestyle of riches, and they end up prioritizing their job. Those who live a more simple life spend their time seeking God and doing His will, no matter what the price is.

Of course, you can serve God while owning a house, a car, and other things. I also know some people come from families with more money, and some people have more education with a higher-paying job; therefore, they can do some things other people cannot do because of their money. I also know that people who do not have much money can sometimes be controlled by money more than the people who have a lot of money.

I know I cannot make a generalization about everyone, but I am saying this to try and help you understand that Mammon has often won over people's faith, focus, and time. If we take the time to read what Jesus says about how Mammon is destroying the Kingdom of God, we can see that He is speaking really radically here. Jesus actually talked more about money than any other subject, and we see many examples in the Bible of how Mammon destroyed people's lives.

One of the first examples we see of this is Judas, one of the twelve disciples. Judas was really close to Jesus. He walked with Jesus and saw many amazing things through Jesus' hands. He was even one of those who had been sent out in Luke 9, but he was still deceived. He was blinded by the love of money, so he made the decision to betray Jesus with a kiss (Luke 22:48). It is crazy to know that he betrayed Jesus for something as pitiful as money.

Judas is not the only one who went wrong when it came to the love of money, but let us look at what happened with him. In Matthew 26:14-16, we read:

> Then one of the Twelve—the one called Judas Iscariot—went to the chief priests and asked, "What are you willing to give me if I deliver him over to you?" So they counted out for him thirty pieces of silver. From then on Judas watched for an opportunity to hand him over.

Luke 22:47-48 states:

> While he was still speaking a crowd came up, and the man who was called Judas, one of the Twelve, was leading them. He approached Jesus to kiss him, but Jesus asked him, "Judas, are you betraying the Son of Man with a kiss?"

As I said, Judas was not the only one who got deceived here. I also want to take some time to discuss the rich, young ruler in Matthew 19. The rich, young ruler was a young man who came to Jesus really wanting to follow Him. He wanted to inherit eternal life, so he asked Jesus what he should do. Although the rich, young ruler wanted eternal life, he did not want it enough to give up his riches, and he ended up walking away from Jesus feeling sad. There are many others in the world like this rich, young ruler, who also, because of their love of money, walk away from the calling God has for their lives.

So we see that the rich, young ruler gave a different response to Jesus' call than Matthew, the tax collector. Matthew was sitting at the tax booth when Jesus told him to leave everything and follow Him. Unlike the rich, young ruler, Matthew was willing to leave everything, and this is exactly what he did. Matthew lived an amazing life with Jesus and received eternal life. The rich young ruler acts as a picture of those of us today who live in the world of Mammon. We all have the same calling to follow Jesus as Matthew and the rich young ruler had, but like the rich young ruler, we often say no because the price is too high. The consequence is often much too high for us because instead of putting our faith in God, we have put our faith in our money and our security. Now, let us read the text about the rich young ruler.

Matthew 19:16-24 states:

Just then a man came up to Jesus and asked, "Teacher, what good thing must I do to get eternal life?" "Why do you ask Me about what is good?" Jesus replied. "There is only One who is good. If you want to enter life, keep the commandments." "Which ones?" he inquired. Jesus replied, "'You shall not murder, you shall not commit adultery, you shall not steal, you shall not give false testimony, honor your father and mother,' and 'love your neighbor as yourself.'" "All these I have kept," the young man said. "What do I still lack?" Jesus answered, "If you want to be perfect, go, sell your possessions and give to the poor, and you will have treasure in heaven. Then come, follow Me." When the young man heard this, he went away sad, because he had great wealth. Then Jesus said to His disciples, "Truly I tell you, it is hard for someone who is rich to enter the kingdom of heaven. Again I tell you, it is easier for a camel to go through the eye of a needle than for someone who is rich to enter the kingdom of God."

Just as we have read in Mark 4 about the four grounds, it is the deceitfulness of riches, worries, and other things that choke the Word and cause most people not to bear fruit. When Jesus called His disciples to follow Him, He was asking them to put their faith and security in Him instead of putting their faith and security in their money or in anything they had to do with. Jesus actually asked many people to leave everything behind in order for them to be able to follow Him. Jesus wanted them to be dependent on God as their Provider, and this is the same for us today. Jesus wants us to have God as our Provider and to seek His kingdom and do His will.

God really wants to teach all of us to be dependent on Him. This is why, in Luke 10:4, He says, *"Do not take a purse or bag or sandals ..."* When Jesus sent out His disciples, He did it in this way because He wanted them to learn to trust God as their Provider. Jesus wanted them to learn to put their faith in God for their daily needs. They needed to learn to seek the Kingdom of God first and do His will in order to see that God would take care of them. This is why Jesus sent His disciples out with the instructions not to take anything with them.

Jesus said something very important that He wanted them to understand as well. Here, in Luke 22:35-37, He states:

Then Jesus asked them, "When I sent you without purse, bag or sandals, did you lack anything?" "Nothing," they answered. He said to them, "But now if you have a purse, take it, and also a bag; and if you do not have a sword, sell your cloak and buy one. It is written: 'And he was numbered with the transgressors;' and I tell you that this must be fulfilled in Me. Yes, what is written about Me is reaching its fulfillment."

What Jesus says in Luke 22:35-37 is very interesting. It is important to understand these verses because it shows how Jesus was thinking and discipling people. What Jesus spoke in these verses shows He does not mean it should be like this for the rest of the disciples' lives, or that they are never again allowed to do anything themselves to provide for what they need, or that they are never, ever again allowed to take anything with them like we read in Luke 10. We see later in Acts that some of the apostles had times where they were working with their hands, and by this they were providing for their own needs and also the needs of others around them.

At the time when Jesus spoke these things we read in Luke 10, He did not want His disciples to take something with them, because He wanted to teach them something. Later in life though, after His disciples learned what Jesus wanted them to learn, it was okay for His disciples to take something with them. This is what many people do not understand. Jesus is not against us owning things, as long as we are not dependent on what we own. But, when Jesus sent His disciples out for the first time, He wanted them to learn to be dependent on God and not on the things they owned. He wanted them to learn something we all need to learn, and that is to trust God.

When God wants us to learn to trust Him, He needs to remove the things from our lives that will keep us from putting our faith in Him. It is difficult to learn to trust that God will provide us with money if we have extra money stored up somewhere. We cannot pray, "God, I really need your help, and if you do not come now and help me, then I need to use the money I have been storing up." We do not need to see how God can intervene and help us if we have extra money stored up in our pockets. We need to first learn to trust God and grow in faith when our money is gone, or when we are in a position where it is no longer fun. This is where we really see how God intervenes and where we hear testimony after testimony of how God provides. It is out there where we really learn to be dependent on God.

As I said before, it is often very difficult to reach that place in our Western world because we have so many different options around us. We often choose the fastest and easiest solution instead of waiting to see what God has in store for us. Because of this, God often needs to let us go through hard times and desert periods, so we can learn to trust Him and Him alone. This is something my family and I needed to learn some years ago. It was in this desert period where we learned to trust God and seek His kingdom first. We also needed to learn to live a simple life and to be happy with what God gave us. We had to learn to be happy when God gave us a lot or when God gave us a little. I clearly remember how that desert period my family and I went through some years ago helped us to grow. During that time, we saw one miracle after another. During that desert period, we learned not to worry about food, clothes, or where we would get money because God led us and provided us with what we needed.

Looking back at this desert period, I can honestly say that it was not always easy. In the beginning it was very hard. We asked ourselves, "Will God come? What if He does not come? Will He take care of us? What if the money does not come in time?" It was often much easier to just give up and get a normal job where we could take money out of the bank and live how most people lived. But, today, we thank God that He controlled the circumstances in our lives, to put us in a place where I could not get a job. We were, therefore, totally dependent on God. He put us in a situation where He closed all the doors and made it so that He was the only thing we had left. I now see that God is doing this with many people today.

I can give many examples of how God provided for us during the desert period. I remember one day how God spoke to me and my family about going to a Bible camp in another city. We packed all of our suitcases and were ready to go. There was only one problem preventing us from going to the Bible camp. We had no money to go. We did not have money to travel there or to stay at the campsite or even money for food. But, as always, God is faithful, and Jesus said we should not worry. The day before we were supposed to go, I got a phone call from a Christian woman in another city. She called me and asked how I was doing. When I told her things were good, she asked how I was doing again. I told her I was doing good and that God was in control. Then I asked her if she was going to the Bible camp, to which she said, "Yes." I told her my family and I were going also, and maybe we could meet her there and talk with her a little more. We said goodbye and hung up the phone.

About ten minutes later she called me again and asked again how I was doing. I told her once again that I was doing good, but she continued saying she felt like something was wrong. She asked me if there was anything she could do for me or if anything was wrong. To these questions she asked, I continued answering, "God is faithful. God is in control." She continued to ask how I was doing and if there was anything I needed. Before we said goodbye and hung up again, she asked if I had money. She heard I was hesitating a little, so she asked if I had money to go to the Bible camp. Again, I said, "God is in control." All of a sudden she shouted, "Hallelujah, I knew there was something!" Then she told me she would like to pay for our trip down to the Bible camp and also for our stay at the campsite. She even said she would like to give us one thousand Danish Krones (150 dollars) for food. When we hung up the phone, I told my wife Lene that everything was in order and that we were ready to go.

It is really amazing to see how God takes care of us when we seek His kingdom first. I remember a conversation I had with some friends when I arrived at the Bible camp. One of our friends told me they felt so sorry for us because we were often struggling with money and we did not have many things. When our friend said this I felt something rise up inside of me, and I said, "No, do not feel sorry for us because if we would have had the money to go to the Bible camp and pay like everyone else, we would not have this testimony to share with you. But, now we have one more testimony about how we can trust God and how we have learned something new."

If you do not live a life where you are really dependent on God, you will not have all those amazing testimonies of how God provides for you time after time. We have more now than we did at that time, but what we learned then was to be dependent on God and to let go. This was an important lesson we needed to learn. Today, we are still dependent on God even though we have more. No matter if we have more or less, we all need to be dependent on God. If you want to experience God providing for you in amazing ways, you need to live a life where you are really dependent on God. There was a reason for Jesus to send His disciples out without anything. He wanted them to learn to trust God and not to rely on what they brought with them. The disciples obeyed Jesus and went out without taking anything for their journey. And, as we know, God took care of them. This is exactly what we ask the students to do in the Pioneer Training School we have. We send them out without a place to stay and without money in their pockets. Oftentimes, when the students come back from their journey, they are very excited and have so many testimonies to share about how God provided food and a place for them to stay. I will share more about this later.

> **If you want to have testimonies about
> how God takes care of your needs, you need
> to live in a place where you are dependent on God
> and not on what you have.**

When I share about trusting God for our needs, I know it is easier said than done. I also know this is a life-long journey and that it is something we need to work on again and again. It is easy to come away from this and start depending again on what we have or do not have. We can fall back into planning our lives by what we have instead of what God wants us to do.

We, as a family, as I have said, have had times when we had almost nothing and times where we had enough or even extra to work with. But, even when we had extra, we still tried to be dependent upon God and seek His will, not just do things because we could.

No matter where you are in your life right now, whether you have a little or a lot, be faithful with it. Understand that everything belongs to God, and do not put your trust in what you have or do not have. Ask God to teach you to be dependent on Him and Him alone. We should all be in God's plan for our lives and be faithful with what we have, whether it is much or little. We should learn to be faithful with the time we have, if we have a family and small kids, or if we are alone with more time to do what we want to do.

I do not say that everyone should sell their house, give everything away, and live like we do. We are not all called to do the same thing, and there is also a season for everything. But, we are all called to seek God and to trust Him with everything in our lives. Let Him speak to you, and do not be afraid if He takes you on a longer journey where you learn the hard way to be fully dependent on Him instead of your money or the people around you. It is not always easy to be in this place, but there is also much freedom in it. It is hard, but it is also something that will change your life forever.

11

DO NOT GREET ANYONE ON THE ROAD

It is so easy to become distracted and to forget to do what Jesus has called us to do. Yes, we can become distracted by even the small things in life that can end up stealing our time, focus, and obedience to God.

When we read these words, *"Do not greet anyone on the road,"* as Jesus says in Luke 10:4, it is so easy to just skim over them. We may read these words, but we do not really understand what Jesus says here and how we should apply it to our lives today. And because we do not understand it or think it is not that important, we often end up skipping over these words.

In the previous chapter, we looked at the first words in Luke 10:4 that say, *"Do not take a purse or bag or sandals ..."* In this chapter we are going to look at the last words in Luke 10:4 that say, *"... Do not greet anyone on the road."* These words can seem strange to us when we do not understand them, but these words are actually very important. Yes, these words are actually Jesus' advice for His disciples during that time and also for us living today. When we follow this advice, it can be such a blessing to us. If we do not listen to it, we can be led away from God and His calling.

So, why did Jesus say these words in Luke 10:4? The reason Jesus said this is not because we are not allowed to greet people we meet. It is good to say "Hi" and greet others. He says it because He did not want His disciples to become distracted and lose focus as to why they were sent out. If you greet people, it can end up that you fall into small talk and forget why you were sent out and what your main purpose is. Jesus wanted them (and you and me) to remain focused on finding the person of peace. He did not want them to waste their time talking with all the people they would meet and then forget why they were sent out. You need to understand it is so easy to become distracted with everything around us, and if we are not on guard, it can happen to all of us. We can end up losing our focus and spending our time on so many other things that are less important. Greeting people does not seem like a bad thing, but as Jesus says, it can still distract us from doing what we are supposed to do. There are so many things in our life that do not seem bad, but that can still distract us and cause us to lose our focus and miss so many things Jesus has called us to do.

As you know, we are put here on earth in Christ's place as His body in order to continue what He has started. If you take the time to look at Jesus, you will see a Man who was really dedicated to His mission here on earth. Jesus did not let Himself be tempted or distracted with what this world had to offer. He was also not led by the needs of the people around Him. He was led by the Spirit of God, and He only did the will of His Father. Of course, we will never be exactly like Jesus, but He is still our Role Model, and our goal in life is to be like Him. Paul, like Jesus, also had a really strong focus in life. Paul was very dedicated, and he knew why he was here on earth. He knew what he needed to do. We can see this in 1 Corinthians 9:24-27, which states:

> Do you not know that in a race all the runners run, but only one gets the prize? Run in such a way as to get the prize. Everyone who competes in the games goes into strict training. They do it to get a crown that will not last, but we do it to get a crown that will last forever. Therefore I do not run like someone running aimlessly; I do not fight like a boxer beating the air. No, I strike a blow to my body

and make it my slave so that after I have preached to others, I myself will not be disqualified for the prize.

Yes, Paul was very focused on the goal. It was not always easy, and it cost him a lot. In Acts 20:23-24, Paul says:

I only know that in every city the Holy Spirit warns me that prison and hardships are facing me. However, I consider my life worth nothing to me; my only aim is to finish the race and complete the task the Lord Jesus has given me—the task of testifying to the good news of God's grace.

These are very strong words. As the Bible says in 1 Corinthians 11:1, we should follow Paul's example, as he follows the example of Christ. But let us look at Christ. From the beginning of Jesus' ministry, we see how the Holy Spirit led Him out into the desert where He was tempted by the devil with everything this world has to offer.
1 John 2:15-17 states:

Do not love the world or anything in the world. If anyone loves the world, love for the Father is not in them. For everything in the world—the lust of the flesh, the lust of the eyes, and the pride of life— comes not from the Father but from the world. The world and its desires pass away, but whoever does the will of God lives forever.

Here we read that everything in this world—the lust of the flesh, the lust of the eyes, and the pride of life—are exactly the things Jesus was tempted with in the desert.
Luke 4:1-13 states:

Jesus, full of the Holy Spirit, left the Jordan and was led by the Spirit into the wilderness, where for forty days He was tempted by the devil. He ate nothing during those days, and at the end of them He was hungry. The devil said to Him, "If you are the Son of God, tell this stone to become bread." Jesus answered, "It is written: 'Man shall not live on bread alone.'" The devil led Him up to a high place and showed Him in an instant all the kingdoms of the world. And he said to Him, "I will give you all their authority and splendor; it has been given to me, and I can give it to anyone I want to. If you worship me, it will all be Yours." Jesus answered, "It is written: 'Worship the Lord your God and serve Him only.'" The devil led Him to Jerusalem and had Him stand on the highest point of the temple. "If you are the Son of God," he said, "throw Yourself down from here. For it is written: "'He will command his angels concerning You to guard You carefully; they will lift You up in their hands, so that You will not strike Your foot against a stone.'" Jesus answered, "It is said: 'Do not put the Lord your God to the test.'" When the devil had finished all this tempting, he left Him until an opportune time.

Jesus resisted temptation when it came to the lust of the flesh, the lust of the eyes, and the pride of this world. We will encounter many temptations like this in our own life, and we need to be strong. We can resist all temptations with the help of Christ. Christ showed us how we should live, and He knew why He was here.

John 4:34 states:

"My food," said Jesus, "Is to do the will of Him who sent Me and to finish His work."

John 5:30 states:

"By Myself I can do nothing; I judge only as I hear, and My judgment is just, for I seek not to please Myself but Him who sent Me."

John 6:38 states:

"For I have come down from heaven not to do my will but to do the will of Him who sent Me."

Yes, it is clear that Jesus knew why He was put here on earth. He was sent here by the Father to do the Father's will. He needed to finish the work He was given. And it was not easy for Him. There were many things in Jesus' life that could have distracted Him from the work He was called to do.

Luke 4:42 states:

At daybreak, Jesus went out to a solitary place. The people were looking for Him and when they came to where He was, they tried to keep Him from leaving them.

In this verse, we read how the people there tried to keep Him from leaving. Wanting to keep Jesus there was not a bad thing. They were hungry for more; therefore, they tried to keep Jesus from leaving.

But Jesus answered them in Luke 4:43-44:

But He said, "I must proclaim the good news of the kingdom of God to the other towns also, because that is why I was sent." And He kept on preaching in the synagogues of Judea."

Jesus was not led by people's needs, and He did not let them distract Him as easily as we often do. He was led by the Spirit. He did what His Father called Him to do, and that should be the goal in our life as well. We read here how Jesus rejected those people who asked Him to stay, even though it might have seemed like a good idea at the moment.

In other places in the Bible, we see that Jesus stayed when they asked Him. For example, in John 4:40 when Jesus met the woman at the well in Samaria, the people there asked Him to stay with them. He stayed there two days longer. It really is about listening to the Holy Spirit and not letting ourselves become distracted by all the things happening around us. When Jesus sent His disciples out saying they should not greet anyone on the road, it does not mean we are never allowed to greet the people we meet on the streets. If God sends you out to find the person of peace, or if He tells you to go to a certain city or place, then do not let anything come in and get you distracted from doing this. It is about listening to the Holy Spirit, and Jesus is an amazing example of this.

When we talk about not being distracted and not losing focus of why we are here and what God has called us to do, distraction can often come from people very close to us. This is not to say that they are evil or that they are going against God's will on purpose. Many of them are not aware this is happening. I have seen many receive the call of Jesus and start to go this way, but then suddenly turn around and start going another way. What happened? What often happens is that someone comes in and gets them to look away from the goal or the call of Jesus. Someone comes in, and their words distract them, so they lose the focus and end up going wrong.

We are the body of Christ. He is the Head.
If a body moves but does not move the way the head
wants it to move, then the body is sick. It is not
about moving randomly; it is about listening to the
Head (Christ) and doing what the Head wants
the body (us) to do.

I remember one time I was in Switzerland doing a kickstart with 300-400 people. After a meeting where I shared the Gospel, a girl came up to me and said she had really been thinking about the words she had heard. She was really convicted of her sins and wanted to get baptized. While she stood there, I felt right away that there would be a big battle for her soul and that the enemy would try to come in and steal this from her. When I felt that very strongly, I looked around to see if there was a place in the church where I could baptize her right away. I wanted to baptize her before something could come in and steal it from her, but there was no place in the church to baptize her. We needed to wait until we could meet down at the sea where the baptism was going to happen. I said to her, "So you will come today to the sea and get baptized?" "Yes," she said, "I will come today and get baptized." I continued, "So, you promise me that you will get baptized today?" She said, "Yes, I promise you that I will get baptized today." But, I felt this was not enough because I knew someone or something would try to hinder her in this baptism and in the freedom God had for her. I asked her one more time, "So, you promise me that no matter what happens in the next few hours, you will come and get baptized today?" "Yes, I promise," she said, "I will get baptized today, and I will not let anything hinder that." So we stopped there and agreed to meet down at the sea.

We all went out to eat and after a break we met down at the sea ready to baptize many from the kickstart. While I was there waiting for her, she came to me and said, "I need to talk to you." We went away from the others, and she said, "I will not get baptized today." It came as a big surprise to me because I was very clear earlier, and she had promised she would get baptized that day no matter what. I asked her, "What has happened so that you do not want to get baptized now? What made you change your mind?" Then she told me how she had spoken with her mom and their priest and that she does not think it is a good idea to get baptized now since she was already baptized as a baby.

When I heard her say this, I said, "I understand. My question to you is: What does God say about it? I am saying you should get baptized, and they are saying you should not get baptized, but what does God say about it? Go and ask Him what He is saying, and then come back in five to ten minutes and let me know what you will do today." Five minutes later, she came back with a big smile on her face and said, "I am going to be baptized today." I was so happy about that because I knew it was the right decision and that God had a new life for her. We went down to the sea, and I baptized her as the first person that day. When she came up from the water, a demon manifested and left. She experienced amazing freedom. Right away, the Holy Spirit came over her in such a beautiful way. There she stood speaking loudly in tongues. It was really amazing, and after this, she helped me baptize the next person. We had an amazing day I will never forget.

When I saw what happened with her and the freedom God had for her, I understood why there was such a fight when it came to her baptism. This is a good reminder to be careful who you are listening to. Do not let anything or anyone take the call of Jesus away from you. Do not be distracted from doing the will of your Father in Heaven, no matter where the distraction comes from. In her case, the distraction came from her own parents and a priest. But she did the right thing, and that was to listen to what God had to say about all this. When the day is over, when this life is over, it is all about what God is saying, and no one else. When you read the words of Jesus and His call that we have been looking at in this book and start to go this way, you can be sure that someone or something will try to distract you. If it is other people or even people you know very closely, do not be surprised. Keep the focus. Yes, it is often more difficult when it is people close to you, but Jesus experienced the same.

One time, when Jesus was together with His disciples, He shared what was going to happen to Him. He shared how He must go to Jerusalem and suffer many things at the hands of the elders, chief priests, and teachers of the law. Jesus shared how they must kill Him and that He would rise up on the third day (Matthew 16:21). When He shared this with His disciples, His good friend Peter rebuked Him and said, "Never, Lord! This shall never happen to you!" (Matthew 16:22). Wow, this is crazy when you think about it. Jesus shared God's perfect will with His very close friends, and Peter, who had walked with Him for three years, tried to hinder Him from doing it, from obeying God, from doing the will of God. We can also experience this in our own life. We can have very sincere people around us who want the best for us but who do not fully understand the will of God, and they can actually, with their words, lead us astray as Peter tried to lead Jesus astray. Peter was in no way evil, and if he had known better, he would not have said what he said. He in no way wanted to go against the perfect will of God, but at that time, he did not understand the will of God. Therefore, he tried to hinder Jesus from doing the will of God, just like the priest and parents tried to hinder the girl I talked about from obeying God and getting baptized. When it happened to Jesus, you could almost believe there was a spirit behind all of this that tried to hinder Jesus from obeying the will of God. When Peter went against the will of God, Jesus did not go against Peter. He went against the spirit behind it by rebuking Satan.

Matthew 16:23 states:

Jesus turned and said to Peter, "Get behind me, Satan! You are a stumbling block to Me; you do not have in mind the concerns of God, but merely human concerns."

Whoa, these are strong words. It is amazing how focused Jesus was. How often are we distracted by the people around us and by the things we see around us? How often do we not hear God speak to us and then listen to a man's wisdom and end up going astray? We really need to listen to Jesus' words and not the advice of man. I am not against listening to advice. I believe advice is good, and we all need people in our lives to confirm what God has spoken to us, but it is important to have the right people around us and to listen to the right people.

> There are so many good things in life, things that have value to us. But, when this life is over, and we stand before God, we will know at that moment what truly has value and what does not.

One of the biggest temptations for many people today, especially young people, is the internet. We can use the internet for a lot of good, and we can use it to help bring people to God. But the internet can also be used to distract people and lead them away from God and away from what God has called them to do. I have seen many people spend much time on Facebook or YouTube. They spend so much time there that they end up only filling themselves with Facebook and YouTube and never obeying the call of Jesus for themselves.

I have seen many people start off good, but end up being distracted and losing focus completely. I know many people who get caught up in a "special" kind of teaching; for example, the end times or different conspiracy theories or false prophets in the church, and they totally forget to obey the call of Jesus. They end up spending so much time in front of the computer watching all these videos that they forget why they are here. To those who are sitting for hours looking at end-times videos, I often say, "Maybe you are correct that Jesus is coming back very soon, but if so, do not let Him find you sitting in front of the TV/computer screen watching end-times videos. Instead, let Him find you busy working in the harvest, making disciples." I have met other people who start off serving God and making disciples, but then start studying the Bible in Greek or Hebrew and suddenly forget to obey what they have learned. I am not against people learning Greek or

Hebrew, and I am not against studying the Bible in different languages, but when we one day stand in front of Jesus, He is going to look at our life. I am sure He will not be as impressed by us knowing Greek or Hebrew as He will be about us obeying Him and making disciples.

When I think about Jesus and how He says in Matthew 28:19, *"Therefore go and make disciples of all nations ..."* I have to admit that we as a church have been distracted. So many mission trips today end up being humanitarian trips. This is not bad; however, giving people clothes and food is not the same as preaching the Gospel and making disciples. I think it is good to give people clothes. I think it is good to give people food. I think it is good to help people with humanitarian aid, but this should never replace the call Jesus has given us to share the Gospel and make disciples.

We have all been trusted to spread the Gospel of Christ to people. We are all called to obey God and His words. When Jesus said to the seventy and to you and me that we should not greet anyone on the road, there was a reason for that. Maybe today Jesus would tell us not to take our cell phones with us but to just go out and listen to the Holy Spirit. And He might tell us not to ask what everyone else is thinking about obeying Jesus or getting baptized, as we have looked at.

I do not know where you are in your life and what you are being distracted by, but you need to get your focus on Jesus and His call. Let God lead you. Seek first the Kingdom of God and do His will. Let's not forget why we are put here on earth and what we are sent out to do. Remind yourself why you are here and what it is Jesus is calling us to, and let us keep doing that. Let's keep it simple and obey Jesus in what He has called us to without being distracted.

12

PERSON OF PEACE

If you do not know what you are looking for, you will not find it. This is the same when it comes to the person of peace whom Jesus has sent you to go out and find. If you do not know what a person of peace is, you will not find them, no matter how long you look.

S o far, we have talked about the harvest being ready and plentiful and about Jesus sending us out like lambs among wolves and about how He is going with us when we take our first steps. We have looked at what we should bring on the trip and how we should not greet everyone on the road. In other words, we should learn to trust God for our needs and not be distracted on the road. We should keep our focus and remember why we are sent out.

Now, the time has come for us to talk about the "person of peace." If there is only one thing you get out of this book, I pray it is learning what a person of peace is and how you find them. And, of course, you need to know what the Gospel is so you can get them soundly saved, which is something we will also look at later. But first, we will look at what a person of peace is.

The question is, what are we supposed to go after, out there in the harvest? Are we just going out to try to save the whole world, or does Jesus have very specific things He wants us to do, or in this case, find? First, you need to know that we are *not* called to just walk out into the harvest blindly, and we are also *not* called to walk out into the harvest with the goal of saving the whole world. This is not our calling. Jesus has given us a much more simple calling, and it is something everyone can do. He has called us to go out into the harvest and find a "person of peace" or "someone who is seeking peace" or a "son of peace," as it is written in Luke 10:5-7. Here, it states:

> *Whatever house you enter, first say, "Peace be to this house!" And if a son of peace is there, your peace will rest upon him. But if not, it will return to you. And remain in the same house, eating and drinking what they provide, for the laborer deserves his wages. Do not go from house to house.*

Here, we read that Jesus sent out His disciples (including you and me) to find a special person, a person who is seeking peace, "a person of peace." Jesus said we should go out and find that person of peace, and when we find that person, we should stay there with them in their house. Jesus also said that we should not be too fast to go from place to place, for we should stay with them and pray that the peace of God will rest upon their house.

What is a person of peace? What is Jesus talking about by saying we should enter into the house, pray that the peace of God will be upon the house, and move on if there is no person of peace in that house? It is so important that we take the time to really look at what Jesus is calling us to do, what He said, and how it looked when the early disciples did this. How did they go out, and how did they find the person of peace, as Jesus called them (and us) to? In Luke 10, we read Jesus sent His disciples out with instructions of what they should do. We read that His disciples came back from their journey rejoicing, but we do not read any examples of what they did when they went out there and found that person of peace. We see, however, many examples of this later in the book of Acts where they continued doing what Jesus called them to do.

Cornelius, in Acts 10, was a clear example of a person of peace. Cornelius was a man who was seeking God with his whole heart. Yes, he was seeking peace with God and peace with man. Because he was seeking God and was a person of peace, we see how God led Peter to him. And when Peter came into Cornelius' house, Cornelius was ready to hear the Gospel and repent. Not only did Cornelius hear the Gospel and repent, but his whole household came to faith. So, a person of peace is someone like Cornelius who is seeking God. A person of peace is someone who is seeking the truth and is ready to receive the Gospel. A person of peace is a person who is seeking peace, whom the Holy Spirit is drawing. A person of peace is not like those out there who are not interested in the Gospel. He is also not someone who only wants to discuss the Gospel and come up with excuses for why they do not believe in God and talk about why religion is so terrible. Things happen more easily when you find a person of peace because God has been drawing their heart, and they are ready to listen to you share the Gospel. Maybe the person of peace is not even aware at the time that God is drawing their heart, but they are seeking the truth and seeking the purpose of life. The person of peace will ask many good questions about your faith and God because they really want to know the truth.

In Acts 16, we find two more examples of persons of peace. We see, like with Cornelius, not only one person comes to faith, but the whole household comes to faith through that one person of peace. The first example we have of this in Acts 16 starts in verse 13 where we read about Lydia. Here, we read how Paul and Silas went to Philippi (led by the Holy Spirit, looking for the person of peace) and found a group of women who were seeking God. We have to understand that these women who were seeking God were still not born again, and they were praying to God according to their understanding of the Old Testament. These women were believers in God, but they were not yet believers in Jesus Christ, nor were they born again. While they were seeking God, Paul and Silas came and talked to the women. Just like in this example, when you share the Gospel with a group of people, you do not always know who the person of peace is before you start talking to them. When you start to share the Gospel with them, you will quickly find out who that person of peace is. As we read here in Acts 16, all of the women listened, but there was one woman (the person of peace) who did more than just listen; her name was Lydia. She not only heard the Word, but God opened her heart so she could receive what she heard. We also read that after Lydia received the message, she invited Paul and Silas to come to her home. This is a good sign that she was a true person of peace. Not only did Lydia come to faith in Jesus Christ, but her household came to faith in Him, too. Yes, Lydia and her whole household came to faith in Jesus Christ, got baptized, and Paul and Silas ended up staying at her house for a long time, exactly like we read in Luke 10.

Something important to understand when we read about Lydia in Acts 16 is that this happened around year fifty, about twenty years after Jesus was on earth and gave His disciples the command in Luke 10. What Jesus commanded His disciples to do in Luke 10 was not something they only did in the short period of time Jesus was on earth, but it was something they continued for a long time after He went to Heaven and sent His Holy Spirit down to earth. Neither was it only for the twelve and the seventy. Paul and Silas were continuing to do what Jesus was saying to the twelve and the seventy in Luke 9 and 10 and Matthew 10. But they, Paul and Silas, were not part of the twelve or the seventy who were sent out by Jesus. What Jesus said to the twelve and the seventy was that they later should go out into the whole world teaching others to obey. This is what we see here with Paul and Silas and what I am teaching you here throughout this book. It is important for us to understand that Jesus still commands us to go out and find a person of peace, to go to their house, and to see their whole household get saved. We should stay there for some time and build fellowships.

In Acts 16, a short time after Lydia and her whole household came to faith, we read how Paul and Silas were thrown into jail where they also shared the Gospel and met the next person of peace. We read that Paul and Silas were sitting in jail worshipping God when, suddenly, God came. Everything shook, God opened the jail door, and all the prisoners were set free in a supernatural way. In the middle of all of this they found the next person of peace—the jailer. The jailer invited Paul and Silas to his home, and in the middle of the night, he and his whole household came to faith, got baptized in water, and received a new life. In the beginning, this situation looked very bad. Paul and Silas were stuck in jail, but through that experience, they found a person of peace. If they had not been thrown into jail, they would not have found the jailer. If they had not found the jailer, they would not have seen his whole household came to faith. From this example, we see how God leads us through many circumstances and how He wants us to be bold, to worship Him, and to find the person of peace.

Acts 16:25-34 states:

About midnight Paul and Silas were praying and singing hymns to God, and the other prisoners were listening to them. Suddenly there was such a violent earthquake that the foundations of the prison were shaken. At once all the prison doors flew open, and everyone's chains came loose. The jailer woke up, and when he saw the prison doors open, he drew his sword and was about to kill himself because he thought the prisoners had escaped. But Paul shouted, "do not harm yourself! We are all here!" The jailer called for lights, rushed in and fell trembling before Paul and Silas. He then brought them out and asked, "Sirs, what must I do to be saved?" They replied, "Believe in the Lord Jesus, and you will be saved—you and your household." Then they spoke the word of the Lord to him and to all the others in his house. At that hour of the night the jailer took them and washed their wounds; then immediately he and all his household were baptized. The jailer brought them into his house and set a meal before them; he was filled with joy because he had come to believe in God— he and his whole household.

We see many different examples in the book of Acts of how the early disciples started doing what Jesus called them to do in Luke 10. They went out into the harvest to find a person of peace, and when they found that person, they stayed there with them in their house and saw how their whole household came to faith. This is what we should do today. Nothing has changed! Jesus is the same yesterday, today, and forever. If we start following what Jesus calls us to do in Luke 10, we will start to see the Kingdom of God growing in a totally different way than ever before. Right now in this very moment, while you are reading this book, there are people in your city and neighborhood who are persons of peace. They are out there. We just need to go out and find them. When we know what to look for, it is not so hard to find, especially when we are being led by the Holy Spirit.

In Acts 22, we read how Paul (also called Saul) came to faith. Paul talks about how, one day, he was on his way to Damascus to get permission to imprison those who believe in Jesus. Suddenly, Paul saw a very bright light come over him, and he heard a voice say, *"Saul, Saul, why do you persecute Me?"* (Acts 9:4). After this incredible experience, Paul was blinded and needed someone to take him by his hand and lead him. He was led to Damascus, where he spent time fasting and seeking God. If you look at Paul at the time he was called by God, you would not believe he was a person of peace. You would not believe he was one seeking God with his whole heart because, at that time, there were many rumors circulating that he was against Jesus and trying to kill Christians. And these rumors were indeed correct. He was against Jesus and trying to kill the Christians. He was against Christians and wanting to kill them, but all this changed in a split second. Yes, suddenly Paul was not against God anymore, and he actually started seeking Him instead. Paul became a person of peace who was fasting, praying, and waiting. He was waiting for something to happen. So, we can see that the harvest truly is out there. It is ready, and it is waiting for the workers to come and get it.

In this example with Paul, we meet a man named Ananias. God spoke to Ananias and told him to go and pray for Paul so that his sight would be restored (Acts 9:11-12). In the beginning, Ananias was afraid because he had heard so many bad things about Paul. You can imagine that he did not believe Paul was a person of peace. But, regardless of Ananias' disbelief, he obeyed God and went to him. To Ananias' surprise, Paul really was a person of peace and was ready to receive the Gospel. So Ananias put his hand on him, and his sight was immediately restored. Ananias then shared the Gospel with him. That night, Paul received the Gospel, repented, got baptized in water, received the Holy Spirit, and a new life.

I believe there are many people out there who are, just like Paul, waiting for someone to come and share the Gospel with them. Maybe they have had something drastic happen in their life like Paul, which

---

Ananias was a disciple, just like you and me. He was not an apostle like the twelve or like the seventy who were sent out by Jesus, but God used him to win Paul for Christ. And God used Paul to travel all over the world to do the work of an apostle. But there would not be a Paul if there was no Ananias. Be an Ananias, and find that person of peace (Paul) in your city.

---

caused them to change their view of life. The people out there need someone like you and me to come and lay hands on them so that they can be healed. They need us to come and share the Gospel with them so they can repent and be born again. The harvest is truly ready and plentiful but the workers are few. There are so many persons of peace out there like Paul, Cornelius, Lydia, and the eunuch (whom Philip shared the Gospel with in Acts 8). Yes, the eunuch was reading and studying the Scriptures. He was a person who was seeking God, but again, he needed someone to come and explain the Gospel to him. And I know there are many people out there who, like the eunuch, are seeking God and reading the Bible but do not understand what they are reading. We need to go out and be led by the Holy Spirit to find these people. I could share many stories about how I, and many others, have been led to a person of peace, just like we see in the Bible.

I would like to share one story with you of how it could look today when we find a person of peace. Some years ago in Denmark, I was on a Christian forum on the internet looking for a special article I had heard about. As I was looking through the forum for this article, I noticed a young woman had asked a question about God. When I saw this question, I just ignored it and continued looking for the article. But, suddenly, I experienced how God stopped me from looking for that article and said, "Go back! She is that person of peace I want you to find today." So I dropped everything about finding the article I was looking for and went back to look for the question the woman had asked. When I found her question I responded to her right away.

In just a short time, I received an answer from her. The woman was very surprised I had written to her. I was the first one to respond to her question, and she had written that question on the forum eight months earlier. By the time I had answered her, she had completely forgotten about the question. So I asked her if she was a Christian, to which she responded, "Yes." Many people today will say "yes" to being a Christian without actually knowing anything about who Jesus is or what it means to be born again. So, I continued writing to her and asked her if she had ever experienced God. She told me she had experienced God one time before, but that she had never told anyone about it. She continued to tell me that some years ago she saw a man on Danish TV who was praying for the sick, and at that time in her life, she had a hearing problem and wore a hearing aid. She told me the man on Danish TV had instructed people to place their hand on the part of their body where they were sick while he prayed. She had done as the man instructed and placed her hand on her ear. Nothing seemed to happen, but the next morning when she woke up everyone around her was speaking so loudly. She went to the doctor to get her hearing aid checked, as she believed her hearing aid was broken. That day, her doctor told her that her hearing aid was not broken. She had been healed!

This was a crazy experience for this young woman. She was totally shocked. She also wrote that she had never shared this with anyone because she did not know if anyone would believe her. I was the first one she had told. When I read this, I wrote back, "Hey, I think it was me who prayed for you that time!" I sent her a YouTube link of when I was on Danish TV praying for the sick. She answered and was totally in shock. To her great surprise, I was actually the man on Danish TV who had prayed for her when she had gotten healed. I asked her where she lived and if she wanted to meet and talk. She said, "Yes," and it turned out she only lived fifteen minutes away from me. The next day, I met with her and her boyfriend. I took the time to share the Gospel with them. A few days later, they came to see me again, this time ready to repent, give their lives to Christ, and to be born again!

Through this woman coming to faith, the doors were opened for her family to also come to faith! The first one we saw come to faith in the family was her sister. She had previously converted to Islam and was at that time living as a radical Muslim. But, when she received the Gospel, she repented and was born again. Then the woman's other sister and her husband came to faith, and then her brother and his girlfriend! It just spread from one person to another and out of this woman's family, a house fellowship started where my family and I attended for some time. It is amazing to see that the whole fellowship started because of one person, the young woman. Today, this woman and the man she was dating at the time are married and have three children. I actually had the honor of marrying them, and they are very good friends of mine.

We need to learn to find these people of peace, and we need to learn what to do when we find them. The first step is to understand that there are people out there whom the Bible calls "persons of peace." If you do not know what this is and that this is what you are looking for, it is unlikely you will find them. I truly believe that this simple message Jesus shared will not only change your life but many others' lives as well. When we all start to look for that person of peace in our everyday lives and know what to do when we find them, the Kingdom of God will grow like never before. There are so many people of peace in your city right now who are waiting for the workers to come and find them. We are called to use the right tools and to go and get these people. And when we find these people of peace (people who are seeking God) they need our help. They need our help like Paul needed Ananias' help and like Cornelius needed Peter's help and like the eunuch needed Philip's help. Yes, they need you and me to share the truth with them so they can understand the truth, repent, and be born again. And when we do this, we will see not only them but often many who are around them come to faith. There are so many people of peace out there. We just need to open our eyes and see that the harvest is, as Jesus says, plentiful.

We must go out and seek them, and we will find them. When you find them, you do not need to take the time to discuss religion, science, evolution, or other things because God is calling those people of peace, and they are ready to receive Jesus. they are ready to give their lives to Him because He is calling them.

Later, we are going to look much more at the person of peace, who they are, how you find them, and what to do when you find them. This is really so important and something our enemy has tried to keep away from the church. It is time now for us to wake up and understand what Jesus is really calling us to.

13

Eat And Drink Whatever They Provide

**Food is an important part of every culture.
It was also an important part of the first church
when it came to having fellowship and
sharing the Gospel. One of the best ways to share
the Gospel is over a coffee table.**

As you have hopefully started to see by now, Jesus is saying many important things in Luke 10. Sadly, many miss these things or do not understand their importance. One more of these things has to do with what Jesus is saying about eating and drinking.

Jesus says in Luke 10:7:

Stay there, eating and drinking whatever they give you, for the worker deserves his wages. Do not move around from house to house.

Let's start by looking at the first part of this verse when Jesus says, "... *eating and drinking whatever they give you, for the worker deserves his wages.*" Jesus is saying here that we are to eat whatever is served. He is also saying that for those who serve God and step out in faith on His words, God will provide for their needs. This is something we have looked at before. Here we see that this often comes by the people out there providing for them. The people who were sent out in the early church often got their provisions and what they needed as gifts, blessings from those they served in the houses they went to.

If we look at the first part when He talks about eating and drinking, food is truly a big part of our daily life, and it is also a big part of the Kingdom of God. When we eat and drink together, we create community and fellowship. This is very important for everyone, especially for us as believers. Yes, the time of eating and drinking is very important for us as believers, as it provides a way for us to come closer together and build real fellowship. Eating and drinking is also an important part of reaching people with the Gospel because when you sit down and eat and drink together you get to know people in a more intimate and personal way.

There is a well-known saying that states, "The way to a man's heart is through his stomach." I actually believe there is some truth behind this. I personally love food, and there is nothing like sitting down with family and friends while eating a good meal. Oftentimes, you can have the best talks with people while you are sitting together and eating with them. Even cultural differences and age are factors that are no longer important to people who are sitting together eating a good meal. Food truly does bring every culture and people of different ages together in a way nothing else can. Whether you are eating while sitting around a coffee table, dinner table, or even on the floor, talking becomes much more natural and relaxed. When you are sitting down to eat with someone, you create an atmosphere that helps people relax and open up their hearts to each other and to the Gospel.

For example, I have met many strangers out on the streets or other places, and oftentimes, as I stand there talking to them, there is a distance, mistrust, and skepticism between us because we do not know each other. But, I know if I can take that person, sit down, and eat and drink something with them, everything would become much more relaxed, and there would be a level of trust that was not there before. When you sit down with someone, you also have that person's full focus, not like if you were standing talking on the street or other places with more people around.

When I am out on the streets and find a person of peace there, I quickly try to find a place where we can sit down and eat something or drink a cup of coffee. I often say something like, "Hey, look, there is a coffee bar. Why don't we go and sit down over coffee?" If the person agrees, I have a greater chance of being able to share the whole Gospel because the conversation will be much more natural, and they will feel more relaxed and open. We will not be easily distracted. Of course, it would be better to meet in a home, but a coffee bar can be a good first step. When you sit down with someone, the whole atmosphere is often so relaxed and natural. It will make talking more open and personal.

Some years ago, I visited a new church. I was standing in the foyer before the service and started talking to the pastor about what God was doing. We had a very natural talk, filled with laughter and interesting stories. But, as soon as he stepped out on stage and stood behind the pulpit to start the service, he completely changed. It was shocking to witness how he changed into a totally different person. His face became very serious, and he spoke in a very formal way. Almost every other word that came from his mouth was "amen" or "hallelujah." While I was listening to him talk, I could not help but ask myself what happened to this man. He behaved and spoke in such a normal way when I was talking to him before the service, but suddenly, he was behaving and speaking in such a strange way.

> **When we behave in a strange way in church,**
> **we will scare people away.**
> **The people we meet on the streets do not know**
> **the church culture, and it is not normal for them**
> **to hear religious talk.**
> **Instead, let us talk about God in the same**
> **natural way that we talk about everything else.**

What I experienced in that church was something I think many of you can recognize. Some people behave and speak in such a weird religious way while they are in church. They talk in a very different way, using special words people outside the church do not understand. People outside the church, because of the way churchgoers behave and speak inside the church, look at churchgoers as weird and wonder what is wrong with them. I have also seen these same changes in Christians out on the street evangelizing. I talk with them before we start telling others about God, and we talk naturally and normally. As soon as they start talking with non-believers about religious things, they start using different words and speaking in a way that is weird for the people who are listening. Something important for us to understand is that the Bible was written in a language that was very natural and normal at that time. We should also use a natural and normal language for our time and culture today when we speak about the Gospel and the Word of God (without using any profanity, of course).

Jesus, in Luke 10, says that when we find a person of peace, we should stay with them. Despite the fact that Jesus says this, we often make the mistake of just inviting that person of peace to church, expecting them to get what they need from the message. This is often a big mistake, and I stopped inviting people of peace to church many years ago. Instead, I started to do what Jesus says to do in Luke 10. I started to sit down with the person of peace and eat and drink with them. When I did this, many opportunities opened up to share the Gospel with them and to pray for them. Today, I often tell people they should stop inviting non-believers to church. Instead, they should sit with them and share the Gospel themselves. It is our job, and not the pastor's, to share the Gospel with them. We should not just invite them to church and let the pastor do it, thinking he is the only one who knows how. If you do not know how, then learn to do it. If you never start, you will never learn.

There was a time in my life when I actually met many people who were open to Jesus. Today, I would call them people of peace. Most of the time, I just invited them to church. Very few of them actually came. It is one thing to be open to hearing about Jesus on the streets but another thing to be open to going to church. I need to say this again so you understand it because this is very important. It is one thing to meet a person of peace out there who is open to hearing the Gospel from you. It is something else to get that person to come to church with you.

Why do you want to invite them to church? You do not see Jesus inviting people to church. No, you do not even see that in the book of Acts. So why not just do what Jesus tells us to do and sit down with the person of peace, eat and drink what they serve us, heal the sick, and preach the Gospel? At that time in my life, I thought it was my job to invite people to church on Sunday and that it was the pastor's job to preach the Gospel to them so they could get saved. Since that time in my life, I have learned many things. One of the first things I learned is that people of peace are very open to hearing about Jesus on the streets, but it is too big of a step for them to go to church. Yes, it is scary for many of them. There were many times that I invited people to church, and on Sunday morning, I stood in front of the church doors waiting and hoping the person of peace would show up. To my great disappointment, they rarely ever came. But who could blame them? Have you ever attended a church where you do not know anyone? If you have, then you know it can be scary.

When I first came to faith, I was very curious (and still am). I tried many things to reach people with the Gospel. One time, I even visited the Jehovah's Witnesses to share the Gospel with them. It is important for me to mention that although I have done this in the past, I would not recommend anyone doing this today because there are deceiving spirits there causing the people to be blinded to the truth. I still remember how difficult it was when I went to the meeting of the Jehovah's Witnesses. My friend and I were supposed to meet before their service and go together. I remember that I had so many questions. I asked myself, "What should I wear? Where should I sit? How should I behave?" It was a totally new world for us. When my friend and I arrived before the service, I wanted to run away, but since we had made the commitment to go together, I decided I was going to be brave and go into the service. When we went into the building, the people were all very nice and welcomed us. But it was very obvious to everyone that we did not belong there. Everyone was staring at us, and we felt like everyone was talking about us. Yes, they were nice, but honestly, if I had not gone with my friend, I would have run away. When it was time for the service to start, we felt totally overwhelmed because we did not know where to sit or how to behave during the service. When the service was finally over, we felt so relieved and happy to leave that building and come out into the "normal" world that we knew. We did not share the Gospel with anyone that day.

Maybe you are thinking to yourself that it is not surprising that I felt out of place there because it was a Jehovah's Witnesses service and not a Christian one. It is true that it was certainly not a Christian service at a Christian church. It was new for us, just like our churches are new for someone attending a Christian church who is not used to going to church. We often forget that many of the things we do in church are natural behaviors for us but totally unnatural for those who have never attended a church before.

A few months after I came to faith, I invited a friend to come to church with me. I remember the church service started with worship, which normally lasted for half an hour. Right away, I closed my eyes and started worshipping God as I would normally do. But, when I opened my eyes and looked at her, she was just standing there looking around at everyone with their arms lifted high and their eyes closed. She even started to glance at her watch, and it was evident that she was beginning to be uncomfortable. So I told her to relax and that the worship (songs she did not know) would soon be finished. Finally, the worship ended, but then someone on stage started to go over all of the information regarding activities in the church. It was a lot of information about meetings, kids activities, and general things about the church. After that, it was time for the offering, time for people to give their money to the church, and on this day, it seemed like they spoke more about money than ever before. I do not think that the church leaders actually talked about money more than they normally did, but I suddenly saw everything through my friend's eyes and realized how weird it must have been for her. I wanted her to have a good experience, but as they continued to talk more and more about money, I saw her eyes get bigger and bigger. It was almost like I could hear thinking, "Oh, this is a sect! It is only about money. I need to get out of here." So, again, I tried to calm her down and explain that the church service was not only about singing and money.

After the offering was finished, I was excited because I thought it was finally time for the preaching to begin. Instead, the musicians started playing again. It was time for more worship. This time it was almost too much for her. She looked like she was ready to leave because she did not understand anything that was going on. Finally, after another half hour of worship, the preaching started. I was so relieved! I thought, "Yes! Come on and preach the Gospel to her so she can get saved!" But, then the pastor started to speak very dramatically about how Abraham took a knife and wanted to offer his son Isaac to God. When the pastor was speaking about this, I saw her eyes get bigger and bigger, and I could tell she was thinking, "What kind of sick place is this? I need to get out of here right now!" I looked at the pastor, thinking to myself, "Stop talking about this! Get to the Gospel! Preach about the Gospel and how she can get saved!" After forty-five minutes of preaching, the pastor finally said that anyone who wanted to accept Jesus into their heart should lift up their hand.

When I look back at this experience, I see that many people of peace have been lost because they were invited to church when, instead, someone should have sat down and shared the whole Gospel with them. I should not have brought her to church because she did not understand it, and she did not hear the Gospel there. The Gospel requires more than five minutes at the end of a sermon where the pastor asks who wants to receive Jesus into their heart. When I took my friend to church, there was no talk about the cross, sin, repentance, baptism in water, or the Holy Spirit. But these things were so important for her to hear. She needed to hear about the cross and why Jesus needed to die for her. I know, for some people, going to church can be a great beginning of repentance and being born again, but for this girl, it was not. She left without understanding who Jesus was. And what she saw at church frightened her so much that she would probably not be a person of peace the next time someone approached her to talk about Jesus.

I would have done so many things differently if I had known back then what I know now. Instead of inviting her to church, I should have taken the time to sit down with her, maybe at her place, my place, or a café, and shared the Gospel. I could have even taken a friend.

When I think back in my life, I have met so many people who were open to God. There were many people of peace whom I could have sat down with at Burger King or McDonald's, or met in a home, and shared the Gospel with them. Instead, I invited them to church. Most of the people I invited to come to church with me did not end up going because Satan had time to scare them and put reasons in their heads as to why they should not go. The few who did come to church with me did not really hear the Gospel there.

I should have sat down with these people and shared the Gospel as Jesus instructed us to do. When you sit at Burger King, McDonald's, or in a private home, you do not need to have a half-hour worship session, you do not need to take up an offering, and you do not need to talk about other things that are not important or relevant to the person you are sitting with. When you sit with them and explain the Gospel yourself, you can give that person your full attention and explain it in a relaxed and natural way. You can explain the Gospel to them in a way they understand, and if they do not understand something, they can ask you for clarification. For example, if they do not understand repentance you can explain it to them again until they do understand.

The problem today is that we use the church as a place where we invite people to come and get saved instead of using it as a place to train disciples to go out into the world and preach the Gospel. Another big problem is that the churches today are becoming more seeker-sensitive. Instead of trying to make more seeker-sensitive churches that focus on bringing in non-believers, the churches should be training believers and sending them out, equipped and able to lead people to Christ. And then when people come to faith, repent, get baptized in water and with the Holy Spirit, we can then invite them to church where they can get solid food and receive the training they need to grow in Christ. It is important for me to tell you that when I started to sit down with people and share the Gospel with them myself, I started to see fruit in my life that I had never seen before. Since then, I have been teaching many other Christians to do the same, and we have seen thousands of people come to Christ.

The harvest is truly ready and plentiful but we should not stand and shout at the harvest to come into the barn (the church). No, we should leave the barn (the church) and go out into the harvest with the tools Jesus has given us. As I have said before, of course we can see people come to faith in church and of course people can meet God there; but I am convinced that we would bring so many more people to Christ if we did it the way Jesus told us to. And I also believe that if we did it the way Jesus told us to, it would help Christians like you to grow and feel satisfied in their lives. It would make you and other Christians happy if you could bring people to God. Yes, it would make you and other Christians feel alive. Then, when you bring a person to Christ, you would have the opportunity to follow up with that person in a natural way. Yes, this is much better than bringing them to a pastor so the pastor can share the Gospel with them. The pastor would likely be busy with many other things, so that they could not find the time to follow up with them.

> **If we start to preach the Gospel and
> reach people the way Jesus did, we would
> see that the harvest is truly great.
> We would see thousands of people come to faith
> in their homes, coffee shops, or wherever they
> hear the Gospel. It would be the beginning of
> a movement that could not be stopped.**

I know many of you are probably thinking, "Yes, this sounds so good, Torben, but I cannot lead people to Christ. It is not natural for me. I have never led anyone to Christ before, and I have also never baptized anyone in water or with the Holy Spirit." To this, I will say I understand you. At one time in my life, I thought the same. It was also not natural for me in the beginning. When I first started, I had never preached the Gospel to someone or baptized anyone in water or with the Holy Spirit. But this is discipleship, and it is why I am writing this book. I am here to help you so that you can learn from me and do it yourself.

We are all called to lead people to Christ. We are not all called to go to Africa and stand in front of fifty-thousand people, but we are all called to live the simple life of finding a person of peace, leading them to Christ, and seeing the Kingdom of God grow. This can also become natural for you. You can learn all of this. Sometimes the best way to learn is to just jump out in it and take the first small steps. I know I am very thankful that, at one time, I took the responsibility myself and decided to go this way. I wanted to learn to walk like Christ has called us to, and I am still learning. If I can learn, then we can all learn to live this life Jesus has called us to.

As I have said before, it is sad to look back and see how many people of peace we have lost because we did not follow what Jesus said to do. So I encourage you, when you do find a person of peace, stay with them. Do not just invite them to church next Sunday. You know Satan will have a lot of time to create fear in them and tell them many reasons they should not go. And if they do go, you never know what they will get there. Instead, do what Jesus has called us to. When we find a person of peace, sit down and eat and drink with them. Get to know them over some food. Build a relationship with them, and then take the time to share the Gospel and heal the sick, like Jesus is saying. If we train Christians to do this simple thing Jesus has called us to, we will see thousands of people come to faith, and we will see a movement we have never seen before.

14

DO NOT MOVE FROM HOUSE TO HOUSE

**We are called not only to
preach the Gospel and see people saved
but also to help people grow into strong disciples.
We should not only see
one person saved here and there, we should
see whole households come to Christ.**

I n the last chapter, we looked at the first part of Luke 10:7, which states, *"Stay there, eating and drinking whatever they give you, for the worker deserves his wages."* Now, we will look at the last part of this verse, *"Do not move around from house to house."* These last few words in Luke 10:7 are very important in reaching the world with the Gospel and making disciples.

As Luke 10:7 states, when you find a person of peace, you should not move on right away in hopes of finding the next one. No, when you find a person of peace who comes to faith, they are new spiritual beings who need milk. They cannot handle solid food yet. This means they are not ready to survive by themselves; they need somebody to feed them (in the spiritual sense). This is why Jesus instructs us to stay in the home of the new believer. It is our job to help teach them, so they can grow up. But, we are not alone here. This is also the job of the Holy Spirit, to teach people and lead them to the truth. John 14:26 states:

But the Advocate, the Holy Spirit, whom the Father will send in My name, will teach you all things and will remind you of everything I have said to you.

Matthew 28:18-20 states:

Then Jesus came to them and said, "All authority in heaven and on earth has been given to Me. Therefore go and make disciples of all nations, baptizing them in the name of the Father and of the Son and of the Holy Spirit, and teaching them to obey everything I have commanded you. And surely I am with you always, to the very end of the age."

It is our job not only to preach the Gospel and baptize people but also to teach them to obey everything Jesus has commanded. Unfortunately, people who are very evangelistic often move on very quickly in hopes of finding the next person they can lead to Christ, to find the next person of peace. Yes, as soon as they see one person give their life to Jesus, they become very excited and want to move on to find the next one right away.

I am definitely more evangelistic than pastoral. It is sometimes very hard for me to sit down with people and listen to their life story for many hours. I find it personally hard to work with the same people and their problems for many years. But, I do not need to be strong in this because I am not alone in this. We are all part of the body, and just like the five fingers on the hand have to work together to open a door or pick up a cup to take a drink, God has given us different ministries that work together. God has given different ministries to His body (His church) for them to work together. Some of those ministries are found in Ephesians when it talks about the five-fold ministry.

Ephesians 4:11-16 states:

So Christ Himself gave the apostles, the prophets, the evangelists, the pastors and teachers, to equip His people for works of service, so that the body of Christ may be built up until we all reach unity in the faith and in the knowledge of the Son of God and become mature, attaining to the whole measure of the fullness of Christ. Then we will no longer be infants, tossed back and forth by the waves, and blown here and there by every wind of teaching and by the cunning and craftiness of people in their deceitful scheming. Instead, speaking the truth in love, we will grow to become in every respect the mature body of Him who is the head, that is, Christ. From Him the whole body, joined and held together by every supporting ligament, grows and builds itself up in love, as each part does its work.

In these verses, we read how the main job of apostles, prophets, evangelists, pastors, and teachers is to equip the saints to do their ministry so they can help people develop into mature Christians who are no longer like babies tossed around by deceiving teachings.

I know many of you have heard numerous teachings about the five-fold ministry, and many of you have also heard teachings about the five-fold ministry that are not biblically sound. I have heard many people speak about the five-fold ministry in a way that puts people in boxes and says, "You are an evangelist, so you should only be out on the streets. My job is to teach people, and your job is to reach people." Sometimes you even hear, "I am a shepherd, so I do not need to evangelize." Or, sometimes you hear, "You are an evangelist, so you are not allowed to start churches." There are many more examples of how people use the five-fold ministry to put people in boxes or to lift themselves up, but I do not believe it was meant to put people in boxes or to make some people more special than others. I also do not believe it was meant to decide what people can or cannot do because people change. Just because you work in one gifting now does not mean you will not work in another gifting later.

We are all called as disciples to follow Jesus, as we read in His Word, but there are some who, when they grow up in Christ, start to work in these different functions and start equipping the saints to serve Jesus in the area they are strong in and called to. Those who work as an evangelist will then go in front when it comes to reaching people and they will also use their gift to equip the saints to be better at reaching people in their everyday lives. Not all are called as an evangelist, but all can learn to evangelize. The same goes with the other gifts. Those who grow up and work as teachers, for example, will then teach and help others to be strong in the Word, so they, too, can teach others in their everyday lives. We are not all called as evangelists, teachers, prophets, and so on, but we can all learn to share Jesus, share the Word, and prophecy wherever we are. There are people in the church who have these special gifts and are very strong in these areas. We need to recognize them and use their gifts to build up the body of Christ.

When I teach about the five-fold ministry in our Pioneer Training School, I often tell people to sit down in the five-fold group where they think their strongest gifting is. I tell them to sit down for either apostles, prophets, evangelists, pastors, or teachers. Then I ask each group, "What do you see as the biggest need in the church today?" When I ask this question, those who are in the group of pastors will often answer, "Oh, the biggest need in the church is that we need to be better at taking care of each other and helping each other more." I ask the group with the teachers the same question, "What do you see as the biggest need in the church today?" They answer, "The biggest need is sound doctrine. We need sound doctrine and to come back to the Word." The people in the prophets' group will say, "No, the biggest need in the church today is that we come back to the voice of God. We need to hear from God. It is important for us to have a relationship with God where we can hear from Him." Then the evangelists interrupt and say, "Yes, that is all important, but the biggest need is to go out and reach the lost people in the world and see people get saved. All the other things are good, but people are lost out there, and we need to do something to reach them." Then all those who are apostles are listening and thinking, "How can we get all those things to work together because we need it all. We need everything these people are saying."

It is interesting how people see this so differently. It is like the DNA in them. We need to recognize that we are not all the same. Yes, we are all called to follow Jesus, but for each of us, some things come more naturally to us than to others, and so on. It is true we need to go out and reach those who are lost, but we also need to help them build a good foundation in Christ. We also need to teach the new people how to hear from God, and we need to take care of each other so we do not fall away. It is clear that all the giftings are needed and must work together for the

Kingdom of God. If the church was only made up of evangelistic people, we would likely reach many people with the Gospel, but they would not mature and would likely fall away. If the church was only made up of pastoral people, we would have a lot of people who could take care of each other and love each other, but nobody would get saved. This is the same for every ministry. God has given everyone unique DNA. We are all different. Some people have a very strong focus on reaching the lost, while some people have a strong focus on helping each other and building each other up. This is great! We all need each other.

No matter what gift God has given you, remember that we all, first and foremost, are called to be disciples. We are called to find the person of peace, lead them to Christ, and build them up in Him. There are some people who are very strong in each of the different areas, so if we can help each other where we are not too strong, it will be much easier for us all. There are some who are strong in the evangelistic ministry and they are very good at finding the person of peace every time they go out on the streets. They can help us become better at reaching people even if we never become as good as they are. The problem is often that the evangelistic people find a person of peace, then move on very fast and try to find the next one. When the evangelistic people move on too fast, the person of peace will often fall away from the faith. Or, when the evangelistic person moves on too fast, sometimes the family and friends of the person of peace will not have the opportunity to hear the Gospel from this evangelistic person. It is a problem when the evangelistic person moves on too fast because we need to remember that new believers are like babies, and they need milk to survive. These new believers need someone around to help them survive, and this could also be an amazing opportunity to reach other people in their network. Yes, the person of peace may have many people around them who need Jesus, and through them, it is possible to reach these people.

**We are not only called to see people
receive Jesus but to build people up in Christ
and teach them to obey everything
Jesus has commanded them to do.**

We need to help new believers lay a foundation in their life. Hebrew 6:1-2 states:

Therefore let us move beyond the elementary teachings about Christ and be taken forward to maturity, not laying again the foundation of repentance from acts that lead to death, and of faith in God, instruction about cleansing rites, the laying on of hands, the resurrection of the dead, and eternal judgment.

The author in these verses talks about a foundation. He speaks about repentance from dead works, faith in God, and so on. Later, Paul also speaks about how he laid down a foundation and how others built on that foundation.

1 Corinthians 3:10 states:

By the grace God has given me, I laid a foundation as a wise builder, and someone else is building on it. But each one should build with care.

We can see from these verses that people need to have a good foundation in their life. However, those who are evangelistic are not always the most effective in building a foundation. This is why I believe we see such a strong relationship between Philip and the apostles in the Bible. In Acts 8, we read how Philip came to Samaria and how he preached the Gospel with boldness.

Acts 8:4-8 states:

Those who had been scattered preached the word wherever they went. Philip went down to a city in Samaria and proclaimed the Messiah there. When the crowds heard Philip and saw the signs he performed, they all paid close attention to what he said. For with shrieks, impure spirits came out of many, and many who were paralyzed or lame were healed. So there was great joy in that city.

Here we read how Philip came to Samaria and how people received the Word. We read how there was great joy in the city. As we continue reading, Acts 8:14-17 states:

When the apostles in Jerusalem heard that Samaria had accepted the word of God, they sent Peter and John to Samaria. When they arrived, they prayed for the new believers there that they might receive the Holy Spirit, because the Holy Spirit had not yet come on any of them; they had simply been baptized in the name of the Lord Jesus. Then Peter and John placed their hands on them, and they received the Holy Spirit.

Here we read how Philip preached the Gospel to many people. We also read how many people received the Gospel and repented. But Philip needed help. He needed someone to come and lay down a foundation, and this is exactly what happened. The apostles went to the people and continued what Philip had already started. Yes, they came and laid hands on people and they received the Holy Spirit. Philip was actually set free and was able to move on in his life when the apostles went to the people and laid down a foundation so they could grow in Christ. Yes, if the apostles had not come and continued what Philip had started, Philip would not have met the eunuch, and maybe the eunuch would have never come to Christ.

We are all important in the kingdom of God, and we need to work together. Try to imagine a world where the different ministries work together, not to build their own church or organization, but to build the kingdom of God. If you are very evangelistic and often see people come to faith, like Philip, you need people around you who can come and help in areas where you are lacking. This will set you free so you can continue to reach people with the Gospel, but you also need to come help the rest of the church to become better at reaching people in their everyday lives. This is the same with every other gift. We need all parts to do what they are good at and also to help us all be better in these areas. We need all parts of the five-fold ministry in order to build up the church and lay down the right foundation.

On October 18, 1999, I received a prophecy that really spoke to me. It made an impact on my life. I still think about it. The word I received was:

"You are going to drive out demons. You are an evangelist. You are going to break down strongholds in people's minds and teach My Word. 'I am going to teach you to teach My Word,' says the Lord.

You are going to learn strategy and develop plans on how to set people free. I am going to train you. You are going to go out from My body and back to My body. Many evangelists have gone independent, but you will walk with an apostolic team. Remember Philip and the apostles' relationship and how people would get saved daily? You will experience miracles, and you will move forward like a big swinging axe. You will win homes and entire cities for the Gospel, and you will experience the power of the world to come."

Wow, what a strong word I received! When I got this word, I thought to myself, "Wow, I am going to be a super evangelist who will travel around the whole world and see stadiums full of people come to faith." Now, however, I understand that this is not how God wanted it to be. I started to understand this word I received in more detail when, a few years later, I got another word that said:

"You are going to lay down a DNA in a new generation, a DNA that is going to go from generation to generation. You are going to raise people up from nothing to spiritual giants, and they are going to win homes and entire cities for the Gospel."

After I heard this word, I realized I was not going to be a super evangelist who was going to, alone, win homes and entire cities for the Gospel. No, I realized that the new DNA (consisting of a strong foundation in Christ and what I am teaching in this book) laid down in a new generation was going to win homes and entire cities for the Gospel.

I really believe the word I received about laying down a new DNA in a new generation is from God. The problem is, we do not recognize each other's giftings, and we do not have the same goal or the same vision. We have gotten far away from what it is that Jesus is truly calling us to do and His vision for the church. We are not here to build the pastor's church or to help the evangelist have evangelistic crusades. We are here to obey Jesus together in what we read in His Word and what we are looking at in this book—to find people of peace and to build them up.

> **If we could recognize each other's
> five-fold giftings and work together in
> accomplishing what Jesus told us to do,
> we would see things most people only dream about.
> We would see homes and entire cities
> come to Christ.**

When we see this, we will also see how we need people who are evangelistic to equip believers. All are called to find people of peace in their everyday lives. Not all are out on the streets all the time as strong evangelists, but all can find a person of peace. Evangelistic people are needed to help train them how. Evangelistic people also need to be out there finding people themselves and letting those with other gifts come and help follow up with those people of peace. This is important if we want to see people not only come to faith but also to build a good foundation and mature in Christ. Working together with the different giftings is important if we want the Gospel to spread throughout the family of the person of peace and the whole city.

Teachers also need to help believers lay a foundation. We need them. We are not all like them. We will not all stand in front of many people to teach them, but we all need the Word in our lives. We can all teach people we meet in our everyday lives in homes and so on. It is the same with every gift. We need them all to be built up and to become all God wants us to be.

If we work together, we will see growth in the kingdom of God like never before. So when you find a person of peace, do what Jesus says and stay with them. It does not matter if you are evangelistic or not because you do not need to do this alone. You can find people who can help in areas where you are weak. Are you very weak when it comes to evangelism? Then find a person who is strong there and work with them. You will both learn from each other, and together you can bear much fruit. Do not just take a person you meet to church right away, and do not just leave them alone. Stay with them and get to know them, and get others to help. You need to know that the people of peace have a whole network of people around them who also need Jesus. If we start doing this, we will not only see single people coming to faith but also homes and eventually entire cities.

One time in Denmark some years ago, I met a young girl at a meeting. She was a person of peace. I prayed for healing for her leg, and she was healed. She was so happy because she loved to play soccer and football, but she had not been able to play for a long time because of her leg. Now, she could play again. After she was healed, I got together with her and her mother and shared the Gospel with them. The young girl who had gotten healed repented, got baptized in water, and received the Holy Spirit. Her mom was also open but was still part of a Lutheran state church, so at that time, she was not born again. When I talked to the mother, I said to her, "How about you invite people to your home, and I can come and share the Gospel and pray for them like I did with your daughter?" She was very excited about this but was not sure anyone would actually come because she had tried many times to invite her friends to attend the Lutheran church with her, and no one ever wanted to join. I told her I understood why her friends did not want to join her in the church. However, I told her it would be different if she invited her friends to her house to hear the Gospel. It is a big step for friends to go to a church where they have never been before. It was not a big step for her friends to come to her house because they had been there many times before. So, she agreed to write an email to all of her friends inviting them to come and hear the Gospel and hear how her daughter had been healed and met God. She sent this email out to seventeen friends, and to her big surprise, sixteen of them came. She was in shock because she tried to invite her friends to church with her many times, but not one of them ever went with her. But now, sixteen people were interested in hearing the Gospel at her house. Why?

As I have already stated, we did not invite them to the church because it would have been too big of a step for them, so we invited them to her house where they had been many times before. This was not a big step for them. It is not a big deal for her friends to go to her house, as they have been there many times before. The only difference was that this time I would be there to share the Gospel. God came with

His power during that meeting. They heard the Gospel, and many people got healed and were set free. It was amazing. The problem was, that at that time in my life, I did not understand that we need the other ministries to work together. I did not have time to follow up on any of them, so there were never any other meetings. I was too busy and had already moved on to find the next person of peace.

Today, I can see that if I had brought people with me who had other giftings in the five-fold ministry, perhaps they would have been able to connect with them better, and we would have seen more fruit come out of this. Instead of just seeing a few people come to faith who now attend other fellowships, we could have started a new fellowship with them. I really believe that what I am teaching is true. It is so exciting because we are starting to see the different ministries working together. We are starting to obey Jesus and stay with people of peace and build fellowships there. So let us find a person of peace and stay with them. Do not move on so fast. Let's work together with all the ministries and have them come together and build up a foundation for the new believers so they can develop into mature disciples of Christ. We need to work together to reach the network of family and friends of each person of peace.

Let's pray that God will put us together with people of other giftings within the five-fold ministry who have the same focus and goal, people who are strong in areas where we are weak. Together, we can more easily obey what Jesus has called us to do and see people and whole households come to faith. Together, we can see entire cities change, and together, we can build them up until they become strong in our Lord Jesus Christ.

15

WIPE OFF THE DUST

> If we truly want to be effective in finding
> a person of peace, we need to do what Jesus says
> when it comes to wiping the dust off our feet
> and moving on when people do not want to
> listen to us. We need to be like a farmer
> who finds the good ground to sow in.

I n the last chapter, we looked at Jesus' words in Luke 10: 7 where He instructs us not to move from house to house. In this chapter, we are going to jump forward and look at verses 10 and 11 where Jesus states, *"But when you enter a town and are not welcomed, go into its streets and say, 'Even the dust of your town we wipe from our feet as a warning to you ...'"* After we look at verses 10 and 11 here, we are going to go back and look much more at verse 9, where Jesus talks about how to heal the sick and preach the Gospel.

The reason we are going to jump to verses 10 and 11 is that these verses are closely connected with finding the person of peace, which we have been focusing on in the last few chapters. In verses 10 and 11, we see what we need to do with those people who are not people of peace.

This is just as important as what we do with the people who *are* people of peace. Let's say it this way: If we do not do what Jesus tells us to do with the people who are *not* people of peace (those who will not receive our message), then we will never be effective in finding those people who *are* people of peace, and we will struggle in seeing the Kingdom of God grow. When we meet someone who is not a person of peace, we should be quick to wipe the dust off our feet and move on. We will meet many people out there who will not receive us and our message. Unfortunately, most of the people we meet out there *will not* receive us and our message.

Sometimes, when I go out on the street to evangelize, I approach forty or fifty people who are not people of peace and will not hear my whole message before I find the one person of peace who is ready to receive it all. If I spent all my time with the first person I met who would not receive my message, I would never have found that person who *was* ready to receive. The truth is, we can use all our time and energy on people who do not want to listen to our message or who only want to discuss or debate, but if we use all our time and energy on those people, we would never find the person the Lord is calling, who is ready to receive. Most of the people I meet on the streets or in my everyday life are not people I would call "people of peace." Oftentimes, I am able to share something with them, but they are not ready to receive it all. And there is a big difference between people who listen to what you have to say because they are nice and those whom God is really calling. As I said before, I can sometimes stop thirty, forty, or even fifty people before I find that one person the Holy Spirit is drawing, the one person who is ready to listen, ready to receive everything I say, and ready to give their life to God.

Many years ago, when I first started telling people about God, I did not know what I know today about all of this. At that time, I did not know what Jesus meant in Luke 10. If I had only known then what I know now about what Jesus says in Luke 10, I would have seen so much more fruit in the work I did for the Kingdom of God. At that time, I did not know what Jesus called us to do. Therefore, I had a lot of zeal for God, and a longing to see the Kingdom of God grow, but I lacked understanding and fruit. If I knew then what I am about to share with you now, I would have seen so much more fruit in my life, and it would have saved me from a lot of discussions and unpleasant experiences. When I first started telling people about God, I thought every person I met needed to have the whole Gospel preached to them whether they wanted it or not. I often preached to people who did not want to listen or receive my message.

As a result, I often ended up in very big discussions. We ended up in many discussions about things like "what religion is best," and "whether or not all religions are the same." Many times, people also wanted to discuss science and evolution and how it was foolish to believe in God. At one time, I thought the reason people did not want to receive my message was because I did not give them the answer they were looking for; therefore, I started to study different subjects. I studied religion, evolution, and the big bang theory. I even studied what Jehovah's Witnesses, Mormons, and Muslims believed. I truly thought that if I could tell people the answer to all their questions and arguments, then they would repent and believe in Jesus. Because I believed this, I spent a lot of time studying different subjects so I would be ready to go out and give them the answers to their questions. But what I discovered was shocking.

I later discovered that they actually did not want to hear the answer at all. When people came with all their arguments as to why my faith and the Bible were not true, they did not do it because they wanted to know the answer. No, they did it as an excuse, so they could continue sinning. The truth is, they were sinners who loved their sin, and they were not interested in repenting. No one got born again from these conversations because they were truly not interested in repenting, only arguing. All of the time I took studying different subjects so I would be ready to answer peoples' questions bore no fruit of any kind.

Today, I never use what I learned from studying those different subjects. To be honest, I have forgotten most of what I studied. Today, though, I see so much more fruit than ever before. Today, I often see people come to faith, and it is because I am much faster in wiping the dust from my feet and moving on to find the people who are truly people of peace. When you meet these people of peace, you do not need to spend time arguing or discussing evolution, science, or religion because the Holy Spirit has been drawing them, and they are truly seeking and ready to receive. People of peace are people who are seeking God and seeking the truth, so when you meet them, you can go straight to the Gospel, and they do not need to know the answer to all the other questions they may have. That will come later after they have found Jesus, and God has opened their eyes. Then they will know the answers a little at a time, but it is not important to them. They have the truth and all they need.

A mistake many people make today when it comes to sharing Jesus is that they only choose a few people to focus on and then try to reach just them with the Gospel for the next five or ten years. Yes, they find a few friends or family members and then spend year after year trying to reach the same few people, people who are often not open or ready to listen. Doing things this way, they spend years on people who will not receive when they could have spent that time trying to reach other people who are ready to receive the message. Jesus says we should wipe the dust off our feet and move on when people do not want to receive our message. He does not say we should spend many years focusing on the same few people who do not want to listen, as most Christians sadly do. This is a big reason so few people are coming to faith in our churches. We are sowing seed in the wrong ground.

Like everything Jesus is saying in Luke chapter 10, we can see how the early disciples continued obeying Him later in the book of Acts. In Acts 13:50-51, we read how Paul and Barnabus did what Jesus said:

But the Jews stirred up the devout and honourable women, and the chief men of the city, and raised persecution against Paul and Barnabas, and expelled them out of their coasts. But they shook off the dust of their feet against them, and came unto Iconium.

Here we see they tried to reach people, but the people there would not receive, and therefore they moved on to the next place. In the next verse, Acts 14:1, we read this:

And it came to pass in Iconium, that they went both together into the synagogue of the Jews, and so spake, that a great multitude both of the Jews and also of the Greeks believed.

Wow. Instead of spending all the time trying with people who did not want to receive, they did like Jesus and moved on. If they had not done that, they would not have seen a great multitude, both of the Jews and also of the Greeks, coming to faith in Iconium.

> **If you want to be effective,
> then take your seed (your time and the
> Word of God) and use it wisely. Do not spend it all
> on the ground that will not bear any fruit.
> When you first use it, it is gone forever.**

You need to understand that when you try to share Jesus with the same people who do not want to listen to you, their hearts become harder and harder against Jesus and the Gospel. So preaching the Gospel to people who do not want to listen will never help them. It will actually harm them. Now, we have millions of people out there who are bitter and hard in their hearts because we did not do what Jesus said we should do. I meet them all over. People who had friends and family who spent years with them, trying to get them saved, not understanding they were not ready for it. Instead, they should have listened to Jesus and given the Holy Spirit time to work in them, so they could become ready. But now, they have hardened their hearts in a way that they will not listen to anyone or anything that has to do with God.

Another big mistake people often make is thinking that a way to win someone over for the Gospel is by becoming their friend. People will try to win someone over for the Gospel by spending years hanging out with them in hopes that they will one day suddenly open up to the Gospel and ask, "What is it you have that I do not have?" And yes, I have heard some stories about people who have accepted the Gospel this way, but I have also heard so many more stories about people who have actually ended up being influenced by the people they were trying to reach with the Gospel. Yes, I have often seen it end that way, where the people who were trying to reach someone with the Gospel ended up compromising and becoming lukewarm and falling away from their faith themselves.

Sadly, I have seen many people fall away from their faith through what we call "friendship evangelizing." "Friendship evangelizing" can be okay if the people being reached are truly seeking the truth. But if born again believers hang out with people who are enemies of the Gospel and who do not want to listen to the Gospel, the born again believer often ends up being influenced by those people instead.

And here I am not only talking about people who are very blatantly against God, but the most dangerous people to be influenced by are often those who seem so nice and say the right things but with their life deny God. If you do not influence the people you are with, they will start to influence you. It is so simple, and something we all need to be aware of. It is extremely important that we do what Jesus has instructed us to do. We need to wipe the dust off our feet and move on, so that we are not influenced by people who love their sin, and so we do not end up falling away from our faith. We need to be better at listening to the Holy Spirit, and doing what God has instructed us to do.

I remember a time when I led a family to Christ. Shortly after I did this, the mother invited me and my family to her home to have dinner with her and her family. She also invited her brother to come to dinner because she hoped I would be able to tell her brother about Jesus and lead him to Christ. So there at dinner, I sat in front of him, and we started to talk about Jesus. But right away, I could see he was not interested. I could tell he was not a person of peace, so instead of continuing to preach to him the whole night and make him more and more irritated, I just changed the subject and talked about other things. After the dinner, I explained to his sister that he was not ready to receive Jesus in his life right now and that it was better for me to change the subject and talk about something else instead of making him feel irritated. I told her we needed to pray for him and give him over to God, and let God work in his life. I also told her that, in the meantime, we should spend our time reaching other people with the Gospel, other people who are ready to receive. One year later, I went back to visit this family, and her brother was there again. This time, everything was different. He was then ready to receive and ready to give everything to Jesus. He was so ready to receive Jesus into his life that he could hardly wait for me to finish sharing the Gospel with him. What happened? Well, in this case, he went through a really hard time that humbled him and brought him to a place in his life where he was ready to receive Jesus. What had happened was that he had left his wife and moved in with another girl. After a short period of time, he regretted his decision and left that girl to return to his wife. His wife was ready to receive him back into her life until she found out the other girl was pregnant with his baby. When his wife found out about the pregnancy, she wanted nothing to do with him, so he had to move into his sister's basement. He was in a very desperate place in his life and realized he needed help. Now, being in a desperate place in his life, he saw that he could not live without Jesus. He saw what his life had become, and he was desperate to be free from sin and desperate to receive Jesus. So that day, this man gave his life to God. He got baptized and received the Holy Spirit, along with a new life!

We need to give God time to work in peoples' lives. We will not see fruit, no matter how much we preach to people, if God is not working in them and if they are not ready to receive. We can keep on preaching to sinners who do not want to repent, but our words will just make their hearts harder and harder, and they will become more closed to the Gospel. Instead of doing this, we need to be quick in discerning where people are in their lives. Yes, we need to be quick to discern whether or not someone is open to God and ready to receive our message. If they are not, then we should be quick to wipe the dust off our feet and move on, but we should stay with the people who are open to God and ready to receive our message. Yes, we should lead these people to Christ and train them in being a disciple.

When I meet people, I tell them a little bit about my faith and what God has done in my life and see how they react to what I say. If they are open and want to hear more, then I tell them more, but if they are not open or interested, I do not share more, and I move on to the next person. Sometimes, I just give them a business card with a link to The Last Reformation movie on it and tell them that if they are interested, they can go and check out the movie. Of course, sometimes you meet people and think, "This is the last time this person has the chance to hear the Gospel." When this happens, you need to listen to what the

Holy Spirit says. The Holy Spirit may tell you to be very direct and clear and let nothing stop you. So we see that every case is different, but in general, I do not spend a lot of time with those who will not listen.

In the past, when I went out to evangelize on the street, I only stopped three to five people within one or two hours because I always had very long discussions. Yes, I had discussions with them about God, evolution, and science, and after our discussions finished, I went home without ever finding the person of peace. I went home thinking there was something wrong with the harvest because those I met were not open. Yes, I thought the harvest was not ready and plentiful like Jesus was saying because I did not see those (few) I talked to wanting to have anything to do with God. This was my experience until I started to wipe the dust off and move on like Jesus said I should. When I did that, I saw that it is actually just like Jesus says. If your experience is that the harvest is not ready and plentiful, you are looking in the wrong place. Maybe it is time to move on and not spend all your time on the wrong people.

Today, I see that the harvest is ready because now when I stop people and see they are not open, I move on very fast. And sometimes I may ask fifty people before I find that person who is ready to receive the Gospel. When I find this person, I sit down with them and we talk. There is something so special about sharing the Gospel with someone God has been working on, who you know will end up becoming a newborn and will follow Jesus for the rest of their lives. I just love this life! I love leading people to Christ. There is truly nothing as special as bearing fruit that will last forever. So do not spend all your time on the wrong people.

Right now, in this very moment, there are people in your neighborhood who are, like Paul, sitting at home "blind." These people, like Paul, have seen the "light" and are seeking to meet a disciple of Christ, like Ananias, who can come and talk with them. Yes, they are looking for a disciple of Christ to come and lay hands on them so they can be healed and receive the Gospel. At one time, I was one of these people. Yes, at one time in my life, I really did not understand who Jesus was. I was baptized and confirmed in the Danish Lutheran Church just like ninety percent of all of the people in Denmark at that time, but it was just religion. It was just tradition and no life. I really did not understand the Bible or who Jesus was. Although I did not understand any of this, I was hungry. When I was eighteen years old, I was ready to receive and find the truth. I remember the first time someone told me the Gospel. I received what they said right away, and I gave my life to Christ, and I have never looked back since then. One week before I heard the Gospel for the first time, I was working a night shift at the bakery when I suddenly looked up into the sky and shouted to God, "God, if you are there, come and take me! I want to know you!" Yes, I desperately wanted to find the truth, but at that time, I did not know that the truth is Jesus. And when I looked up into the sky and said this, I thought maybe a UFO would come and beam me up and fly away with me. I even thought maybe a big angel would appear, or that writing would suddenly appear on the wall. I truly did not know what I was seeking, but I was seeking the truth. I was seeking something that was real. I was seeking the purpose of life. When I look back at this time in my life, I can see that the Holy Spirit, without me knowing it, was drawing me and making me ready. All I needed was for someone to come and tell me about Jesus. And God did that. He sent someone to me to tell me about Jesus, and that person was my friend who had also just given his life to God. As soon as my friend told me the Gospel, I received it, and gave my life to Christ. Why did I do this? Because I was a person of peace. And there are more people out there right now, who are just like I was at that time in my life.

I was not brought up in a Christian family, and at that time in my life, I had never met anyone who was born again. No, I did not know anything else other than religion and the Lutheran Church. Later on, as I grew up, I found out there were many Christians in the city I was living in, and that there was even a Bible school. Yes, I later found out that I had grown up living in the city with probably the most Christians in all of Denmark. But sadly, no one ever approached me to tell me about God. Why? This is likely because the Christians were so busy with all their church activities and meeting with their friends. In spite of this, God still sent someone to tell me the Gospel, and on April 5, 1995, I gave my life to Christ. I was so ready, but I am also sure that if someone would have approached me to tell me about God a month earlier or even years earlier, I still would have been ready at that time.

There are millions of people
out there right now who are seeking.
They are seeking something, but they are
not sure what it is. They are seeking God,
and they need you to come and
help them find Him.

Yes, I was actually ready to give my life to Christ for a long time.

I want to say that there are many people out there now, who are ready to give their lives to Christ, like I was. But if all the Christians choose only three or four friends to focus on over the next five to ten years, what about those who are not "lucky" enough to have a friend who can tell them about Jesus?

If we use all our time on the same people, we will not do what the Bible says when it comes to wiping the dust off our feet and moving on. We will not find those people out there who are truly seeking the truth and who are people of peace. Remember, if you want to be effective in finding the person of peace, and if you want to be effective in the Kingdom of God, then you need to obey Jesus' words to wipe the dust off your feet when people reject your message. Do not spend five or ten years on people who do not want to listen to your message. The harvest is truly ripe and plentiful, and there are those who are hungry and waiting for your arrival.

16

HEAL THE SICK
AND PREACH THE GOSPEL

**Jesus is the same yesterday, today, and forever.
When Jesus walked on the earth, He went
to people's homes because the sick needed a doctor
and the sinners needed forgiveness.
Now, you and I are His body, bringing healing
and forgiveness to people.**

The harvest is great but the workers are few, and we should pray to the Lord of the harvest to send out workers into the harvest. Jesus says many times what two things we should do when we go out into the harvest. These two things are to preach the Gospel and to heal the sick (or in the order Luke 10 states it: heal the sick and preach the Gospel). Yes, we need to bring healing and forgiveness to the world. Jesus paid a high price on the cross in order for us to be able to bring healing to the sick bodies and forgiveness to the souls. This is what Jesus did, what He died for, and what He now continues doing through you and me, His body.

We have already looked at the harvest and how it is ready and full of people of peace. We have also looked at how we will meet many people out there who will not receive our message, and how we should wipe the dust off our feet and move on when that happens. In the next chapters, we are going to look at what Jesus says when it comes to preaching the Gospel and healing the sick.

Luke 10:9 is an important verse to look at. It states, *"Heal the sick who are there and tell them, 'The kingdom of God has come near to you.'"* What Jesus says here is actually very interesting. Jesus says to heal the sick, and then preach that the Kingdom of God has come near; therefore, He is saying to heal the sick first, and then preach the Gospel second. This is so interesting because oftentimes we think we should do it in another order. We often believe we need to preach the Gospel first, and then pray for people, but what Jesus is saying in Luke 10 is the opposite, and it is also the opposite to what many churches believe and are doing today.

Many years ago, I went to a church where the pastor needed to preach forty-five minutes to one hour before anyone could pray for the sick. I have since found out it does not need to be that way. No, it is not necessary to preach or create faith in people first before you can pray for them. Actually, today, I often start with praying for healing for the sick, and then after they are healed, I tell them the Gospel and explain what has just happened to them. I see many positive things in healing first and preaching second. Yes, when people experience healing themselves, they are very open to listening to what you have to say. And there is no better way to get someone's attention than when they have just experienced healing or deliverance in their own body. It is really amazing to preach the Gospel to someone who has just experienced healing because everything becomes so much more alive and real to them.

Maybe you are thinking *yes, but what happens when you pray for people who do not get healed?* Maybe you think it would make it more difficult for them to listen to the Gospel if they are not healed, right then and there. But no, it is not like that. Even just showing them you are willing to pray for them is a big testimony, even if they do not experience healing. When we step out in faith to pray for someone who is not healed, we show that we believe in this, and that it is real to us.

I do not want to build a big theology on the order of how we should do things, whether we heal the sick first or preach the Gospel first, because every place and every person is different, and we need to be led every time. Yes, it can be different from one time to another. Therefore, we need to be led by the Holy Spirit. In different places in the Bible, Jesus said we should heal the sick first and preach the Gospel second, but we can also find places in the Bible where Jesus says we should preach the Gospel first and heal the sick second. Overall, the order of how we do it is not of great importance. It is, however, very important that we do both things and do what Jesus has called us to do. There is no place in the New Testament where you find Jesus only calling us to preach the Gospel, or only calling us to heal the sick. No, He is calling us to do both things, and we can see throughout the whole New Testament that healing and preaching often go hand in hand. When it comes to healing the sick and preaching the Gospel, it is not just a suggestion, so that if we want to, we are welcome to do it, but if not, then we do not have to. This is not something we only do if we want to because it is a command. Jesus has commanded us, those who love Him and follow Him, to obey His words, and healing the sick and preaching the Gospel are some of those. You cannot say you love Jesus if you do not keep His commands (John 14:15). We, as disciples of Jesus, can be bold when we pray for the sick because we know it is God's will for us to do this. We can be bold because we know it is what Jesus has commanded us to do. Jesus has commanded us to do both, to both heal the sick and preach the Gospel.

Throughout the entire New Testament, we see Jesus' command to us, is to both heal the sick and preach the Gospel, and we need to realize how both of these things go hand in hand. Healing the sick and preaching the Gospel are two areas Jesus paid for with His life when He died on the cross so we could overcome sin, and so we could be healed by His stripes.

Isaiah 53:1-6 states:

Who has believed our message and to whom has the arm of the Lord been revealed? He grew up before him like a tender shoot, and like a root out of dry ground. He had no beauty or majesty to attract us to Him, nothing in His appearance that we should desire Him. He was despised and rejected by mankind, a Man of suffering, and familiar with pain. Like one from whom people hide their faces He was despised, and we held Him in low esteem. Surely He took up our pain and bore our suffering, yet we considered Him punished by God, stricken by Him, and afflicted. But He was pierced for our transgressions, He was crushed for our iniquities; the punishment that brought us peace was upon Him, and by His wounds we are healed. We all, like sheep, have gone astray, each of us has turned to our own way; and the Lord has laid on Him the iniquity of us all.

I am not someone who goes totally crazy over healings, in a way that I am a fanatic, reading all the books and only wanting to see healing. I do not read every book out there about how to heal the sick, nor do I listen to all the teachings about it. Healing is not one of those areas that interests me most. I am much more interested in areas like the Gospel and discipleship. I have read so many more books on the Gospel and discipleship than I have on how to heal the sick, but I love Jesus and want to be a good and faithful servant to Him. I want to be a disciple He can count on, and that is why I pray for the sick. That is why healing the sick is a part of my life and ministry. I love Jesus Therefore, I obey His command. 1 John 2:4 states, *"Whoever says, 'I know Him,' but does not what He commands is a liar, and the truth is not in that person."* So I pray for the sick and preach the Gospel because I love Jesus, and I want to obey Him. Healing the sick and preaching the Gospel are not special callings for a few select people out there. It is part of obeying Jesus. If you take the time to read through the gospels, you will see that healing the sick and casting out demons was not just a small part of Jesus' life. I believe when you look at Jesus and see how He was living, how much time He was using on healing and deliverance, and how much time He was using on teaching and spreading the Gospel, you will see how we should do it. I am not saying everyone should travel around the world and do things exactly like Jesus. I know there are different ministries, but we are all called to be Jesus' body where we are. Praying for the sick and preaching the Gospel is a call for everyone.

Before I move on, if you are thinking to yourself that you are not the kind of person who can just preach the Gospel and heal the sick, I want to tell you it was also very difficult for me to start doing all of this in the beginning. Yes, it was very frightening for me, but you know what? Today it is so much easier. So just give it time and let God work in your life. I want to remind you of Matthew 11:28-30, which states, *"Come to me, all you who are weary and burdened, and I will give you rest. Take My yoke upon you and learn from Me, for I am gentle and humble in heart, and you will find rest for your souls. For My yoke is easy and My burden is light."* Yes, His yoke is easy and His burden is light even when it comes to healing the sick and preaching the Gospel.

We need to die to ourselves. This is part of discipleship. Are you willing to die to yourself? Are you willing to be a disciple? Are you willing to learn and take things step by step? If so, then just relax. Healing the sick and preaching the Gospel can be as natural for you as it is for me and many other people. You are not alone in this. We are here to help you, but first you need to understand that healing the sick and preaching the Gospel are a part of Jesus' call to all of His disciples. Our enemy Satan has been so busy leading God's people astray and has created a lot of wrong teaching when it comes to how to heal the sick and how to preach the Gospel. When it comes to how to heal the sick, our enemy has made many people believe that we, as Christians or disciples, need a very special gift before we can heal the sick, and that there are only a few of us that have that gift.

Now let us look at what the Bible says about the gift of healing. 1 Corinthians 12:30 states, *"Do all have gifts of healing? Do all speak in tongues? Do all interpret?"* In this verse, we read "gifts of healing", and if we read it in context, it is clear that not all have the gift talked about here. Not everyone has the gift of healing, but that does not mean you cannot heal the sick even if you do not have the gift. You do not need the gift of healing to be able to heal the sick, and this is what many people have misunderstood when it comes to this gift.

From reading 1 Corinthians 12:30, it is clear that not everyone has the gift of healing, but as I have said, that does not mean we cannot heal the sick. If we look at Luke 9, Luke 10, and Matthew 10, we read about how Jesus sent the twelve and the seventy disciples out and how they all got the commandment to go and heal the sick. Does that mean those twelve and seventy disciples all had the special gift of healing? No, of course not.

Mark 16:15-18 states:

He said to them, "Go into all the world and preach the gospel to all creation. Whoever believes and is baptized will be saved, but whoever does not believe will be condemned. And these signs will accompany those who believe: In My name they will drive out demons; they will speak in new tongues; they will pick up snakes with their hands; and when they drink deadly poison, it will not hurt them at all; they will place their hands on sick people, and they will get well."

So here we read that these signs follow those who believe. Yes, healing, speaking in tongues, and casting out demons are signs that follow those people who believe. It does not say those signs follow only a few who have a special gift. Let me explain how this works. We read about different giftings and ministries in Corinthians and Ephesians. In Ephesians, we read about the different ministries, and also what the purpose is. The purpose of the different ministries is to equip the saints to do ministry, so they can build up the body. Ephesians 4:12 states, *"For the perfecting of the saints, for the work of the ministry, for the edifying of the body of Christ."*

God has given us, the church, these different giftings and ministries, so we can be equipped to be like Jesus, and help reconcile people to God. He gave us these giftings and ministries so we can be His disciples, and His body here on earth. The giftings and ministries are there to equip us to evangelize, prophesy, help people, heal the sick, teach, and so on. So it is correct that not everyone is a prophet, or has the gift of healing, and so on, but the Bible is very clear that everyone can prophesy, learn to heal the sick, learn to teach people, and so on.

Try to imagine you were only able to do whatever you have a special gifting for. Yes, imagine if someone asked you, "Can you help me in the kitchen?" and you answered, "No, sorry, I cannot help you because I do not have the gift of helping." Or imagine if someone asked you, "Can you give money to this work or organization?" and you answered, "No, sorry, I cannot give any money because I do not have the gift of giving." Or again, imagine if someone asked you, "Can you help the kids with their homework?" and you answered, "No, sorry, I do not have the gift of teaching." Are you understanding the point? These are some of the gifts we read about in the Bible: helping, giving, and so on.

Try to imagine you could only do the one thing you have a gifting for. The world would look very different. This is not how it should be because the giftings are there to equip the saints to do ministry; they are not there to limit us. So we are capable of doing every gift because we have the Holy Spirit, but if we want to learn to prophecy, for example, God has put people on earth who are very strong prophets, and they can help us learn to prophesy. If you want to, for example, learn to love people more, God has put people on earth who are like shepherds, and who can help teach you to love people more. If you want to, for example, learn to reach out to people, God put people on earth who are evangelists, and they can help equip you to reach out to people. So let us focus on Jesus, and do what we read in the Bible. Yes, you can heal the sick, preach the Gospel, cast out demons, teach people, and do everything in Jesus Christ who strengthens you. Maybe you will become so good at a particular gifting that you start to train and teach others how to do the same, and if this happens, we can say that you are gifted in that gifting. So when it comes to healing the sick, you do not need the gift of healing. You just need to do it. You just need to believe in the Word of God, step out, and pray for the sick. When you step out and do this, you will see God's Word is true, and you will see people be healed.

Many Christians are standing in their churches, waiting for a special gifting or feeling, but they need to stop waiting around, and step out and do it. They need to listen to the Word of God, and step out and do it. If this is you, maybe you think it is very difficult to step out in faith and do what Jesus says, but you can always find people around you who can train you and help equip you, so you can be an effective worker in the Kingdom of God. When you meet people who are sick, be bold and pray for them, and you will see how God heals. Yes, we will also pray for people who do not get healed, just like Jesus' disciples also experienced, but remember we are just a disciple. We are here to learn, and become more and more like our Master, Jesus, and we must take one day at a time. Matthew 10:24 states, *"A disciple is not above his teacher, nor a servant above his master. It is enough for the disciple to be like his teacher, and the servant like his master..."* And here in Luke 6:40, he says this, *"The student is not above the teacher, but everyone who is fully trained will be like their teacher."* So we are not above Jesus, but when we have gone through training and discipleship, we will be like Him.

Later on in Matthew, we read that Jesus' disciples prayed for a boy with a demon, and they were unable to cast the demon out. When Jesus came and saw that His disciples were unable to cast out the demon, He rebuked His disciples for their lack of faith, and set the boy with the demon free.

Matthew 17:14-20 (NIV) states:

> *When they came to the crowd, a man approached Jesus and knelt before Him. "Lord, have mercy on my son," he said. "He has seizures and is suffering greatly. He often falls into the fire or into the water. I brought him to Your disciples, but they could not heal him."*

> *"You unbelieving and perverse generation," Jesus replied, "how long shall I stay with you? How long shall I put up with you? Bring the boy here to Me." Jesus rebuked the demon, and it came out of the boy, and he was healed at that moment.*

> *Then the disciples came to Jesus in private and asked, "Why couldn't we drive it out?"*

> *He replied, "Because you have so little faith. Truly I tell you, if you have faith as small as a mustard seed, you can say to this mountain, 'Move from here to there,' and it will move. Nothing will be impossible for you."*

Verse 21 (KJV)*
Howbeit this kind goeth not out but by prayer and fasting.
  *Verse 21 is not included in all translations.

So it really comes down to simple faith. If we believe, nothing will be impossible. But we need to train our faith muscle. We need to take steps and use the faith we have. If we are faithful in the small things, God will give us more. So, instead of thinking it is all about some special gifting, we should be focusing on discipleship because we can do everything through Jesus Christ, who strengthens us. When I read in Matthew 17 how Jesus' disciples could not cast out the demon and how Jesus rebuked them, I think back to the time when I was an apprentice at a bakery. Yes, I think back to the time when I made mistakes, and how my boss shouted at me in frustration, as Jesus did with His disciples. But you know what? I learned. And you know what else? The disciples also learned. Yes, the disciples in the Bible grew, and we read later that everyone who came to the disciples was healed. I believe it is the same today. We need to start where we are and grow in our faith, obedience, and relationship with God. In the beginning, we will pray for many people who do not get healed, but then we will learn and grow, and we will become stronger.

My theology is very simple when it comes to faith. I truly believe it is always God's will to heal, just like it is always His will to save people. When Jesus' disciples could not cast out the demon, they could have come up with many excuses as to why that boy was not set free. Yes, they could have said, "Oh, maybe he has sin in his life and that is why he was not set free", or "Maybe it is not God's will to heal." Or, they could have said, "Maybe healing is not for today." They could have come up with so many excuses, just like people often do today, but at that time, Jesus was still physically here on earth, and He rebuked His disciples for their lack of faith, and He set the boy free. The problem today is that Jesus is no longer physically walking around on earth as He did at that time; therefore, today, when people do not get healed, we start to come up with a lot of false theology as to why it did not happen. There are many books out today that say why healings do not happen, but much of what is being taught is not biblical. If Jesus physically came down to earth today, He would heal everyone just like He did before, and we would all have to change our theology, and throw away all those books and false teachings about healing. So I have a simple theology. Jesus wants to heal everyone, and everyone who came to Jesus was healed. Not everyone came to Him, but of those people who did come to Him, all of them were healed.

Many will say this is not correct because Jesus could not heal many in His home city because of their unbelief, but as I said before, Jesus healed everyone who came to Him. In some places, many were brought to Him, and He healed them all. Other places, like in His hometown, they looked at Him like, "Is this Jesus, the son of Joseph?" and therefore only brought to Him few, but those few, He laid His hands on, and they all got healed.

Mark 6:4-6 states:

> But Jesus said unto them, "A prophet is not without honour, but in his own country, and among his own kin, and in his own house." And He could there do no mighty work, save that he laid His hands upon a few sick folk, and healed them. And He marvelled because of their unbelief. And He went round about the villages, teaching.

So here we read, like in all the other places in the Bible, that Jesus always healed all He laid His hands on. All whom Jesus prayed for were healed. In some places, they brought to Him many because of their faith, and other places, like here in His hometown, they only brought few to Him because of their unbelief.

This is our goal today, to be like Jesus. We are not there yet, but if we continue to grow and learn, I believe that one day, we will reach the point where we as the body of Christ, can see everyone healed, like we see in Act 5:14-16:

> Nevertheless, more and more men and women believed in the Lord and were added to their number. As a result, people brought the sick into the streets and laid them on beds and mats so that at least Peter's shadow might fall on some of them as he passed by. Crowds gathered also from the towns around Jerusalem, bringing their sick and those tormented by impure spirits, and all of them were healed.

In the last chapter of the book of Acts, we read that Paul came to Malta, and he first healed one old man. When the rest of the island heard this, they all came and got healed. Acts 28:8-9:

> His father was sick in bed, suffering from fever and dysentery. Paul went in to see him and, after prayer, placed his hands on him and healed him. When this had happened, the rest of the sick on the island came and were cured.

It is actually very simple. When we pray for people who do not get healed, I do not believe it is their fault because they have sin in their life or anything else like that. I also do not believe it is God's fault. I actually think it is our fault. We, as the body of Christ, are not where we are supposed to be today. We have much learning and growing to do. As I have said, we do not look exactly like Christ now, or like the early disciples in the book of Acts. We do not look like Christ now, but we should look more like Christ now than we did last year. And for me, it is okay when I pray for people, and they do not get healed. It is okay with me when it is my fault that they are not healed because of my lack of faith, and it is also okay that I am not where I am supposed to be because I know I am just a disciple who needs to grow and learn more. God knows we are disciples, and He knows we will make mistakes, and that we need to grow. This is how it always is. Our job is to be faithful in the small things God has given us, and when we do this, He will give us more.

It is okay to make mistakes, but it is not okay to not try. Look at yourself as a disciple or an apprentice who is not yet like your master, but also as one who is learning and becoming more and more like your Master every day. This is what I love about Matthew 17. Here you read that Jesus' disciples were unable to cast out the demon, but later in Acts, we read again and again that everyone who came to Jesus' disciples were healed. So we can see, from Matthew and Acts, the disciples learned and did greater things later in their lives than they did in the beginning. I know when people read Matthew 17, many think Jesus was talking about a certain kind of demon that could only come out through prayer and fasting, but we see this is not true when we read the book of Acts or the rest of Scripture. You never read that there are special kinds of demons that only come out through prayer and fasting. Jesus, in Matthew 17, did not need to stop, pray, and fast before He could cast out that demon. No, Jesus had already prayed and fasted in the beginning of His ministry, and He did not have the unbelief many of us have. The demon could not come out because of the disciples' unbelief. When Jesus said this kind only comes out through prayer and fasting, the kind He was talking about was not a demon; the kind He was talking about was unbelief. Sometimes we come to a place in our life where we have so much doubt and unbelief that we need to do what Jesus said: take some time in prayer and fasting and let God set you free from that spirit of unbelief.

After six years of being a Christian, I had never healed the sick or cast out a demon, but then I did what the Word says. I took time to fast. I did a forty-day fast, and after that fast, I saw the breakthrough I needed in my life. Yes, I started to see people getting healed and demons getting cast out of people. This breakthrough did not happen because I suddenly got a special gift through fasting, but the fasting helped me get set free from the unbelief in my life. The fasting helped me to step out and see things I had not seen before. So I want to encourage you that when you find a person to pray for, do it. Yes, be bold, pray for them, and cast out the demon if they have one. This is what Jesus commanded us to do. And when you pray for people and they do not get healed the first time, you should pray again. If they are not healed the second time you pray for them, then you should pray again. We should continue praying for them until they get healed or until they do not want you to pray for them anymore. But never give up because the people who keep going and continue praying are those who will see healing.

In the beginning, when you first start to see people being healed, you will start to grow in your faith, and it will become easier, and you will start to see greater healings. So, no, you do not need a special gift to heal the sick. You just need to step out on God's Word, lay hands on the sick, and they shall be healed. If you become so good at it that you start to teach and disciple other people how to heal the sick, then we can say you have a gift of healing. This "gift" of healing is not something that should put you in a position over other people, but it is a function in the body of Christ meant to equip and train others to do the same as you.

If you come to a point in your life where you feel you cannot break through, then I recommend you take a time of prayer and fasting. I can see in my life that the times I have fasted forty days have been times where I have seen a breakthrough in my personal life and have really grown in my faith.

We read that Jesus went around healing the sick, casting out demons, and preaching the Gospel of the Kingdom. But the harvest is great and the workers are few. He first called twelve, and then seventy, and now you and me. No place in the Bible do you find that we should only preach, or that we should only heal the sick, or that we should only cast out demons. No, we should do it all. Mark 16:15-18 tells us the signs that should follow us who believe:

> *He said to them, "Go into all the world and preach the gospel to all creation. Whoever believes and is baptized will be saved, but whoever does not believe will be condemned. And these signs will accompany those who believe: In My name they will drive out demons; they will speak in new tongues; they will pick up snakes with their hands; and when they drink deadly poison, it will not hurt them at all; they will place their hands on sick people, and they will get well."*

Yes, here we read it all. Let's go out and preach the Gospel, and we will see these signs follow us. We shall cast out demons, heal the sick, and speak in new tongues. Yes, if something happens and a snake bites us, like Paul in Acts 28:5, we should just shake it off, and if we should drink deadly poison, God will protect us. These are signs that follow all those who believe. Do you believe? Then let us go out and do it, and we will experience that this is the truth. The signs really follow!

17

THE KINGDOM OF GOD IS NEAR YOU

**We should never be ashamed of the
Gospel of Jesus Christ, for it is the power
of salvation for everyone who believes in it.
The Gospel of Jesus Christ is the only power
that can ever transform a person
from the inside out.**

S atan has managed to deceive many in the church when it comes
to the Gospel. Sadly, there are many people, both inside and
outside of the churches today, who have never properly understood the Gospel. They may have heard that Jesus died on a cross for
them, but for many people, it stops there. Many people do not actually
understand why Jesus needed to die on the cross, and they do not
understand what they need to do to receive His forgiveness. Many
people in churches today have heard numerous sermons, but they still
do not understand what faith really is, and what it really means to be
born again. The truth is, you can attend church Sunday after Sunday
without really hearing the Gospel. You can attend church Sunday after
Sunday and think you believe and are born again, but the truth is, you

have been deceived, deceived by something that sounds like the Gospel, but is not. Or you have heard the Gospel of Christ, but when it comes to what you need to do to receive it, you have been told a lie.

In the last few years, I have seen countless Christians being born again and experiencing a brand new life. Yes, you are reading this correctly. I have seen countless Christians being born again and receiving a new life, and these Christians I am speaking about are people who've been in church for years, reading their Bible and hearing preaching, without ever really understanding what it means to be born again. It is really frightening to think about how many people in churches today are not born again. The truth is, we are living in a time where preaching about sin, repentance and the cross is being replaced with a feel-good message. You can hear a feel-good message and receive it without really being changed. you have probably heard it said before, "You do not become a Christian by sitting in church on Sunday, just like, in that same way, you do not become a burger by sitting at McDonald's." I want to add to this that if you sit at McDonald's long enough and eat what they serve, you can end up looking like a burger.

It is truly an amazing transformation to see a Christian who has been sitting in church for years finally understand the Gospel, repent, and become born again. When this happens, it is such a visible transformation that the other Christians around them start to ask what happened to them. We have a big mission field in front of us, and our mission field is not only *outside* the church, it is also *inside* the church. We need to understand that the goal is not to get people to come inside the church for a few hours every Sunday, but that it is to make disciples who follow Christ every day. Our goal is to see people being born again and following Jesus with everything in them. Jesus is the only one who can save. He should not only be our Savior, but also our Lord. We should love Him with all our heart, and together with Him, reach out to the dying world around us.

The Pharisees, at the time of Jesus, did what many church leaders are still doing today. Yes, they give a lot of teachings and rules, but no salvation. They serve religion instead of having a personal relationship with Jesus Christ. Jesus, in Matthew 23:25 states, *"Woe to you, teachers of the law and Pharisees, you hypocrites! You clean the outside of the cup and dish, but inside they are full of greed and self-indulgence."* Like Jesus is saying here, the religious Pharisees (and also many Christians today), were so busy with their outside appearance; however, Jesus did not come to transform the outside: He came to transform the inside. Yes, He came to make a new creation inside, that would be visible on the outside. Jesus came to give us a totally new life, and that comes through a true relationship with God. This is a 24/7 life, not just something you live or do two hours every Sunday. Jesus did not have much compassion for the Pharisees. He was very harsh to the Pharisees because He saw they were hindering people from entering the kingdom of God. Matthew 23:13 states, *"Woe to you, teachers of the law and Pharisees, you hypocrites! You shut the door of the kingdom of heaven in people's faces. You yourselves do not enter, nor will you let those enter who are trying to."* Jesus continues afterward in Matthew 23:25-27:

> *Woe to you, teachers of the law and Pharisees, you hypocrites! You clean the outside of the cup and dish, but inside they are full of greed and self-indulgence. Blind Pharisee! First clean the inside of the cup and dish, and then the outside also will be clean. Woe to you, teachers of the law and Pharisees, you hypocrites! You are like whitewashed tombs, which look beautiful on the outside but on the inside are full of the bones of the dead and everything unclean.*

Yes, these are just some of the things Jesus said to the religious leaders at that time. The truth is that we, in many ways, have lost the Gospel. We are preaching something that is tickling people's ears— something that is not the Gospel, and something that is not transforming lives. The truth is, many today, in the same way as at the time of Jesus, are "shutting the door of the kingdom of heaven in people's faces" by their teaching. They possibly do not know it themselves, and are like the blind leading the blind. Yes, many are blind today when it comes to the Gospel, and what I am sharing here might come across as something new to you, even though it is not new, but actually just what we see in the Bible. For many it will seem strange and new, but do not take my word for it. Take your Bible and see for yourself if what I am sharing is not the truth. Do not be blind like the Pharisees at the time of Jesus.

Let's take the time to look at what the Gospel truly is. If I ask people today, "Where in the Bible do you find the Gospel preached the way we should preach it today?", many people would make the mistake of answering, "In the gospels. We find the Gospel preached in the gospels of Matthew, Mark, Luke, and John." People might think that is the right answer because these four books are called "the gospels," but that is a wrong answer, because we do not find the full Gospel preached in the gospels the way we should preach the Gospel today. When Jesus, in Luke 10, sent out His disciples, they did not share the Gospel the way we should share it today. At that time, they did not share that Jesus died on the cross and that He rose again, because it had not happened yet. At that point in time, they also did not understand the cross the way we do today. Yes, even right after Jesus died and rose up again, the disciples still did not fully understand what God was doing, and they doubted it was truly Jesus who had risen. They also did not understand Jesus needed to die for them on the cross. Yes, before the cross, Peter, in the Garden of Gethsemane, tried to tell Jesus not to go to the cross, but Jesus knew what God's will was, so He rebuked Peter. We have to understand, when Jesus sent out His disciples in Luke 10, He sent them out to preach that God's Kingdom has come near; He did not send them out to preach the Gospel of the Good News of the cross, and how Jesus died for their sins and rose up again. That came later.

If you ask people today what the Gospel is, many people will quote 1 Corinthians 15:3-4 where Paul says, *"For what I received I passed on to you as of first importance: that Christ died for our sins -according to the Scriptures, that he was buried, that he was raised on the third day according to the Scriptures..."* Yes, this is the center of the Gospel that we need to preach today, but you do not find this preached in the four gospels because they were before the cross, and they were still talking about the gospel of the kingdom. The Gospel is about the kingdom, and the King is Jesus.

The disciples at the time of Jesus did not yet understand the full picture, as we can today, and they did not preach the cross as we should today. They were preaching that the kingdom of God was near. They preached that people needed to repent for their sins, and that the kingdom of God had come near to them. They were preaching about

Jesus and how we should all follow Him as His disciples. So at that time, they could only preach that the Kingdom was near, but today we can preach that the kingdom of God is here now, and that is a big difference. We need to understand, the four gospels were all during the time of the Old Testament, and it was a special time between the time of the old and new covenants. In the four gospels, we see a transition happening between the old and new covenants. We see Jesus sometimes talked to people under the law who were still under the old covenant. At other times, He taught about the new covenant, and about what will happen later, in the time in which we are living today. So again, when Jesus sent out His disciples in Luke 9 and 10, they did not preach the same as we should preach today, because they lived before the cross, and we live after the cross.

> **The cross made all the difference. When Jesus died and rose again, something new began. It is so important that we as believers understand what covenant we are under, and what context the verses in the Bible are written in.**

When Jesus sent out His disciples in Luke 9 and 10, He did not call them to go out and preach the cross, and to baptize people in Jesus' name, in water and with the Holy Spirit, as we see later in Acts 2, 8, 10 and 19. Jesus could not send them out to do this because it was before the cross, and they did not have the baptism in Jesus' name, and the Holy Spirit at that time, as we do now. In Luke 9 and 10, when Jesus sent them out, He did not lay hands on them and give them the Holy Spirit before sending them out. The reason, as I said, is very simple. He couldn't do that because it was before the cross, and before the Holy Spirit was sent to earth like we read later in the beginning of the book of Acts. Instead, at that time, He gave them authority for that special moment, to do what they needed to do.

Luke 9:1-2 states, *"When Jesus had called the Twelve together, he gave them power and authority to drive out all demons and to cure diseases, and he sent them out to proclaim the kingdom of God and to heal the sick."* So why did not Jesus baptise them with the Holy Spirit? The four gospels were all before the cross, and before the Holy Spirit was poured out on the earth. But today, we can all receive the Holy Spirit, and in Him, we have the same authority that the disciples were given.

When the disciples were sent out to share the Gospel in Luke 9 and 10, they did not baptize anyone in water to Jesus Christ, because there was no water baptism to Jesus, in Jesus' name, as we have today. There was no one in the four Gospels who was baptized to Jesus, and there was also no one in the four gospels who got baptized in the Holy Spirit. There was also no one in the four gospels who went around preaching the cross, and about how Jesus died for them and rose again.

But today, after the Cross, and after the Holy Spirit has come down, we can and should preach from Acts 2:38, which states, *"...Repent and be baptized, every one of you, in the name of Jesus Christ for the forgiveness of your sins. And you will receive the gift of the Holy Spirit."* Yes, today is the day of salvation, and today you can be born again. The kingdom of God is now here. So although Jesus could not baptize people in water in His name or baptize people with the Holy Spirit, He could teach about it. And Jesus often spoke about the Holy Spirit, which His disciples and many others would one day receive. After Jesus rose up again, He said to His disciples, in Acts 1:4-5:

> *On one occasion, while He was eating with them, He gave them this command: "Do not leave Jerusalem, but wait for the gift My Father promised, which you have heard Me speak about. For John baptized with water, but in a few days you will be baptized with the Holy Spirit."*

Today, we do not need to tell people they need to wait in Jerusalem or any other place, to receive the Holy Spirit, because the Holy Spirit is already here. We do not need to wait anymore. The Holy Spirit is here, and you can receive Him today. As I have said before, they could not baptize people in Jesus' name because the baptism in Jesus' name into Christ is a symbol of the cross. Yes, in baptism we die with Christ, we are buried with Christ, and we rise with Christ (Romans 6). In the

Gospel, they did not baptize to Jesus, but they did baptize people with John's baptism. The people who got baptized with John's baptism later got re-baptized with the "right" baptism, which we read about in Acts 19. In the same way you see that no one in the Gospels got baptized in Jesus' name before the cross, you see everyone who comes to faith got baptized right away to Jesus, in Jesus' name after the cross.

When I tell people it is necessary for someone to be baptized to Christ, people ask me again and again, "Yes, but what about the robber on the cross? He did not get baptized so it cannot be so important." To this, I want to say that yes, it is correct the thief on the cross did not get baptized to Jesus, just like the woman at the well, and just like everyone else we read about in the gospels, or in the Old Testament. None of those people got baptized to Christ, or received the baptism with the Holy Spirit, because it was before the cross. But, we see that everyone who came to faith after the cross all got baptized to Christ right away, and so should you, and that the gift of the Holy Spirit is for everyone.

The first words Jesus spoke were in Mark 1:15, *"The time has come,"* *he said. "The kingdom of God has come near. Repent and believe the good news!"* In John 3, Jesus taught about the Kingdom of God, and that if someone wants to enter into the Kingdom, they must be born again of water (be baptized in water) and of Spirit (be baptized with the Holy Spirit). John 3:1-7 states:

Now there was a Pharisee, a man named Nicodemus who was a member of the Jewish ruling council. He came to Jesus at night and said, "Rabbi, we know that you are a teacher who has come from God. For no one could perform the signs you are doing if God were not with him." Jesus replied, "Very truly I tell you, no one can see the kingdom of God unless they are born again. How can someone be born when they are old?" Nicodemus asked. "Surely they cannot enter a second time into their mother's womb to be born!" Jesus answered, "Very truly I tell you, no one can enter the kingdom of God unless they are born of water and the Spirit. Flesh gives birth to flesh, but the Spirit gives birth to spirit. You should not be surprised at My saying, 'You must be born again.' "

Here in these verses, we see Jesus talk for the first time about the new birth, and what we need to do to enter the kingdom of God. We need to repent, as He said, and then we need to be born again, or *"born from above,"* which is what is written in Greek. We need to be born out of water and Spirit, which is baptism in water and baptism in the Holy Spirit. Many today are teaching that the water Jesus is talking about here is the natural birth because a baby comes out of water from the mother's womb. They say baptism in water is not important for the new birth and to enter the kingdom of God, and they also teach that the Holy Spirit is given to us automatically when we come to faith. Sadly, this is a normal teaching today, but it is not biblical and is not in line with the rest of the New Testament. We will look at this later.

The problem with being deceived, is that you do not see you are deceived. Let's not be afraid to take the Bible and believe it as it is written, no matter our tradition or what people around us think or say.

It makes no sense if Jesus, in John 3, was talking about the natural birth where a baby is coming out of the water in the mother's womb. Then Jesus would actually be saying this, "Very truly I tell you, no one can enter the kingdom of God unless they are born (in the natural) and the Spirit." Why should He say it was important to be born in the natural first, and then in the Spirit to enter into the kingdom of God. Everyone who heard Him, and everyone who will ever read His words, are already born in the natural from their mother's womb. No one who ever heard these words is not already born in the natural. If that was so, then Jesus should have just said, "Very truly I tell you, no one can enter the kingdom of God unless they are born of the Spirit." Yes, this would have been the correct way because it does not make any sense to say to someone who is already born (by the mother) that they need to be born (by the mother) to enter the kingdom of God.

What do we see after the cross when the new covenant started? After the cross, and after Jesus sent His Holy Spirit down to earth, we start to see all of this come together for the first time. When the people asked Peter and the other disciples what they should do, Peter replied, in Acts 2:38, *"Repent and be baptized, every one of you, in the name of Jesus Christ for the forgiveness of your sins. And you will receive the gift of the Holy Spirit."* This is amazing. Here we can see, for the first time, the Gospel being preached the way we should preach it today. Yes, here we see what Jesus was talking about, that we need to first repent and then be born again out of baptismal water and Spirit.

It is so beautiful to see how the new covenant was established, and how everything got started. Peter continues, in Acts 2:39 saying, *"The promise is for you and your children and for all who are far off—for all whom the Lord our God will call."* Those whom the Lord will call include you and me.

We need to first recognize our sins and repent to the Father. Then we need to get baptized into the Son, Jesus Christ, and receive the Holy Spirit. Satan has been lying and trying to confuse people when it comes to the Gospel. Satan has tricked many people today into thinking baptism is just a symbol, that the Holy Spirit is not for everyone, and that you automatically receive the Holy Spirit the moment you believe or pray the sinner's prayer.

I have met many people who are so fast to pray a prayer with people, and right away, after they have finished the prayer, they tell them, "Congratulations, you are born again." But this is found nowhere in the Bible. We do not find people who pray a "sinner's prayer," as many call it. The idea that people pray a special prayer and are then suddenly born again is an idea that has existed for only a few hundred years. You do not see this anywhere in the Bible. Maybe you are thinking, "Yes, but in Romans 10, it says you should ask Jesus into your heart." Romans 10:9 states:

If you declare with your mouth, "Jesus is Lord," and believe in your heart that God raised Him from the dead, you will be saved. For it is with your heart that you believe and are justified, and it is with your mouth that you profess your faith and are saved.

Yes, it could look like that is what Romans 10 is saying, but that would be taking these words out of context. Yes, you need to understand that these words are not written to sinners out on the street who do not know the Gospel. These words are written to Christians. They are written to people who have already been baptized in water (Romans 6), and who have already received the Holy Spirit (Romans 8). Paul, in Romans 10, encourages the Christians to continue believing and to continue confessing that Jesus is Lord. If the followers of Christ do this, they shall one day be saved. This is how Romans 10:9 should be understood. But no matter how you see it, if you look at the book of Acts, you will see how the early church was preaching the Gospel to other people, and you will never find the "sinner's prayer."

As I have previously mentioned, the sinner's prayer is only a few hundred years old. The idea of the sinner's prayer started with Charles Finney (1792-1875) and Dwight Moody (1837-1899). Later, it became more known through Billy Graham and the Campus Crusades for Christ. Now, almost everyone practices the sinner's prayer. I am not saying that God cannot use a prayer like that, and I am not saying it cannot be the beginning of a new life with God, but it is wrong to say to people who have just prayed that prayer, "Congratulations, you are now born again" because this is not biblical, and it was not something they did in the early church. When you study the early church and how they were preaching the Gospel of Christ, you can see how Satan has brought the church far away from the truth.

Despite Satan misleading the church and causing it to be built on a wrong foundation, we praise God because He is taking people back to the true Gospel as it is written in the Bible. We are up against some strong traditions in the church that have been there for many years, and it is not always easy to change these traditions. For example, baby baptism is an important part of the Lutheran church I grew up in. When you look at a church tradition like this, it would be very hard or almost impossible for the church to let go of that tradition. It would split the church, although this is the wrong foundation to build on.

When I was a baby, I was baptized in the Lutheran church in Denmark, just like ninety percent of the other people in Denmark at that time. Growing up, we all believed we were born again because we were baptized as a baby in the Lutheran church. Why did I get baptized as a baby? Is it written in the Bible that babies should be baptized? No.

No, it is not written in the Bible, but hundreds of years ago, a Roman emperor, Constantine, laid down the foundation of what became the Catholic church, and throughout the years, the Catholic church became what we know it to be today. At one time, they changed baptism from full immersion in water to sprinkling of water on the forehead. They also changed it from adults and bigger children, who were baptized on their own faith, to babies, as we see today. Later on, in 1517, Martin Luther went against the Catholic church, and it resulted in the start of the Lutheran church. Although Martin Luther went against some of the heresies in the Catholic church, he never changed the baby baptism back to what we see in the Bible. So I, along with many others, got baptized as a baby because of Constantine, Martin Luther, and hundreds of years of history. But if we go back to the time of Jesus and the early disciples, there was no Catholic church, Lutheran church, or baby baptisms. Many of the traditions we see in churches today did not exist during that time, but they did have the Gospel. (For more study on this, read Matthew 15:1-9, Mark 7:8 and 13.) The early disciples had an amazing life following Jesus, and they saw that He was alive and among them through the Holy Spirit.

Today, it is difficult for many people to truly understand the Bible the way that it should be understood because of their strong tradition, and what I call the "religious glasses." We read the Bible through our "glasses" of what we have been taught throughout the years.

Another area our enemy Satan has really managed to destroy the way we read or understand the Bible is by the chapters and verses. When the Bible was written, it was written book by book and letter by letter without chapters and verses, and it was never meant to have chapters and verses. We were never supposed to take out a verse like John 3:16 or Romans 10:9 and make a sermon with the verses. I am not against quoting verses from the Bible, but we always need to understand the context in which the verses were written. Many people today do not understand the context in which the verses were written, and many Christians are living what I call a "copy and paste Christianity," where people find a few verses from the Bible, take them out of context, and then put them together to get the Bible to say what they want to hear. But again, the Bible was never meant to be read like that. We need to understand the big picture. We need to understand the Bible from the beginning to the end. So, in the next chapters, we are going to take some time to look at the Bible and what the Gospel is, so that we preach the true Gospel, the Gospel that can transform a person not only on the outside, but also on the inside.

18

THE BOOK OF THE APOSTLES

**We are living in an amazing time, a time the
prophets in the old days were looking forward to.
Yes, we are living in a time they were prophesying
about, but a time they never experienced. We are
living in a time where we can walk around here on
earth as disciples of Christ, filled with the Holy
Spirit, healing the sick and casting out demons,
saying the kingdom of God is here!**

"*It is finished*." Those were the last words that came out of Jesus'
mouth before He gave up His life on the cross (John 19:30). When
Jesus breathed His last breath and died, this marked the beginning
of the new and amazing time we are living in today. Yes, we are living
in the time the prophets in the Old Testament were prophesying about
but never got to experience themselves. We are living in a time Ezekiel
and Jeremiah prophesied about five hundred years ago before Christ.
Ezekiel prophesied in Ezekiel 11:19-20:

> "*I will give them an undivided heart and put a new spirit in them; I
> will remove from them their heart of stone and give them a heart of*

191

flesh. Then they will follow My decrees and be careful to keep My laws. They will be My people, and I will be their God."

Jeremiah prophesied in Jeremiah 31:33-34:

"This is the covenant I will make with the people of Israel after that time," declares the Lord. "I will put My law in their minds and write it on their hearts. I will be their God, and they will be My people. No longer will they teach their neighbor, or say to one another, 'Know the Lord,' because they will all know Me, from the least of them to the greatest," declares the Lord. "For I will forgive their wickedness and will remember their sins no more."

Whoa, we are living in a time when we can be born again and experience God replacing our stony heart with a heart of flesh, and we can experience His Holy Spirit within us. We can have this life today, a life where we can know and walk with God. This is the Gospel Paul was unashamedly preaching.

I would like to share something about the book of Acts and how we can learn so much about this new life from this book. The book of Acts is a special book because it is the first book after the cross, and it is also the only book where we really see the new covenant being lived out by the first disciples.

The apostles, at the time of the book of Acts, had walked with Jesus for three years and experienced many amazing things. They heard Jesus speak about the kingdom of God, and He sent them out to people around them for them to later come back to Jesus and learn even more. They were in true discipleship with Jesus for over three years.

They were there when Jesus was crucified, when He rose from the grave, and later ascended into Heaven. They were there when the Holy Spirit came down and filled them all. They were there in the beginning of the new covenant that was prophesied about five hundred years earlier. They were all there, and the book of Acts shows how they lived this new life. It shows the early beginning of the true disciples of Jesus. It is the only book in the entire Bible where we really see how the people who were there in the beginning were living, and how they were working with Jesus, being led by the Holy Spirit, preaching the Gospel of the kingdom that had come, and how people were being born again. We can learn a lot from the book of Acts.

One thing we can see in Acts, which we cannot see in any other book, is how they preached the Gospel, how people responded to what they heard, and what they did to be born again. We do not find this in any other book of the Bible. It is therefore important for us, when we read the book of Acts, to pay attention to how they shared Jesus and how people reacted to hearing the Gospel. We can learn so much by looking at what they preached to others and also how people responded to the Gospel. Sometimes we cannot see what they were saying in detail, but we can get a better idea of what was said from the response they got.

If we look for examples, we can find in Acts 8 about Philip and the Ethiopian eunuch. Here, we do not read in detail what Philip was preaching to the eunuch, but we read how the eunuch responded to what he heard. And out of his response, we can learn a lot and get a good picture of what was said. We read here how the Holy Spirit said to Philip that he should go to Gaza, and this is where Philip met the eunuch who was sitting in a carriage reading the prophet Isaiah.

Acts 8:26-39 states:

Now an angel of the Lord said to Philip, "Go south to the road—the desert road—that goes down from Jerusalem to Gaza." So he started out, and on his way he met an Ethiopian eunuch, an important official in charge of all the treasury of the Kandake (which means "queen of the Ethiopians"). This man had gone to Jerusalem to worship, and on his way home was sitting in his chariot reading the Book of Isaiah the prophet. The Spirit told Philip, "Go to that chariot and stay near it." Then Philip ran up to the chariot and heard the man reading Isaiah the prophet. "Do you understand what you are reading?" Philip asked. "How can I," he said, "unless someone explains it to me?" So he invited Philip to come up and sit with him. This is the passage of Scripture the eunuch was reading: "He was led like a sheep to the slaughter, and as a lamb before its shearer is silent, so He did not open his mouth. In His humiliation He was deprived of justice. Who can speak of His descendants? For His life was taken from the earth." The eunuch asked Philip, "Tell me, please, who is the prophet talking about, himself or someone else?" Then Philip began

with that very passage of Scripture and told him the good news about
Jesus. As they traveled along the road, they came to some water and
the eunuch said, "Look, here is water. What can stand in the way of
my being baptized?" And he gave orders to stop the chariot. Then
both Philip and the eunuch went down into the water and Philip
baptized him. When they came up out of the water, the Spirit of the
Lord suddenly took Philip away, and the eunuch did not see him
again, but went on his way rejoicing."

This is a good example of how we can learn so much from the book
of Acts. In Acts 8, we do not see Philip preaching about Jesus and the
cross. However, in verse 35, he begins with the same Scripture and tells
him the good news about Jesus. That is all that we read here. We do not
read exactly what he preached, but from the response the eunuch gave,
we can make an assumption about what he preached. Yes, we can see
that Philip preached a Gospel that led into baptism because the eunuch
saw water and wanted to get baptized right away. Yes, the response he
gave was the same response people gave all throughout the book of Acts,
and it is still the response we should see today.

We need to ask ourselves how often we hear of the Gospel being
preached to a person today where they have the same response as the
eunuch, who wanted to get baptized right away. Everyone in the book
of Acts who came to faith had the same response, getting baptized right
away. If we do not see this today, there is something wrong, and it is
not the Bible. There are also other places in the book of Acts where we
see a little more detail about what they were preaching, and the
responses people gave to what they heard.

If we take the whole book of Acts and all the experiences we read
about—what was said, and how people responded to what they
heard—and put it all together, we end up with a very clear picture of
how the early church was sharing the Gospel. Yes, we end up with a
more clear picture of how the early church was living, how they were
persecuted, how they loved each other and lived together preaching
the Gospel, and how people responded to what they heard.

So the book of Acts is a very unique book. It is not a book of
theology, but it is a book that shows the life they were living, a life we
should be living today. As I have said before, I truly believe that Jesus

is the same yesterday, today, and forever and that the Holy Spirit is also the same yesterday, today, and forever. So what the disciples did in the book of Acts is what we should still be doing today.

I am very inspired by how the early disciples lived in the book of Acts because we can see the real life there before it got destroyed by all of our tradition. They were living in a time before the Catholic church, the Lutheran church, the Baptist church, and so on. They were living in a time before hundreds of years of church history, and before all our traditions of man came in and took us away from the simple and strong life in Jesus. In the book of Acts, you see a purity, and a real life I believe we should imitate today.

> **God has given us the book of Acts as a glimpse of the life the early disciples lived. Here, we can see how they preached, and people's responses to their preaching. This should be the same today.**

In Acts 2, I love how three thousand people got baptized in one day. In Acts 8, I love how Philip came to Samaria, and people got healed, set free, and a small revival broke out. I love Acts 10, where you read how Peter went to the house of Cornelius, and how Cornelius and his whole family came to faith. I also love what happened in Acts 16 with Paul and Silas being let out of jail supernaturally, and how the jailor and his whole household came to faith and were baptized in the middle of the night. I love it when Paul came to Ephesus in Acts 19. There he met some disciples, and asked them if they had received the Holy Spirit when they came to faith. When they said no, Paul baptized them in water, in Jesus' name, right there. He then laid his hands on them, and they were baptized with the Holy Spirit and spoke in tongues and prophesied. I love the whole book of Acts, and I love all these examples that give a good picture of how they obeyed the call of Jesus and what we should experience today. I love to take all these chapters and put them together, so it gives an even clearer picture of what happened in the time of the early disciples. It gives a very clear picture of how people at the time came to faith in Christ by repenting from their sins, getting baptized in water, and receiving the Holy Spirit.

We can also learn a lot from the book of Acts by seeing what they did not do. For example, we do not find anyone who prayed "the sinner's (or salvation) prayer," asking Jesus into their heart. We also do not see anyone waiting to be baptized in water until they have been in church longer or received some extra teaching. Yes, there are many things we do today that are just not biblical. It is not biblical to get people to pray a "sinner's prayer," or to "ask Jesus to come into their heart." No, the response they gave in the Bible was turning away from their sins, immediately getting baptized in water, and receiving the Holy Spirit. They took Jesus' words seriously when He said, in Mark 16:16, *"Whoever believes and is baptized will be saved, but whoever does not believe will be condemned."*

The book of Acts is special because it is the only book in the New Testament where we see that they did what Jesus called them to do in Luke 10, and so on. All other New Testament books are teaching and letters written to people who are already believers. They were all written to people who were already born again. When they started writing a letter, they often started off by addressing "the saints," which means the believers in that city. In Philippians 1:1, we read, *"Paul and Timothy, servants of Christ Jesus, to all the saints in Christ Jesus that are at Philippi, with the bishops and deacons: Grace to you and peace from God our Father and the Lord Jesus Christ."* And in Colossians 1:2, we read, *"To the saints and faithful brethren in Christ that are at Colossae: Grace to you and peace from God our Father."*

We see that the letters were written to those who were already believers; therefore, we do not go to the letters to see how the early church was preaching the Gospel, or how people came to faith in Jesus. The letters were more of teaching that was meant to equip the already-born-again believers. The letters are as important as the book of Acts, but we see things in the book of Acts that we do not see in the letters, and vice versa. For what I am teaching in this book that you are holding in your hands, how we are to obey Jesus' call in Luke 10, the book of Acts is unique.

If we look at the church today, we are sadly seeing many people who believe, but without having a full understanding of the Gospel, and without being born again. Yes, I have met many people who believe in God; however, their faith alone cannot save them. Satan also believes in God, and he is not saved. I have met many people who believe that Jesus is the Son of God and that He died on a cross, but that kind of faith is not going to save them because they have not yet responded biblically to what they have heard, and they are continuing in sin. Satan and the demons also believe that Jesus is the Son of God, and they know He died on a cross, but they still live in rebellion against Him and His Word. The faith that saves us is a faith that not only believes "about" Jesus, but it is a faith that believes and trusts "in" Jesus and what He says. This faith believes Jesus and His words but also acts on His words. If someone today says something to you and you believe them, you will act on what they say.

If you are standing in the middle of the road and a person standing on the side of the road sees a truck coming toward you, they would shout, "A truck is coming! Move! A truck is coming!" If you believe them (not only about them as a person, but truly believe in them and what they are saying), you will move. You will not keep standing there on the road unless you have a death wish. Faith without obedience is dead. I want you to read the following verse from James, and when you read this verse about deeds or works, you have to understand that James is not talking about works by the law, like the law of Moses, but he is talking about obedience by faith. And faith without obedience is, as James says here, dead.

James 2:14-26 states:

What good is it, my brothers and sisters, if someone claims to have faith but has no deeds? Can such faith save them? Suppose a brother or a sister is without clothes and daily food. If one of you says to them, "Go in peace; keep warm and well fed," but does nothing about their physical needs, what good is it? In the same way, faith by itself, if it is not accompanied by action, is dead. But someone will say, "You have faith; I have deeds." Show me your faith without deeds, and I will show you my faith by my deeds. You believe that there is one God. Good! Even the demons believe that—and shudder. You foolish person, do you want evidence that faith without deeds is useless? Was not our father Abraham considered righteous for what he did when he offered his son Isaac on the altar? You see that his faith and his actions were working together, and his faith was made complete by what he did. And the scripture was fulfilled that says, "Abraham believed God, and it was credited to him as righteousness," and he was called God's friend. You see that a person is considered righteous by what they do and not by faith alone. In the same way, was not even Rahab the prostitute considered righteous for what she did when she gave lodging to the spies and sent them off in a different direction? As the body without the spirit is dead, so faith without deeds is dead.

James is not talking about works by the law, but he is talking about (works) obedience by faith. If you truly believe in Christ, you believe Him, trust in Him and what He is saying, and you will therefore do what He says. If you do not do what He says, then you do not truly believe in Him. You can see if a person truly believes in Christ by looking at the way that person lives. It is actually so simple, and in the book of Acts, we can really see their faith. We can see what they truly believed by what they did and how they lived.

> We should not only believe *about* Jesus, but we should believe *in* Jesus. We should believe His words and what He says to us in the same way we believe other people around us and what they are saying to us. There is only one way we can show and prove we believe in Jesus' words, and that is through our actions and our works.

I have met many people who believe they believe, but it is clear by the way they live that they do not. The faith that the Bible is talking about is a faith that is visible in the choices a person makes. It is not about keeping the law of Moses, but it is about living in obedience to Jesus and His words. Jesus' first words were to repent, and later He said to repent and be baptized. If we believe Jesus, then we should repent and be baptized. It is so simple.

I have also met many people who believe and say they love Jesus and are very sincere in their faith, but because of their lack of understanding of the Gospel and discipleship, they are not free and do not live a life according to what we read in the Bible. Some of them have not yet truly repented and been baptized in water, so they are still struggling with sin in their lives, or they have not yet received the Holy Spirit, so they lack the power and the life that comes with the Holy Spirit.

I love the way Paul met people, like he did in Acts 19 when he came to some disciples in Ephesus. He met some believers there, and it was not clear from the verses if they were disciples of John or disciples of Jesus, but they had faith. One thing was for certain, they needed to be born again. When Paul met them, he did not ask what church denomination they came from because that was not important. (Yes, I know there were no church denominations at that time, but it is not important what church denomination people are from. You can meet someone from a Baptist background who has received the Holy Spirit and a new life, and you can meet someone from a Pentecostal background who has not.)

When Paul met the people in Ephesus, he asked them if they had received the Holy Spirit when they believed. This is a weird question for many today who believe they automatically received the Holy Spirit the moment they believed, but this passage, and Acts 8, show it is not like that. You can repent, believe, and even be baptized without receiving the Holy Spirit. Here, Paul talked with them about the new birth, and right then, they got baptized into Christ. After they were baptized, Paul laid his hands on them, and they received the Holy Spirit. It should still be like this today. When we meet people today who believe in God, we should ask them, "Did you receive the Holy Spirit when you believed?" If the answer is no, we should lay hands on them and pray for them to receive the Holy Spirit.

Acts 19:1-7 states:

While Apollos was at Corinth, Paul took the road through the interior and arrived at Ephesus. There he found some disciples and asked them, "Did you receive the Holy Spirit when you believed?" They answered, "No, we have not even heard that there is a Holy Spirit." So Paul asked, "Then what baptism did you receive?" "John's baptism," they replied. Paul said, "John's baptism was a baptism of

repentance. He told the people to believe in the one coming after him,
that is, in Jesus." On hearing this, they were baptized in the name of
the Lord Jesus. When Paul placed his hands on them, the Holy Spirit
came on them, and they spoke in tongues and prophesied. There were
about twelve men in all.

In the next chapters, I want to use more time to look at the Gospel
of the kingdom. I want to give you the big picture from the beginning
to the end, and help you understand what people need to do to be born
again and enter into this kingdom Jesus came with. Later, I will put it
all together so you can go out on Jesus' words and, as we read in Luke
10, find a person of peace and lead them to Christ.

The Gospel is the power of salvation, and we should not have this
wrong. We can do everything Jesus is saying in Luke 10, but if the
Gospel of the kingdom you are preaching is wrong, it does not matter
if you get the rest right. This is the reason we will spend more time on
what the Gospel is about and what it is that Jesus has called us to go
out and preach.

19

THE WHOLE STORY

**Some things in life are more important
than others, but when it comes to why we are here,
how our sins separate us from God, and what
Jesus did on the cross, there is absolutely nothing
more important than this. We need to take the
time to explain this to people. We need to
tell them the whole story.**

"*What shall we do?*" (Acts 2:37). This is what the people asked Peter and the other apostles after they heard Peter share the Gospel. His words stung them deeply in their hearts. Acts 2:37 states, "*When the people heard this, they were cut to the heart and said to Peter and the other apostles, 'Brothers, what shall we do?'*" There have been many times when I have sat down in front of a person of peace and shared the Gospel with them. Oftentimes, they have asked me, "What shall I do?" "How can I meet God?" Or "I want to be born again." It is wonderful to hear people ask these questions, and it is so important that we give them the right answers.

Peter's response to the people's question is shown in Acts 2:38-39:

"Repent and be baptized, every one of you, in the name of Jesus Christ for the forgiveness of your sins. And you will receive the gift of the Holy Spirit. The promise is for you and your children and for all who are far off—for all whom the Lord our God will call."

But Peter did not stop there, and neither should we stop there. Acts 2:40-41 states,

"With many other words he warned them; and he pleaded with them, 'Save yourselves from this corrupt generation.' Those who accepted his message were baptized, and about three thousand were added to their number that day."

So Peter and the other disciples took their time to explain to the people that they needed to be saved from this corrupt generation, and, after that, they took the time to explain the Gospel and baptize them.

We have been looking at the call of Jesus in Luke chapter 10. We have seen His mission and how He wants us to reach the lost people around us, finding the person of peace. But as I have said before, if we do all this but get the Gospel wrong, we will get everything wrong. We will deceive ourselves and those who are listening to us.

One thing I have needed to change over the years has been my understanding of the Gospel, and how to share it. Many years ago, I was traveling as an evangelist and asking people in churches to come up and "ask Jesus into their hearts," and to pray the "sinner's prayer." I saw many "accept Jesus" like this. For a few, this became the beginning of a new life, and they later got baptized and received the Holy Spirit, but for most of them, there was not a real, everlasting transformation.

Then, God started taking me on a journey where I took the time to really study how the early church was preaching, and what the Bible, not our tradition, was saying about the Gospel. Then, wow, everything changed. After this long journey, when I started to share like we see here, everything changed. The fruit I saw was so different. I started to see amazing trust. I started to see what we see in the book of Acts. I started to see how people repented, got baptized, and received the Holy Spirit, sometimes all on the same day, and they really became strong disciples of Christ.

I plead with you to listen to what I want to share here, and take your Bible and see if this is not the truth. Put away your tradition and what you have previously learned, and with new eyes, join me on this journey as I take the time to explain how I share the Gospel, and how I talk about sin, the cross, repentance, baptism in water, and the baptism with the Holy Spirit.

Maybe you will also find out that something is missing in your life. Hebrews 4:12 tells us:

"For the Word of God is alive and active, sharper than any double-edged sword, it penetrates even to dividing soul and spirit, joints and marrow; it judges the thoughts and attitudes of the heart."

When you learn the Gospel and share it with others, it cuts both ways. I have seen many, as they are learning to share the Gospel, finding out that they themselves have never fully repented, or they needed to get baptized again on their own faith, not like when they did it because their parents wanted them to do it, or everyone else expected it from them. So be ready to examine your own life when we look at the Gospel.

As I have said before, when we find a person of peace, I believe it is very important for us to take the time to explain the Gospel and show them how they need to respond to what they have just heard. When I sit in front of a person of peace and share the Gospel with them, I often start from the very beginning, where everything went wrong with Adam and Eve. I start in the very beginning because I want people to understand what sin is, and why the world looks the way it does today. It is important for people to see their sin and why they need Jesus as their Savior. We should not serve the solution to the problem before people understand the problem. We should not try to make people take their medicine before they even know they are sick. We should not try to give Jesus to someone who does not see their sin and their need for salvation. They will not understand it. They will not see the sense in it all and will reject it right away.

Try to imagine a doctor who has a patient with cancer, and this doctor has a treatment that can cure cancer, but it will only work if the patient follows the treatment plan one hundred percent. Imagine this doctor starts by explaining to the patient the seriousness of the sickness, and the patient becomes visibly uncomfortable and upset while hearing this. Although this news makes the patient uncomfortable and upset, it actually helps to prepare the patient to accept the treatment the doctor later presents because, after the doctor explains how sick the patient is and how he is going to die, the patient is desperate to hear how this treatment can save him. At that moment, the patient is so ready and excited not only to receive the treatment, but also to follow the treatment exactly as the doctor prescribes it. Yes, as soon as people see their sins, they will see their need for a Savior, and what Jesus did on the cross will suddenly make sense. And when they hear what they need to do to receive that Savior, they are excited and ready to do what is needed.

> **The more people see their sins, the more thankful they are to Jesus for what He did for them. And the more they are forgiven, the more they will love Him. We all have sinned, but not everyone sees how much they have been forgiven.**

I hope you are ready to go through the Gospel with me the way I normally share it. I normally do not share where the verses are written in the Bible when I share the Gospel, but I will do that now because it will give you the opportunity to look at the verses for yourself. So now, let us start at the beginning.

In the beginning of the Bible, we read how God created the heavens and the earth and how He said everything He created was very good (Genesis 1:31). Yes, everything God created was very good. It was perfect. In Genesis 2, we read in more detail how God created man and how He put man in the Garden of Eden.

Genesis 2:9, 15-17 states:

The LORD God made all kinds of trees grow out of the ground—trees that were pleasing to the eye and good for food. In the middle of the garden were the tree of life and the tree of the knowledge of good and evil.

The Lord God took the man and put him in the Garden of Eden to work it and take care of it. And the Lord God commanded the man, "You are free to eat from any tree in the garden; but you must not eat from the tree of the knowledge of good and evil, for when you eat from it you will certainly die."

This was God's plan. God created Adam and Eve, and they walked with Him in the Garden. It was a perfect world. They were free to eat from the Tree of Life. The world God created was a world without sickness, wars, rape, or murder. Yes, everything was good, and man walked with God and had close communion with Him. Try to imagine this: a life without all the evil we see around us today, a perfect world in fellowship with God where there is no sin, sickness, and so on. But it is not like that today if we look at the world we are in. Just look at the news and see all the terrible things happening around us. It is clear that this is not a perfect world and that it is only going to get worse.

The world God created was good, and it was supposed to continue to be good. Everything changed when Adam and Eve ate from the wrong tree, the Tree of the Knowledge of Good and Evil. They ate from the forbidden tree, and that changed everything.

Genesis 3:22-23 states:

And the Lord God said, "The man has now become like one of Us, knowing good and evil. He must not be allowed to reach out his hand and take also from the tree of life and eat, and live forever." So the Lord God banished him from the Garden of Eden to work the ground from which he had been taken.

When Adam and Eve ate from the wrong tree, they sinned against God, and their eyes were immediately opened. When they did this, God did not want them to eat from the Tree of Life and live forever in their fallen state. If they had eaten from the Tree of Life and lived forever, we would always have a problem with sin. Therefore, God drove them out of the Garden of Eden, away from the Tree of Life, and away from having close fellowship with Him.

After Adam and Eve were cast out of the Garden of Eden, they had a son who murdered his own brother, which we see in the story of Cain and Abel. Yes, this was the first murder ever, but not the last because when Adam and Eve ate from the wrong tree, the world became a very different world than the one God had created. I have heard many people say, "I cannot believe in a good God with all of the evil in the world today." To these people, I would say, "Try and read the Bible because all of the evil we see in the world today is exactly what we read would happen, and it will only get worse. But, it is not God's fault." God did not create the world this way. Yes, He hates it more than we do. God regretted that He had made man because of their evil deeds.

Genesis 6:5-6 states:

The Lord saw how great the wickedness of the human race had become on the earth, and that every inclination of the thoughts of the human heart was only evil all the time. The Lord regretted that He had made human beings on the earth, and His heart was deeply troubled.

We need to understand that none of this evil is God's fault. God hates evil, even more than we do. This was never God's plan. Although we read how God regretted making man, He found Noah and his family. Genesis 6:8-9 states, *"But Noah found favor in the eyes of the Lord. This is the account of Noah and his family. Noah was a righteous man, blameless among the people of his time, and he walked faithfully with God."* So God found Noah, a righteous man, and told him to build an ark, which God used to judge the world for their evil deeds. God flooded the world, and only Noah and his family survived in the Ark, together with some of the animals.

However, as soon as Noah and his family came out of the ark, there was a problem again. Yes, Noah got drunk, and everything went wrong again. Why? This is because sin is not only in the world, but it is also inside of man. Yes, sin is in our nature, and unfortunately, it is a big part of us. So instead of creating a new earth and putting the old man on the new earth, letting them destroy it again, as He did with Noah and the Ark, God decided to first create a New Man, and then later put this New Man on the new earth. This is where Jesus comes in.

Jesus is our Savior. He came to save us from our sins and our sinful nature. Jesus came so we could be born again, so we could become new.

Before we talk about Jesus and what He did for us so we could be born again and receive eternal life, we first need to talk about sin.

Maybe you think you are not so bad because you have grown up in church and have never been to jail or taken drugs, and so on. But if you are thinking like this, you have a problem, and your problem is your self-righteousness. Self-righteousness is when you think you are so good that you do not need forgiveness, or that you only need a little forgiveness and then can do the rest yourself. But the truth is, you are *not* good enough. Ecclesiastes 7:20 states, *"Indeed, there is no one on earth who is righteous, no one who does what is right and never sins."* And Romans 3:23 states, *"... For all have sinned and fall short of the glory of God."* So now, let us look at sin, and what standard we should be living. This is what Jesus says about anger.

Matthew 5:21-22 states:

You have heard that it was said to the people long ago, "You shall not murder, and anyone who murders will be subject to judgment." But I tell you that anyone who is angry with a brother or sister will be subject to judgment. Again, anyone who says to a brother or sister, "Raca," is answerable to the court. And anyone who says, "You fool!" will be in danger of the fire of hell.

These are strong words spoken by Jesus. He then continues, by talking about lust.

Matthew 5:27-30 states:

You have heard that it was said, "You shall not commit adultery." But I tell you that anyone who looks at a woman lustfully has already committed adultery with her in his heart. If your right eye causes you to stumble, gouge it out and throw it away. It is better for you to lose one part of your body than for your whole body to be thrown into hell. And if your right hand causes you to stumble, cut it off and throw it away. It is better for you to lose one part of your body than for your whole body to go into hell.

Do I need to say more? If you look lustfully at someone, you have already committed adultery with that person in your heart. And what about lying? Have you ever lied? Or have you ever stolen something? The question is not if you are a good person. The question is, are you good enough? Or, let me ask it this way. Are you perfect? Have you always kept God's law? James states, in James 2:20, *"For whoever keeps the whole law and yet stumbles at just one point is guilty of breaking all of it."*

I want to make it even more clear how far you have fallen. Try to imagine that I have a special camera, and this special camera has been filming your whole life. Now, imagine that I put together a five-minute video clip of you and published this video on Facebook and YouTube for everyone to see. This camera has been following you for your whole life without you knowing it. Yes, this camera has filmed everything. It has filmed the times you have looked around and thought no one was seeing what you were doing or what you were looking at. And this camera has even filmed what you have been thinking. It has also recorded how you have been looking at people with lust and all those sexual thoughts, the times you have looked with lust at others, or had hate in your heart. Yes, this camera has filmed everything.

Well, not everything. It has never filmed anything good you have done in your life. No, none of the good things you have done has been filmed on this camera, because you need to understand that the good things you have done do not count. The good things are not pluses on your account, and the bad things you have done are not minuses on your account. No, the good things you have done are not a plus, but a zero. The good things you and I have done are not a plus, because the good things we do have been expected from us from the very beginning. Therefore, your good deeds can never justify the wrong things you have done.

**The idea that good deeds can justify
the wrong deeds is deeply ingrained in all of us.
No, sin has consequences, and it demands blood.
And this was the price that Jesus paid.
He died so we could go free.**

So now imagine I have recorded a five minute video of your life. Yes, a video where we see all of your sexual thoughts and deeds, all of your selfish thoughts and deeds, all of your evil thoughts and deeds, and so on. Now imagine I show this video to everyone out there, to your friends, your family, and to the whole world. How would you feel if this happened? Would you still think you are a good person? The truth is, you would be so ashamed if everyone knew all the terrible things you have done, and if people saw the real truth about you, and what you have been doing, looking at, or thinking about other people and God. If this all came out for everyone to see, you would be so ashamed that you would run away as fast as possible, never showing yourself to anyone again. I know I would. Yes, we would be so ashamed if others knew about us and about what we have been doing.

Then try to imagine how ashamed you would feel standing totally alone, naked, in front of a holy and righteous God who saw everything. On the day, when you stand in front of God, you will not be able to justify yourselves to Him and say, "Oh, I am not so bad. What about her, or him?" or "What about them, they are worse than me." No, on that day, you will only know one thing, that you are guilty and deserve hell because God is good, and you are not. But on that day it will be too late. The truth is, God could send every one of us to hell and still be good, loving, and righteous because He is not the problem. We are. We all have sinned.

I hope you understand now that no one can become righteous in front of God by their own deeds. No one can become righteous by keeping the law. Romans 3:20 states, *"Therefore no one will be declared righteous in God's sight by the works of the law; rather, through the law we become conscious of our sin."* So God could send all of us to hell and still be good, loving, and righteous because He is not the problem. We are. But in the middle of all this, God did something amazing. God did not need to do it, but He did it anyway. He sent His only Son Jesus to die for you and me, so that we, in Him, can experience forgiveness and get a whole new life. This is the good news, the Gospel of Jesus Christ, and that is what we are going to look at in the next chapter.

20

JESUS, OUR SAVIOR

It is possible to fall in love with Jesus over and over again. When you take the time to see how lost you were without Him and what He did for you, you will want to love Him and serve Him for the rest of your life.

In the previous chapter, we looked at how God created a perfect world and how He made man to walk with Him and to have fellowship with Him. It was a perfect world, without all of the bad things we see in the world today, and man walked in close fellowship with God. It should have been like that forever, but then Adam and Eve sinned, and they were thrown out of the Garden of Eden so they could no longer eat from the Tree of Life and live forever.

Man sinned, and because of our sin, we were separated from God, and the world was forever changed. We are now living in this fallen world. Because of our sin, God could send every one of us to hell and still be a good, loving, and righteous God because He is not the problem. We are. Instead of doing this, though, He did something amazing, and this is where John 3:16-18 truly becomes wonderful news.

John 3:16-18 states:

For God so loved the world that He gave His one and only Son, that whoever believes in Him shall not perish but have eternal life. For God did not send His Son into the world to condemn the world, but to save the world through Him. Whoever believes in Him is not condemned, but whoever does not believe stands condemned already because they have not believed in the name of God's one and only Son.

When you are able to see your sin and how far you have fallen, the good news of Jesus really does suddenly become the *good news*. Let's continue now to look at what Jesus did for us, and what we need to do to receive His forgiveness. What do we need to do to experience forgiveness and to walk with God as we were created to do?

First, let us look at what we need to do to be born again.

Matthew 1:21 states about Mary, *"She will give birth to a Son, and you are to give Him the name Jesus, because He will save His people from their sins."* Jesus walked here on earth among people, but where we all have sinned, He was without sin. When He was thirty years old, He was baptized in water and when He came out of the water, the Holy Spirit came over Him. Matthew 3:16-17 states, *"As soon as Jesus was baptized, He went up out of the water. At that moment heaven was opened, and He saw the Spirit of God descending like a dove and alighting on Him. And a voice from heaven said, 'This is My Son, whom I love; with Him I am well pleased.'"*

After Jesus was baptized and the Holy Spirit came over Him, the Holy Spirit led Him out into the desert where He fasted for forty days and was tempted by Satan. After forty days, when Jesus came out of the desert, He started His ministry where He walked around healing the sick and preaching the Gospel of the kingdom. We can see this in Matthew 4:17, which states, *"From that time on Jesus began to preach, 'Repent, for the kingdom of heaven has come near.'"* We also see this in Matthew 4:23, which states, *"Jesus went throughout Galilee, teaching in their synagogues, proclaiming the good news of the kingdom, and healing every disease and sickness among the people."* So Jesus preached the good news of the kingdom, and told people they need to repent and be born again. We see this in John 3:5-7, which states,

Jesus answered, "Very truly I tell you, no one can enter the kingdom of God unless they are born of water and the Spirit. Flesh gives birth to flesh, but the Spirit gives birth to spirit. You should not be surprised at My saying, 'You must be born again.' "

When Jesus walked on earth preaching the Gospel, He told people how they should follow Him as His disciples.
Matthew 16:24-25 states:

Then Jesus said to His disciples, "Whoever wants to be My disciple must deny themselves and take up their cross and follow Me. For whoever wants to save their life will lose it, but whoever loses their life for Me will find it."

And Matthew 10:34-39 states:

Do not suppose that I have come to bring peace to the earth. I did not come to bring peace, but a sword. For I have come to turn a man against his father, a daughter against her mother, a daughter-in-law against her mother-in-law— a man's enemies will be the members of his own household. Anyone who loves their father or mother more than Me is not worthy of Me; anyone who loves their son or daughter more than Me is not worthy of Me. Whoever does not take up their cross and follow Me is not worthy of Me. Whoever finds their life will lose it, and whoever loses their life for my sake will find it.

Yes, Jesus was very radical. After He walked around on earth for about three years preaching the Kingdom, healing the sick, casting out demons, telling people what they need to do to follow Him as His disciples, and how they should repent and be born again out of water and Spirit, He died on the cross. He died for you and for me, so that we could live. He died to save us from our sins, and from what is separating us from God, our sins that bring death and destruction.

In Matthew 27, we read what they did with Jesus before they crucified Him.

214 The Call of Jesus

Matthew 27:28-31 states:

They stripped Him and put a scarlet robe on Him, and then twisted together a crown of thorns and set it on His head. They put a staff in His right hand. Then they knelt in front of Him and mocked Him. "Hail, king of the Jews!" they said. They spit on Him, and took the staff and struck Him on the head again and again. After they had mocked Him, they took off the robe and put His own clothes on Him. Then they led Him away to crucify Him.

Yes, Jesus was truly our King, not only for the Jews, but also for everyone in the whole world. After Jesus experienced all that pain and mockery, they took Him and hung Him on a cross, the most terrifying way to die. There, He hung, totally naked, and He gave up His life.
Matthew 27:46 and 50 state:

About three in the afternoon Jesus cried out in a loud voice, "Eli, Eli, lemasabachthani? (which means 'My God, my God, why have you forsaken Me?').

And when Jesus had cried out again in a loud voice, He gave up His spirit.

We also read, in John 19:30, that just before giving up His spirit, He shouted, *"It is finished."*

Our sin was put on Him, and He paid the price no one else could pay. He gave His life for you and me so that we, in Him, can go free. Then they took His body down from the cross and buried it. Because He was without sin, death could not hold Him, and through His death He conquered sin. He died and rose up on the third day. Jesus conquered death and, by His blood, paid the price to forgive and wash away our sins. If He even just one time had lied, stolen, or looked with lust at someone like we all have done, He would have been guilty just like you and me, and His death would not have changed anything. But because Jesus was the only Man without sin, death could not hold Him. He rose up again, and by Him we can experience forgiveness for our sins and a whole new life. This is the good news we preach today.

1 Corinthians 15:1-4 states:

Now, brothers and sisters, I want to remind you of the gospel I preached to you, which you received and on which you have taken your stand. By this gospel you are saved, if you hold firmly to the word I preached to you. Otherwise, you have believed in vain. For what I received I passed on to you as of first importance: that Christ died for our sins according to the Scriptures, that He was buried, that He was raised on the third day according to the Scriptures...

After Jesus rose again and showed Himself to His disciples, He spoke to them about the Kingdom of God. He also commanded His disciples not to leave Jerusalem because they should wait for the promise of the Holy Spirit, the promise the Father had given.

Acts 1:4 states:

On one occasion, while He was eating with them, He gave them this command: "Do not leave Jerusalem, but wait for the gift My Father promised, which you have heard Me speak about."

Shortly after Jesus said this, He went to Heaven, and the Holy Spirit was sent to earth as God had promised, and as it had been prophesied hundreds of years before.

**Jesus did what no one else could do.
He gave His life in our place. He paid the price
so we could go free, and this is something
we should never forget or take for granted.
We should be thankful to Him for all eternity.**

We can then read in Act 2:2-4 how the Holy Spirit came and filled 120 people who were gathered.

Suddenly a sound like the blowing of a violent wind came from heaven and filled the whole house where they were sitting. They saw what seemed to be tongues of fire that separated and came to rest on each of them. All of them were filled with the Holy Spirit and began to speak in other tongues as the Spirit enabled them.

After the Holy Spirit came and filled the first disciples, we read how Peter and the other apostles stood up and started preaching. We see this in Acts 2:36-39, which states:

"Therefore let all Israel be assured of this: God has made this Jesus, whom you crucified, both Lord and Messiah." When the people heard this, they were cut to the heart and said to Peter and the other apostles, "Brothers, what shall we do?" Peter replied, "Repent and be baptized, every one of you, in the name of Jesus Christ for the forgiveness of your sins. And you will receive the gift of the Holy Spirit." The promise is for you and your children and for all who are far off—for all whom the Lord our God will call."

This is what we still need to hear and see today. We need to hear the full Gospel, and understand how we have sinned, how God has raised Jesus from the grave, and that we can get born again today. We all need to repent toward God, get baptized into Jesus for the forgiveness of our sins, and we shall also receive the promise of the Holy Spirit.

The first thing we read here, is that we need to repent. 2 Corinthians 7:10 states, *"Godly sorrow brings repentance that leads to salvation and leaves no regret, but worldly sorrow brings death."* We need to understand that we have sinned against a holy and righteous God. Before people see that they have sinned against a holy and righteous God, they cannot repent and experience forgiveness. How can you repent of your sins if you do not acknowledge that you have sinned? So, first, people need to see their sins and that they have broken God's law. They need to come to the point that they feel sorry for their sins and really want to turn away from them and live a new life. When a person really recognizes their sins, feels sorry, and realizes they have sinned against God, then they can turn away from their sins and put their faith in Jesus and what He did on the cross. Yes, then God will come and take out their stony heart, and give them a new heart. We read in Ezekiel 36:26: *"I will give you a new heart and put a new spirit in you; I will remove from you your heart of stone and give you a heart of flesh."*

But confessing your sins and turning away from them and getting the new heart is not enough. The person also needs to be baptized in water, and they need to receive the Holy Spirit, as we read. Repentance and baptism in water go hand in hand with faith in Jesus. Mark 16:16 states, *"Whoever believes and is baptized will be saved, but whoever does not believe will be condemned."* Jesus did not only say the one who believes shall be saved, but He said the one who believes and is baptized shall be saved. Acts 2:41 states, *"Those who accepted his message were baptized, and about three thousand were added to their number that day."*

Baptism is so important. It is not just a symbol, as many churches sadly are preaching today. Because of this, many in the churches are still struggling with their sins. They are not free and truly born again because they have not buried their old life or understood the freedom we have in Christ. Jesus did not come just to save us *in* our sins. He came to save us *from* our sins, as we read. Here are some verses from the Bible about baptism.

Romans 6:3-4 and 12-14 state:

Or do not you know that all of us who were baptized into Christ Jesus were baptized into His death? We were therefore buried with Him through baptism into death in order that, just as Christ was raised from the dead through the glory of the Father, we too may live a new life.

Therefore do not let sin reign in your mortal body so that you obey its evil desires. Do not offer any part of yourself to sin as an instrument of wickedness, but rather offer yourselves to God as those who have been brought from death to life; and offer every part of yourself to Him as an instrument of righteousness. For sin shall no longer be your master, because you are not under the law, but under grace.

Galatians 3:26-37 states:

So in Christ Jesus you are all children of God through faith, for all of you who were baptized into Christ have clothed yourselves with Christ.

When we are baptized into Christ, we clothe ourselves with Christ, or "put on Christ," as some translations say. Yes, we are the children of God through faith. When we are baptized, we are then in Christ. It is no longer I that lives, but Christ in me, or I in him. In baptism, we bury the old life and start all over. In baptism, we wash away our sins. We experience forgiveness of our sins, as Peter is preaching in Acts 2:38:

Repent and be baptized, every one of you, in the name of Jesus Christ for the forgiveness of your sins. And you will receive the gift of the Holy Spirit.

If you take the Bible and look at every place it talks about baptism in water, it is very clear that baptism is not just a symbol. You will not find anywhere in the Bible that it says baptism is "an outward expression of an inward faith," as many churches are preaching today. In the early church, they preached baptism as a part of salvation, and when people heard the Gospel, they got baptized right away, not a week or two after, not as a symbol, but as a part of salvation and as something that was truly life changing.

Water baptism is necessary to follow Christ, and I encourage everyone to take the time to really study what the Bible says about baptism because there is so much more about baptism than I am presenting here. Find all of the Scriptures in the Bible about baptism, and look at what the early church was preaching/teaching about it and how they did it. They got baptized as a response to the Gospel.

As necessary as repentance and baptism are, they are still not enough to live as a disciple of Jesus Christ. We also need the baptism of the Holy Spirit. In the Gospel of John, Jesus says this about the Holy Spirit:

"If you love me, keep My commands. And I will ask the Father, and He will give you another Advocate to help you and be with you forever—the Spirit of truth. The world cannot accept Him, because it neither sees Him nor knows Him." (John 14:15)
"But the Advocate, the Holy Spirit, whom the Father will send in My name, will teach you all things and will remind you of everything I have said to you. Peace I leave with you; My peace I give you. I do not give to you as the world gives. Do not let your hearts be troubled and do not be afraid." (John 14-26-27)

"But very truly I tell you, it is for your good that I am going away. Unless I go away, the Advocate will not come to you; but if I go, I will send Him to you. When He comes, He will prove the world to be in the wrong about sin and righteousness and judgment: about sin, because people do not believe in Me; about righteousness, because I am going to the Father, where you can see Me no longer; and about judgment, because the prince of this world now stands condemned. I have much more to say to you, more than you can now bear. But when He, the Spirit of truth, comes, He will guide you into all the truth. He will not speak on His own; He will speak only what He hears, and He will tell you what is yet to come. He will glorify Me because it is from Me that He will receive what He will make known to you. All that belongs to the Father is Mine. That is why I said the Spirit will receive from Me what He will make known to you." (John 16:7-15)

Often, people received the Holy Spirit by other people laying their hands on them and praying for them to receive Him. Acts 8:17 states, *"Then Peter and John placed their hands on them, and they received the Holy Spirit."* Acts 19:6 states, *"When Paul placed his hands on them, the Holy Spirit came on them, and they spoke in tongues and prophesied."* So when you repent, get baptized in water, and receive the Holy Spirit, you become the body of Christ here on earth. Yes, you and I are now Christ's body here on earth, and Jesus is the Head. We are His body, filled with the same Spirit who raised Jesus from the grave. We are now here in Christ's place to continue what He has started. Now, you and I are Jesus' disciples who are walking around here on earth, preaching the Gospel, leading people to repentance, baptizing them in water and with the Holy Spirit, and seeing the Kingdom of God grow. And one day soon, Jesus is going to come back and judge the world.

We read in Hebrews 9:27-28, *"Just as people are destined to die once, and after that to face judgment, so Christ was sacrificed once to take away the sins of many; and He will appear a second time, not to bear sin, but to bring salvation to those who are waiting for Him."* Matthew 25:33 states, *"He will put the sheep on His right and the goats on His left."* So God is going to come and judge the world, and divide the sheep from the goats. And we who are born again, who are cleansed and washed clean by the blood of Jesus, will then be with

Him forever in the New Jerusalem.

Revelation 22:3-5 states:

No longer will there be any curse. The throne of God and of the Lamb will be in the city, and His servants will serve Him. They will see His face, and His name will be on their foreheads. There will be no more night. They will not need the light of a lamp or the light of the sun, for the Lord God will give them light. And they will reign for ever and ever.

And Revelation 22:14 states:

Blessed are those who wash their robes, that they may have the right to the tree of life and may go through the gates into the city.

Amen! These verses are so amazing. I get so excited every time I think of this, that we, because of the blood of Jesus and the salvation He gives us, will one day stand there in the new Jerusalem. We will eat from the Tree of Life and live forever. How amazing is that? We can again eat of the Tree of Life because there will no longer be any sin and all will again be so good and perfect, just as God created it to be. And that is the Gospel, from the beginning to the end.

So, in summary, sin came into the world through Adam and Eve. It was because of their sin that they were sent out of the Garden of Eden, so they could not eat of the Tree of Life and live forever in their fallen state. Death has now come to all of us because we all have sinned. And Jesus came as the new Adam to save us from our sins. He paid the price at the cross so we could be saved from our sins. Yes, He died on the cross, rose up again, went to heaven, is sitting at God's right hand, and has sent His Holy Spirit down here to earth. We can now be saved from our sins. We can now be born again. We can have our robes washed clean by the blood of Jesus. And those who are born again will one day sit in the new Jerusalem and eat from the Tree of Life and live forever and ever. One more time, everything will be so good and perfect, as God created it to be. Hallelujah! That is so amazing!

This is the story from beginning to end. Jesus is the Second Adam. He is the firstborn of many. He came so we, in Him, can get a new life and live forever. But for people to enter into the new earth and live forever in the new heaven and earth, it is not enough that they only believe in God and go to a church. No, they also need to be born again and experience this new birth. They need to say yes to following Jesus, as we read in the Bible. This is the good news of the kingdom, the kingdom that is here and also yet to come, the new heaven and earth.

> **There is really nothing more wonderful than to hear the Gospel, how God sent His Son Jesus to earth to die for us, and how we, in Him, can get eternal life. Yes, this should make us so thankful because, without Him, we are all lost.**

I would like to make it clear to those of you who are reading this that it is not enough to hear or read about this. You need to believe it and turn away from your sins and be born again! You need to live as a disciple of Jesus. The Gospel is not, "Hey, God loves you and has a wonderful plan for your life, and if you pray this prayer, you are saved, and nothing can take it away." No, the Gospel is what I have just shared, and we need to remain in Christ and continue in Him until the day we are standing in the New Jerusalem and can eat from the Tree of Life.

I wanted to use the last two chapters to share the Gospel with you, so you can hear it and receive it, and also so you can preach it to other people. So take the time to go deeper into what the Gospel is and get better at sharing the Gospel of the kingdom with others around you. Yes, show the people their sins, what Jesus did on the cross, how they need to repent, be baptized in water, be baptized with the Holy Spirit, and how they need to die to themselves and follow Jesus with their whole heart. Tell them how they can experience the new life, and how they need to continue walking in Christ as His disciple.

Maybe you have not heard the Gospel like this before. Maybe you still have a stony heart and still live in sin. If so, you need to repent for your sins, be baptized in water, and be filled with the Holy Spirit. Or maybe you believe and have already repented and received a heart of flesh, but you are still fighting with your sins because you have never buried the old life through water baptism. Because of that, you are not living in the freedom we read about in Romans 6. If this is you, your next step is to be water baptized, and experience the freedom of God. Or, maybe you have already repented and been baptized in water, but you have not received the Holy Spirit yet, and therefore, do not live a supernatural life as we read about in the Bible. If this is you, your next step is to get baptized with the Holy Spirit. Find someone who can pray for you so you can receive the Holy Spirit. Yes, I know that sometimes people receive the Holy Spirit before their baptism in water, and I want to say that the order in which it is done is not what is important. The most important thing is that you repent and are baptized in water and with the Holy Spirit.

No matter where you are, we are sure there are others near you who can help. If you need help, you are welcome to go to our map at www.TLRmap.com and find someone near you who is ready to help. On our YouTube channel, I also have many other videos where I explain more about all of this and how you can learn to understand the Gospel and share it with others.

In the next chapter, I will share some testimonies from Luke 10, and then we will start to put it all together. I believe this will do something in you when you see this all come together, and see that it is true for all of us today. We can all experience this life we read about in Luke 10 and throughout the New Testament.

21

Luke 10 Testimonies

> **It is one thing to read about it, and it is
> something else to do it. Jesus' words for us
> in Luke 10 are not only for us to read, but also
> for us to obey. When we start to live what we read
> in Luke 10, it will not only change our lives
> but also the lives of the people around us.**

We have now gone through what Jesus says in Luke 10 and looked at how He wants us to obey Him today. We have looked at Luke 10 verse by verse, and we have looked at the Gospel and how we need to lead people to repentance, baptism in water and with the Holy Spirit. We have shown that people need this to be able to follow Jesus as His disciples. In this chapter, I will share different Luke 10 testimonies, so it will become even more clear how this can look today.

I am convinced that if we follow Jesus' call in Luke 10, everything will change. I am also convinced that if we, as the body of Christ, take His Word seriously, it will be the beginning of a movement that the church has been longing for, a movement that will change the world. It could be the beginning of a movement where we see the whole body of Christ become active and built up in Christ Who is the Head of the Body.

It is time to obey what Jesus has called us to do, not only to read or listen to His words but also to obey them. We do not need to wait. Many believers have a lack of knowledge and a misunderstanding that God will one day give us a special calling, and then we can start to serve Him. We already know what Jesus wants us to do and how He wants us to do it. It is time now for us to go out and do it.

When you step out on Jesus' words and start to obey the call He has given, you will not only experience the excitement of serving Him, but you will also experience that the harvest is big, and it is ready. There are people out there who are just waiting to get saved and follow Jesus. I have already seen the fruit of this, not only in my life, but in everyone else's lives who have begun to step out on Jesus' words in Luke 10. I would now like to share some testimonies from my own life to give you some more practical examples of how it can look today when you obey Jesus' call in Luke 10.

The first testimony I would like to share shows how important it is that we don't give up. This is a testimony about a girl named Maria. Maria is in our first movie, "The Last Reformation: The Beginning." In this movie, you can see how I met Maria in a shopping center in Canada. She later comes to our hotel, gets baptized in water, and receives the Holy Spirit. You can also see how, the next day, she was sitting in the hotel telling people about what God has done in her life and that she has found what she had been searching for. I would like to share more about this amazing story.

On the day I met Maria, I was doing a kickstart meeting (training people how to obey what we read in Luke 10) in Canada. I took a few people out with me to a shopping center to show them how to approach people to pray for the sick and share the Gospel. What most people don't know is that on that day when I took those people out to the shopping center, it was a very difficult time. It was so hard. No one wanted to stop and talk with us. I think I was there trying to stop and talk to people for around forty minutes. I tried to stop at least twenty or thirty people, and no one wanted to talk with us. No one wanted us to pray for them. It was one of those days when I thought to myself, "The harvest is not ready. The harvest is not plentiful." Yes, it was one of those days when I just wanted to give up, and eventually I did give up.

I said to one of my friends, "Let's stop and try to find another place to go because no one here is open. No one wants to listen to us." But my friend did not want to give up, and today I am so thankful for that. My friend said, "Hmm … let's try one more." He then stopped the next person who came through the door into the shopping center. That person was Maria.

When my friend stopped Maria and asked her if she had something we could pray for, she immediately said, "Yes!" She took hold of my friend's arm and took him to the side where I was standing. She then told us that she really wanted us to pray for her. In the beginning, she did not tell us exactly what she wanted us to pray for, so we just laid our hands on her and started to pray. When we started to pray for her, the Holy Spirit came over her and touched her very deeply. She started to cry!

We decided to go outside the shopping center where we could talk some more and pray for her again. When we got outside the mall, she told us that in recent days she had experienced that God had been drawing her. She told us that on her way to the shopping center, she had been listening to a Christian radio station and that God really spoke to her through a song she heard. She told us she was reminded of when she was a child, and of the time she had believed in God. She told us that while she was listening to the song, she realized how she was so far away from God. She suddenly felt so guilty for all of the things she had done. Maria was truly a person of peace. God had been calling her and opening her eyes to see her sins. She was ready to repent and receive a new life with Jesus. We took her phone number. She came to the meeting that night at the hotel, and we prayed for her a little more. The next day, Maria came to the hotel, ready to be baptized. She got baptized in water and received the Holy Spirit. And, wow, her life changed dramatically!

Maria's story is really an amazing one and truly shows the power of the Gospel. Today, Maria loves Jesus and has told many people about God and what He has done in her life. Her story is an amazing reminder that we should never give up, no matter how hard it is. If we had stopped that day, like I actually wanted to, we would never have met Maria. Even though the day started off extremely hard, it ended up being a very fruitful time. The harvest is truly ready and out there waiting for us. We need to keep going and not give up when it looks hard.

Had we stopped that day, it would have been a terrible day, one that I just wanted to forget. But because we kept going and found the person of peace, it became an amazing day that I never want to forget. I have experienced this again and again since then. I have learned the importance of not giving up and to keep going until I find that person. Sometimes it may be an hour or two. Sometimes it is several days. It truly is those who keep seeking who will find. Let's not give up when it looks like the harvest is not ready because the harvest is truly ready and plentiful, as Jesus state in His Word.

> **If we give up too early, we will not experience
> that the harvest is ready and plentiful, as Jesus says.
> The people who do not give up and who keep on
> searching are those who will experience that the
> harvest is ready and plentiful.**

I would like to share another testimony with you. I love sharing this testimony because here we can clearly see how the Holy Spirit leads and takes care of our daily needs when we step out on Jesus' Word.

When we share testimonies like this, it is important to understand that God can do the same for us as we hear He did for others. The Bible says in Revelation 12:11 that we overcome our enemy by the blood of the Lamb and by the word of our testimony. The ancient root meaning of the word "testimony" means to "do it again/repeat." When we share testimonies, we are not only sharing information but also power. There is power in a testimony for the event to be repeated again: "What God did for them, He can also do for me!" This brings faith and boldness to us.

We are all called by Jesus, and He has promised to be with us all. It does not matter who we are. If you are very strong and this comes very natural for you, or if you are new to this and are learning to take the first small steps, God wants to use us all, no matter where we are right now in our walk with Him. He can only use those who are willing to step out in faith on His Word and obey Him. When we do this, we will see that God is not a respecter of persons. He will use everyone who is willing, man or woman, young or old.

When I share testimonies like this, you need to remember that God can do the same in your life and in the lives of everyone around you. It is not because I am very special that I experience these things. On the other hand, yes, I am very special, but so are you if you have the Spirit of God inside you. We are all very special, and we are all called to walk like Christ here on earth.

Why do some experience this and others do not? Because some are willing to step out on Jesus' words, and others are not. It has so much more to do with that than if we have the totally right theology and can quote the Bible the right way and so on. It is important to have a good Bible foundation, but do not wait until you have that. Start in faith where you are, and you will grow while you are walking out on Jesus' words.

When you listen to testimonies that people are sharing, know that what God can do for them or through them, He can also do for or through you.

One day, I shared a testimony with a friend about how we had just seen a boy who was blind in one eye since birth get healed on the street. When my friend heard this he said, "Wow! I've never seen that happen before." But one week later, he stood in front of a man who was blind in one eye and remembered the testimony and thought, "If God can do it there, He can do it here." He got boldness to pray for the man, and God healed him. Yes, if he had not heard the testimony, he would not have prayed for him in faith, and it would not have happened. That is the power of a testimony. What we saw happen was repeated because we shared it as a testimony. So remember, if God can do it there, He can do it here.

Some years ago, I got a very strong dream from God. In the dream, I was fishing. Every time I cast my line into the water, I caught a fish. I remember the first fish I caught was a very unique fish. It did not look like a fish you would normally see. The fish had a different shape and funny colors. So, in my dream, I stood there looking at the fish in my hand and thinking to myself, "What a strange fish." Then I laid the fish down beside me and cast the line into the water again. As soon as my line touched the water, I caught a new fish. When I saw the fish, I thought to myself, "Whoa, what a strange fish!" Again, the fish had a unique shape and color. It was not a fish I recognized. So I laid the fish down beside the first fish I caught and thought to myself, "What strange fish these are." I continued casting the line into the water, and I caught a total of five fish just like the first two. At the end of my dream, I looked at the fish and thought to myself, "I am now starting to recognize these fish." The fish were no longer strange to me because they were starting to feel more and more familiar.

As soon as I woke up from the dream, God spoke to me and said that the dream meant I should catch people from other cultures and nations. I went for a walk that morning to pray and thank God for the dream. As I was walking, I was thinking about the dream and what it would mean for the future. Suddenly, I got an email from a young Pakistani man who was living in Copenhagen, the capital of Denmark. This man sent me a message to thank me for my website. When I read the email, I knew this was a person of peace and one of the "strange fish" I had dreamed about. I wrote him back right away and asked if he wanted to meet with me. He replied that his name was Ronald and that he would love to meet. He explained that the day before he wrote to me, he had sat down and started thinking about life and God. He asked Jesus to show him if He was real, and right away the television turned on and off. This shocked him, so he had written to me and asked if that could be a sign that Jesus is real. It was all very new to him, even though he called himself a Christian. For him, though, Christianity was more of a cultural thing than real Christianity.

I wrote back to Ronald, and we decided I would visit him the following Friday. It was about a four-hour drive for me to get to where he lived in Copenhagen. I was so excited about the dream God had given me, and that God had led me to this young man and that I was not only going to meet Ronald but also his family.

On the Monday before I was supposed to visit him, I had a problem. My family and I did not have any money. The reason for this is that a short time before, I had cut down on the hours I worked at my job so I could spend more time with God. By that Monday, we did not have any money left. To make matters worse, we had a bill of one thousand, eight hundred Danish Krones (two hundred and seventy dollars) that needed to be paid that day. What do you do when you cannot pay a bill? You pray. So I went for a walk and prayed. I started to thank God for the dream He gave me and for the contact with Ronald. I said to God, "God, I am really looking forward to visiting Ronald on Friday, but I don't have any money, and I have a bill that has to be paid today. I don't have any money for the gasoline needed to drive to Copenhagen or any money to pay the bridge toll to get to Copenhagen." Yes, when you want to drive to Copenhagen, you have to cross a bridge that has a toll of two hundred and forty Danish Krones (thirty-five dollars each way)!

As I continued to walk and pray, a man with a dog suddenly walked in front of me. We turned down the same path, walking in the same direction. This man and his dog were walking right in front of me, and to be honest, I was very frustrated and thought to myself, "Go away! Why are you walking right in front of me? I am praying, and I want to be alone with God." But the man and his dog continued to walk directly in front of me.

Then I suddenly got a thought, "Go on this road instead." So I decided to walk down a different path than I normally walked on, and I eventually reached a road. After walking down the road for about forty or fifty feet, I stopped and looked around and thought to myself, "Hmm, I've never been here before. Maybe I should just turn back because now the man with the dog is gone, and I can go back onto the path I normally walk on." So I turned around and was about to start walking back when I thought, "No. God, You want me to walk here." I felt like God wanted me to continue walking on the road that I did not know. As I walked along the road, I asked God, "Why do You want me to walk on this road?"

Suddenly, while I was asking God this question, a car came and stopped right in front of me. The man driving rolled down his window and said, "Hey, Torben! Come here!" I had seen this man a few times before but did not know his name. I walked over to his car, and he asked me how I was doing. I told him I was doing fine. I also told him about the dream God had given me and that I was going to go to Copenhagen on Friday. When I told him all of this he said, "Whoa!

Torben, do you have any money?" When he asked me this question, I was so surprised. I answered him, "Uh … God provides." I continued telling him about the dream and about what I expected God would do on Friday. He interrupted me and said, "Torben, I feel like I should give you some money. I feel like I should give you two thousand Danish Krones."

I looked at him in shock and said, "Yes, if you want to …" When I said this, he was so excited and said, "Yes, I will give you two thousand Danish Krones! I will just go and park the car, and I will give you the money!" Whoa! I was so surprised because he did not know about the bill I had to pay that day or about what I had just been praying.

The man parked his car, came over to me, gave me five hundred Danish Krones (seventy-five dollars), and said, "Here's the first part of the money." I thanked him and stared down at the money in my hand. I excitedly told him about my situation and how God had used him in an amazing way. He smiled when he heard this, looked at the five hundred Danish Krones in my hand and said to me, "Keep the money. You can give me the bill, and I'll pay for that, too." He asked where I lived and said he would be at my house in three hours to pick up the bill and that he would go and pay it.

When he got in his car and drove off, I stood there on the side of the road with five hundred Danish Krones in my hand, knowing the bill was going to be paid. That was a moment I will never forget. When I got back home, I told the whole story to my wife, and we were so happy. Three hours later, he came and got the bill, gave me two thousand Danish Krones (three hundred dollars) more and then he left. Suddenly, I stood there with two thousand, five hundred Danish Krones (three hundred and seventy-five dollars) in my hand, and the bill had been taken care of, too. It was amazing how God provided for me, just like He said in His Word. With this much more, I had more than enough money to drive to and from Copenhagen, and to buy food there.

On Friday, some friends and I drove to Copenhagen to meet Ronald and his family. While we were driving, Romans 1:11-12 came to my mind. *"I long to see you so that I may impart to you some spiritual gift to make you strong—that is, that you and I may be mutually encouraged by each other's faith."* I did not fully understand why or what God was trying to tell me.

When we arrived in Copenhagen, my friends and I got some pizza (since we had some money). Then we went to Ronald's apartment. I did not know much about Ronald's family, as he had only written a few words to me in an email. All I knew was that they called themselves Christians but that it was more of a cultural thing. I also want to add that I grew up in a small city, so going to the middle of Copenhagen and meeting someone from Pakistan was all very new to me. I was a little nervous.

When we arrived at Ronald's apartment, he, his mom, and his sister greeted us. They welcomed us and told us they had food for us. So we sat down to eat in front of a big table filled with food. Yes, we had just eaten pizza and were very full, but I remembered the word Jesus spoke in Luke, that we should sit and eat and drink whatever they serve, so that is what we did. As we ate and drank what they served, the family stood around watching us eat. That was so different for us. We truly were with people from another culture.

After we finished eating, I asked Ronald's mother, "Can you tell us a little bit about who you are? Are you Christian?" She said, "Yes, my family and I are the only Christians from Pakistan who are living in Denmark." As I have mentioned before in this book, "Christian" can mean many things. For many people, the word "Christian" is just a religion or part of a culture. So, again, I asked Ronald's mother, "What about the Holy Spirit? Do you have the Holy Spirit and speak in tongues?" I will never forget her answer. She said, "No, we don't, and that's why you are here." Wow, what an answer! And in that moment, I was reminded of the verse God gave me while I was driving to Copenhagen. I was reminded of Romans 1:11-12 which states, *"I long to see you so that I may impart to you some spiritual gift to make you strong—that is, that you and I may be mutually encouraged by each other's faith."*

Then Ronald's mother said to my friends and me, "Come. Now we are going to go to my daughter's apartment in the next flat where we have gathered some people." So we all went to the next apartment. I will never forget what I saw when I stepped into that apartment. It was a small apartment with fifteen or twenty people crowded around. Several of the people gathered in the apartment were of Muslim faith, and the rest were cultural Christians who were not born again. It was so crowded in the apartment's small living room that there was almost no room for me, so I was actually standing behind the door. At one point, there was a man sitting on the floor, playing a small drum and singing something I did not understand. I looked around at all the people in the room and thought to myself, "Whoa! What funny fish. God is amazing. A week ago I had a dream about the 'strange fish' I should catch, and now I am here in Copenhagen with 15 to 20 people I have never seen before. Wow! What a God we serve!"

I was reminded of the story of Peter and Cornelius in Acts 10. Cornelius was a God-fearing man who was praying to God, but he did not understand the full Gospel. Cornelius received a vision of an angel who said he should send someone to Joppa and ask for a man named Simon, called Peter. God spoke to Peter and said some people were coming to find him. When they found him, Peter followed them to the house of Cornelius. And we read what happened when Peter came to Cornelius' house in Acts 10:44-48, which states:

While Peter was still speaking these words, the Holy Spirit came on all who heard the message. The circumcised believers who had come with Peter were astonished that the gift of the Holy Spirit had been poured out even on Gentiles. For they heard them speaking in tongues and praising God. Then Peter said, "Surely no one can stand in the way of their being baptized with water. They have received the Holy Spirit just as we have." So he ordered that they be baptized in the name of Jesus Christ. Then they asked Peter to stay with them for a few days.

**Today, we can also experience
what Peter, Paul, and the others experienced
at that time. The Spirit is the same, Jesus is the
same, and our life should also resemble
what we read in the Bible.**

So there I stood in the apartment with fifteen or twenty people from Pakistan. That night, God came. I shared the Gospel and talked about who God is, and then I started to pray for people. I remember one woman I prayed for. While I prayed for her, she stood up against the door, and suddenly, her face changed. Yes, you could almost see the demon in her face, and she started to manifest. I continued praying and cast out the demon. You could see the change in her face and the freedom she now had. After I finished praying for her, she told me what she had experienced while I was praying for her. She told me she saw a face come up from her stomach with two black eyes looking at her. She told me she could also hear me from far away, shouting, "Come out, in the name of Jesus!" Then she felt the demon leave her. I also prayed for a man who fell down. When he stood up again, he told me he had a tumor in his body, and when I prayed for him, he saw in a vision that a cloud came over him, and out of that cloud came a hand that touched him. Then he saw a light and fell down. When he stood up again, the tumor was gone.

We truly saw God work that night in amazing ways. Many people were healed and set free. At midnight, we went to the ocean and baptized seven people in water and with the Holy Spirit. One of the people we baptized in water saw a vision of angels standing all over the place. It was so amazing. One week later, I went back to them again. We baptized six more people in water. They also received the Holy Spirit and were healed of different illnesses. While we were in the apartment, one man who received the Holy Spirit started shouting in tongues, holding one finger pointing at the wall. He told us afterward that when someone prayed for him to receive the gift of tongues, he saw a hand writing on the wall. He read what the hand was writing, and that is when he started speaking in tongues. Wow!

To see how everything in Luke 10 came together so perfectly, this is what Jesus is talking about in Luke 10, and like we read later in Acts. Ronald was truly the person of peace that God led us to. God provided for our needs and was with us there. We saw people healed, set free, and receive Jesus Christ and the Gospel of the kingdom. I love this story! And this is just one of many amazing experiences I have had since then. What Jesus is saying in Luke 10, and what I have been trying to share in this book is really real. And, it is for all of us today!

Today, Ronald and his family are our Pakistani family in Christ. Church is like a family. That is our real family. Today, they all love Jesus and have started one fellowship in Copenhagen and one fellowship in Pakistan. I just love serving Jesus, and I love His Word. I love this testimony because it reminds us of Jesus' call in Luke 10 and what we read in Acts 10 with Peter and the house of Cornelius.

There are many differences, of course, between the testimony with Ronald and the story of Peter in Acts 10. One of the differences is that I received an email and drove a car to Ronald. whereas in Acts 10, people were sent to find Peter, and they walked the whole way to him and back to Cornelius, which took them several days. Why did Cornelius not email Peter? Why did he not call Peter? Why did Peter not drive a car to Cornelius' house? Because there were no emails, phones, or cars at that time! They did not have the technology we have today. But, the Holy Spirit is the same, Jesus is the same, His call is the same, and the Gospel is the same. This is what I want to share with you. We are living in a time that is very different from the time we read about in the book of Acts, but what we have to understand is that the call of Jesus, the Holy Spirit, and the Gospel are still the same. And what they experienced during the time of the Bible is also what we can experience today. Our life should look like the life we read about in the book of Acts. I could tell many stories like this, not only my own testimonies, but also testimonies from other people.

Every time we do our Pioneer Training Schools, we send people out on a Luke 10 trip. They are sent out for two days, often without any money, without a plan, and without a place to stay. They are sent out on the call of Jesus alone to find a person of peace. Many people come back telling about the amazing things that happened and how God led them by the Holy Spirit to find the person of peace. Many people share how God provided food for them to eat and a place to stay for the night. They often say the trip was life-changing. I hope you are starting to understand that what Jesus says in Luke 10 is still for you today. We are not only called to share about Jesus. We are called to do it the way He says in His Word. We are called to find the person of peace, like Ronald here, go to their house, eat and drink what they serve, heal the sick, share the Gospel, and see the whole household get born again. And when that happens, do not just go to the next house right away. Help them grow in Christ, and they will start to do the same, as we see with Ronald and his family.

This is so simple and biblical, but it is still so far away from many Christians today. When the church starts to see this, though, and starts to live it out, we will see thousands of new fellowships like this pop up everywhere. Remember the prophecy I got many years ago. We should lay a new DNA (or let's say an old DNA that has been lost) into a new generation, and see homes and entire cities coming to faith. This is the beginning of that prophesy. Let's obey what Jesus is saying in His Word and start to see this more and more.

22

FINDING THE PERSON OF PEACE

**When it comes to finding the person of peace,
start with those around you.
You already know people who need repentance,
baptism in water, baptism with the Holy Spirit,
or who need to get kickstarted.
If you start to love those around you and
give them what they need, you will see great things.**

When we read Paul's letters, it is very clear that he had a great heart when it came to following Jesus. He was ready to give up everything to follow Him. He also had a great heart when it came to reaching the lost with the Gospel and seeing people repent and follow Jesus. He was willing to give up everything to save souls. Paul did not get the heart and focus for reaching the lost from a stranger. We see this same heart and focus in Jesus. In this chapter, I will talk more about reaching the lost and how to find a person of peace. In the next few chapters, I will talk about how to build them up when we find them.

First, let's keep the focus and do a little summary. We know from

Jesus' words that the harvest is ready and plentiful. There are so many people out there waiting for us to go and get that harvest into the barn. The harvest (or people) will not just come to us by itself (themselves). No, we as workers need to go out as lambs among wolves. It is sometimes a scary thing to talk about God and Jesus to people, but when we go, He is with us and will provide what we need on the way. We go, led by the Holy Spirit, and the goal is to find that person of peace that God is calling. We are to heal the sick, preach the good news of the kingdom of God, and to build them up into mature people in Christ. The focus, and why Jesus sends us out, is not to save the whole world, but to be obedient and find that person of peace. We will now look at some more practical ideas on how to start doing this, and then we will look more at how we can build them up to Christ.

Jesus knew why He was here on earth. He was not here just to have fun. He was not here for His own sake. He was here to do the will of God, His Father. He was here to save us. His goal was, of course, to do God's will, which was to die on the cross for us. But before He died on the cross, He was very active in sharing the Gospel and seeking and saving those who were lost. When He walked around here on earth, His focus was to reach the lost. Jesus said things like, *"For the Son of Man came to seek and to save the lost"* (Luke 19:10). He talked about the lost sheep and about how to find the lost. When He shared the parable about the lost sheep, He really showed His heart and how He was willing to do everything needed to save that one that was lost.

Matthew 18:10-14 states:

> *"See that you do not despise one of these little ones. For I tell you that their angels in heaven always see the face of My Father in heaven. What do you think? If a man owns a hundred sheep, and one of them wanders away, will he not leave the ninety-nine on the hills and go to look for the one that wandered off? And if he finds it, truly I tell you, he is happier about that one sheep than about the ninety-nine that did not wander off. In the same way your Father in heaven is not willing that any of these little ones should perish."*

In this parable, when Jesus talked about the ninety-nine and how He left the ninety-nine to go after that one that was lost, it was not only something He was teaching us, it was something He was living Himself. This showed His heart. In another place in the Bible, you can read that there were many people around Jesus who wanted Him to stay with them and not leave. But even though Jesus loved those people around Him, His heart was always for the ones who were lost. He loved His brothers, but He knew why He was here on earth.

Luke 4:42-43 states:

At daybreak, Jesus went out to a solitary place. The people were looking for Him and when they came to where He was, they tried to keep Him from leaving them. But He said, "I must proclaim the good news of the kingdom of God to the other towns also, because that is why I was sent."

Jesus knew why He was sent down here to earth. He was here to save the one who was lost. He came with a goal, and He knew what that meant. He knew that meant He would die on a cross, and that He needed to pay the price, so we could experience forgiveness from our sins and receive a new life.

Jesus' ministry started a long time before the cross, and throughout His life, He showed us how we should live today. Jesus spent a lot of time with sinners, so He could bring healing and salvation to them, which is something you do not see when it comes to the Pharisees. The Pharisees in Jesus' time were very busy studying Scriptures and putting burdens on people. They often kept a far distance from sinners. It almost sounds like something we can experience in the church today. I believe it is very important to study the Scriptures, but we should not forget why we are here.

There are so many people today who are busy criticizing those who try to reach out to the world, but they themselves are not ready to raise one finger to obey the call of Jesus. This is very sad. And this is what the Pharisees of Jesus' time were also like. They only wanted to criticize people. The Pharisees were busy criticizing Jesus for what He was doing while they were not willing to put any effort into reaching the lost themselves. We see how Jesus walked on earth, how He found people of peace, how He went to their homes, invited their friends and family, and brought healing and forgiveness to them. Jesus did not teach us to do anything that He did not do Himself.

In Matthew 5, we read that Jesus was out walking and met a man named Matthew. Matthew was a person of peace. Matthew invited Jesus to his home and gathered as many people as he knew to come and listen to Jesus. So Jesus sat in Matthew's home, shared the kingdom, and brought healing and forgiveness. Meanwhile, the religious Pharisees were outside, criticizing Jesus for spending time with sinners. But what Jesus said to them was perfect. He really showed God's heart and His mission here on earth in His answers to them. He was not here on earth just to have fun and spend time on Himself and what He wanted in life. He was here to bring healing and forgiveness to those who wanted it. Let's read Matthew 9:9-13, which states:

> As Jesus went on from there, He saw a man named Matthew sitting at the tax collector's booth. "Follow Me," He told him, and Matthew got up and followed Him. While Jesus was having dinner at Matthew's house, many tax collectors and sinners came and ate with Him and His disciples. When the Pharisees saw this, they asked His disciples, "Why does your Teacher eat with tax collectors and sinners?" On hearing this, Jesus said, "It is not the healthy who need a doctor, but the sick. But go and learn what this means: 'I desire mercy, not sacrifice.' For I have not come to call the righteous, but sinners."

Jesus was here to seek and to save those who were lost, and Matthew is a clear example of a person of peace like Jesus tells us to find in Luke 10. But Jesus at that time had a problem with the religious people in the same way we often do today. What we read here in Matthew really reveals God's heart. We are called to be out there among the people, among the sinners and the wolves. We are called to love God with our whole heart and to love our neighbor as ourselves. Although we love to be together with the ninety-nine sheep who are *not* lost (our brothers and sisters in Christ), we should not forget the ones who *are* lost. Those are the ones who are really on Jesus' heart. And how can we say that we love God if we do not reach out to the lost people Jesus died for? How can we say we love our neighbor if we are not willing to share the good news with them? Jesus wants to invade every home with the Kingdom of God.

When Jesus walked here on earth, there was so much work to be done. He said, many times, that the harvest is plentiful but the workers are few. Now He is in heaven, sitting at the right hand of the Father and has sent His Spirit down here. Now we are the Body, and Christ is the Head, and as His Body, we are called to continue doing what Jesus did. We are called to find the person of peace, to go to their home, and to bring healing and salvation like Jesus did with Matthew and Matthew's network of friends and family. Paul had the same focus when it came to reaching the lost. He had the same love for the people around him. He was willing to lay down his life to save as many people as possible. Paul worked as much as he could to reach people with the Gospel. Like Jesus, Paul preached the Gospel publicly, and like Jesus, he also went from home to home.

Acts 20:19-21 states:

I served the Lord with great humility and with tears and in the midst of severe testing by the plots of my Jewish opponents. You know that I have not hesitated to preach anything that would be helpful to you but have taught you publicly and from house to house. I have declared to both Jews and Greeks that they must turn to God in repentance and have faith in our Lord Jesus.

Paul knew what his call was. He was very radical, and he said things we do not often hear people say today. For example, let's read what Paul said in 1 Corinthians 9:16-19, which I am sure is something that is not preached a lot in the churches today.

1 Corinthians 9:16-19 states:

For when I preach the gospel, I cannot boast, since I am compelled to preach. Woe to me if I do not preach the gospel! If I preach voluntarily, I have a reward; if not voluntarily, I am simply discharging the trust committed to me. What then is my reward?

It is very radical what Paul is saying here. Paul uses the words "compelled to preach," and how terrible it would be if he did not do it. Where do we hear something like this today? Paul knew he needed to do it. He was ready to lay down his life to save as many as possible,

just as Jesus was ready to lay down His life. Paul was ready to be a
servant to everyone, so He could win as many people as possible. He
continues in 1 Corinthians 9:20-23, by saying:

> *To the Jews I became like a Jew, to win the Jews. To those under the*
> *law I became like one under the law (though I myself am not under*
> *the law), so as to win those under the law. To those not having the*
> *law I became like one not having the law (though I am not free from*
> *God's law but am under Christ's law), so as to win those not having*
> *the law. To the weak I became weak, to win the weak. I have become*
> *all things to all people so that by all possible means I might save some.*
> *I do all this for the sake of the gospel, that I may share in its blessings.*

Would it not it be wonderful if we could have the same heart as
Jesus? Or if we could have the same heart and focus as Paul? If we did,
then we would be willing, in the same way, to lay down our lives to
save as many people as possible. But the question is, "Are we there
where we have that same heart and focus in our lives?" If not, then let's
seek God and ask Him to give us the heart, focus, and a real zeal for
the people around us.

I have often gone to a public place filled with many people just to
sit down and look at everyone. And while I look at everyone, I pray to
God and ask that He would give me a heart for all the people around
me. Yes, I have prayed for the Holy Spirit to open my eyes that I might
see how lost all the people are around me, to see them like Jesus saw
them, and to be willing, like He was, to do something about it. All of
these lost people around me are heading for judgment, and I am sitting
there with the answer.

When you trust God and do something like this, it can make you
feel uncomfortable. It can feel overwhelming when you look around
and see how many people are lost and to know that you have the
solution. Even though it can feel overwhelming and uncomfortable, it
is still the truth. It would be wrong to turn a blind eye and pretend that
all is good when it is not.

We also need to know that it is not our job to save the whole world.
Saving the world is too big of a burden for any one of us to carry. There
is only one Person who can carry that burden. That is Jesus, and He

has already done it. It is now our job to find the person of peace. We have the responsibility of finding the person of peace, as He has called us to. We can not just close our eyes and pretend everything is good. We need to open our eyes and ask God to give us a zeal for all those who are lost. We need to pray that the Lord of the harvest will send out more workers, and then love God and the people around us. We need to come to the point where we are willing, like Paul, to do anything that is needed to save those God has called us to save.

> **Jesus was driven by compassion.**
> **He did not close His eyes and ignore the people**
> **who were lost without God. He knew how lost**
> **they were, and that drove Him to do**
> **what He needed to do.**

If you do not have the love or compassion that is needed to reach people with the Gospel, pray that God will open your eyes and fill you with the love Jesus had while He walked here on earth. If you need love and compassion, you should go and do what I said. Go to a public place and look at all the lost people. You need to understand that you have been given the truth and that it is something you are commanded to share with the people around you. So let us obey Jesus by being workers in His harvest field.

Do not be afraid to open your eyes and to understand that people are lost and that you have a responsibility. You must be careful, though, not to end up in fear and works because this is not where we should end up. You should also not close your eyes and pretend that people are not lost. The truth is that you and I have a responsibility. Remember that our responsibility is not to save the whole world. Our responsibility is to obey Jesus and find the person of peace, to be led by His Spirit, to go when He says, "Go," and to stay when He says, "Stay." So, in love, take one step at a time and ask God to open your eyes and give you the same heart Christ and His disciple Paul had.

When it comes to reaching people, start with those people who are around you. Right now, you probably already know two or three people around you who are ready to give their life to God, or who are ready to listen to what you have to share. Right now, you may know people who are thinking about life and seeking the truth. You may also know people who have repented, but are not yet baptized in water, or with the Holy Spirit. Or maybe you know people who have repented, been baptized in water and with the Holy Spirit, but who need to be shown how to preach the Gospel and heal the sick, as Jesus has commanded us to do.

So, start with the people around you. Meet the people around you to pray for them, share the Gospel with them, and kickstart them by taking them out on the street to train them in obeying Jesus. If you do not feel ready to share the Gospel or kickstart people, then I have some advice for you. Do it anyway. It will become easier the more you do it. Every start is difficult in the beginning, and no one ever feels ready for the first time, but if you do it, it will become easier and easier. If you really do not have the courage to do any of these things by yourself, then take someone with you who can help you. You do not need to do it by yourself because there are other people around you who can help.

There is truly no excuse when it comes to obeying Jesus. If you do not feel confident and ready to share the Gospel, then learn how to share it. That is how I started. I did not feel ready to share the Gospel in the beginning, but then I learned how to do it. I became better and better, and the fear disappeared. I spent hours listening to teaching and practicing alone, by myself, to learn how to share the Gospel. It is so simple. The more you do something the better you become at doing it.

You are also welcome to use The Last Reformation YouTube videos or our free movies where the Gospel is shown clearly. You could, for example, invite people to your house, put on The Last Reformation movies or YouTube videos where I share the Gospel, and let the movies or videos explain the Gospel to the people you have invited over. I have heard so many amazing testimonies of how people have done that and seen lives changed. I have heard how people invited people to their home to play The Last Reformation movies and then afterward prayed for them and baptized them in water and with the Holy Spirit, something they had never done before. Then they do it again, and in the end, they are the ones sharing the Gospel with people. When I am out doing our TLR Kickstart weekends, I often tell people how they can invite people over to their home to see the movies, and that all they really need is a lot of Coca-Cola, popcorn, and a place to baptize afterwards.

I am sharing this with you because there are so many options out there to help you see the kingdom grow. Start with what you have. Find someone who can help you if you need it, and use the materials out there that are free to use. Pray to God to show you who you should start with. Ask God to remind you of a person or a family you should start with. Then be bold, and do something about it. Take the telephone and call and invite them over, or send a message through Facebook. The worst thing that can happen is that they are not interested in what you are saying. If that's the case, then you should move on to the next person until you find the person of peace who is ready to receive.

We are all called to share the Gospel and to make disciples. We are not all called to go to a foreign country and stand on a platform and preach, but we are all called to use the platform we have in our everyday lives. You can use many different places to share the Gospel, like the dinner table, garden, living room, local café, or other places. Start with the people around you. The person of peace in your life could be a family member, a work colleague, a neighbor, or a friend. If you do not know a person of peace, then take a trip down to Walmart or another public place, and ask God to lead you to the person of peace there.

I would like to tell you that God has made us all unique. Yes, He has made the harvest ripe and plentiful, and He has also made different kinds of workers. He did not only make people who are very evangelistic and comfortable approaching strangers to talk about God. He also made people who are more introverted, who are really good at listening. He has made us all different. And just like we as disciples are all different, the harvest of souls that we meet are also different. What I really love about the call of Jesus is that it is for everyone. You do not need to have experience. It will come with time. You do not need to be ordained or a priest because, as the Bible says, we are of a "royal priesthood" (1 Peter 2:9).

**Just like we are all different, the people
we are going to meet are also different.
So there is a need for you in the harvest field.
You are created with a purpose, and that purpose is
to reach those whom God has put you among.**

Many years ago, I had a very wrong idea when it came to making disciples. At that time in my life, when I met people who were already in a church, I thought that I could not disciple them because they somehow belonged to the pastor there. I thought it was wrong if I tried to help them without first talking to the pastor or doing it through the church. I know today that this sounds crazy, but it is what I was thinking at the time. I truly believed it was their pastor's responsibility to help the people in the church, and I would be going against the pastor and God if I tried to disciple "his" sheep. I have since met others who think like this or who somehow push the responsibility away because they think that if a person is already in a church, it is the responsibility of the pastor or the church to take care of them.

Today, God has really set me free from this wrong way of thinking, and I pray He sets you free, too, if you think like this. I am free now to disciple everyone I meet without needing to know if they are in a church or not. Today, I see only one church, and no matter where people come from or if they are in a church or not, I am ready to disciple them if that is what they need. I am ready to baptize them if they need to be baptized, no matter what church they are from. I am ready to lay hands on them and pray for them to receive the Holy Spirit, no matter if the pastor and church believe in that or not. I am also ready to take people out on the streets to kickstart them, no matter what other people around them think about it.

I have met many pastors and Christians who think I should not baptize or disciple other church members and that it is stepping over a line that is wrong if I do. But let me ask you, what is more important? Is it more important that a person gets baptized and receives the Holy Spirit, or is it more important to make the pastor and a few leaders happy? I am not writing this to provoke you or create problems. If the pastors and leaders of the church did their job in the first place, I would not need to do anything. But, because they have not done what they are supposed to do, I am ready to step in. I know that what I am saying here may seem disrespectful, but that is not how I want it to be received. I know many pastors out there are really trying to do the best they can, and I do not want to say these things to create anarchy. We need to respect each other. But, I do believe it is more important to help people and give them what they need than it is to respect the man-made boxes and the system the church has created. This way of seeing things has given me a lot of problems, but when I see all of the fruit that has come out of it, I get so excited. I get excited when I see the joy a person experiences when they receive the Holy Spirit or when they get set free from something that has been binding them for years.

It is so worth it, even though I have pastors or leaders looking down on me because I am praying for or baptizing their sheep. I do not actually believe that pastors or leaders have any sheep. They do not have any sheep because all the sheep belong to one Shepherd, and that is Jesus Christ. This understanding that there is only one Shepherd, that we are all His sheep, and that we are all called to make disciples of people no matter what church they attend has really set me free. It has set me free to help people without worrying what church they are from and how people around them will react. The fruit I have seen from this has been amazing. I love it! I am not saying this to create rebelliousness in people. I am saying this to set people free.

I truly believe we need to respect each other. It is not easy to be in leadership or to be a pastor in a church, but I am convinced that if we all experience this freedom and start to disciple each other wherever we are, not only in church on Sunday, we will see it grow like never before. God has not put us in boxes according to the church denomination we come from. I am thankful to know that some pastors and leaders do not have a problem with me discipling "their" people; however, I know many do have a problem with what I do. We should respect people but also obey Jesus and do what He has called us to do. We are all called to make disciples and lead people to Christ in our everyday life. We are all called to go and make disciples and even baptize people in our homes. If the church has another tradition and another way of doing it, then we should try to help the people in the church to understand what Jesus has called us to do. If they cannot understand it or agree with it, should we then stop obeying Jesus because of this? No, we obey Jesus and maybe find another church to attend.

Yes, I know it is not easy, but it also was not easy in Jesus' time. There were people around Him who did not like His way of doing things either. I want to say that you are free, and you are called and ordained by our Lord Jesus Christ to make disciples of everyone, no matter what church or denomination they belong to. It can be people who have never heard the Gospel or people who have heard but never really understood it. It can also be people who have already repented and received a new heart but need baptism in water or baptism with the Holy Spirit, or who need to be kickstarted.

As I said before, I have seen so many people in churches who have faith in Christ, but who are not truly free. They sometimes need baptism in water or baptism with the Holy Spirit. Sometimes they need to be kickstarted and set free from their fear of sharing the Gospel. When the person receives what they are lacking, their life and the lives of many others around them will also change. Some of the best fruit I have seen is actually from people who have been sitting in church for years without seeing any fruit in their lives, people who are not free. When these people experience true freedom through salvation in Christ, they start to obey Jesus and lead others to Christ, and suddenly, ten or twenty people will be saved through them, even people who have never been to church before.

So, some very important advice for you if you would like to obey Jesus and see fruit in your life is to start with the people around you, whether they are Christian or not. Recognize where there is a need, and then do something about it. You will see the kingdom of God grow like never before. If you attend a church where they have a different way of doing things, then respect them and talk with the leadership. Try to explain and help them understand the call of Jesus. In the end, we must obey the call of Jesus whether people agree with it or not.

Sometimes I see people take this and bring transformation and reformation to their church. Other times, the leadership asks them to stop, or they get so busy making disciples in their everyday life that they do not have the same need to go to church every Sunday.

In the end, it is not about building our churches but about making disciples and obeying Jesus. We can do that inside a church building or outside. We can do that with a pastor or without. Just start where you are, take one person at the time, and let Jesus build His church. We do not need to worry about how it will end up, or if the church will accept or reject it.

23

WE ALL NEED FAMILY

**A family
with a father, mother, brothers, and sisters
is God's natural design for us to grow up
from being a helpless baby into a mother or father
who has children of their own. In the same way
that a family is God's design for us to grow in the
physical sense, a spiritual family (the church)
is God's design for us to grow spiritually.**

I n the great commission, Jesus said we should go into all the world and disciple all nations, baptizing them and teaching them to obey everything He has commanded. Thus far, we have looked at how we should do this according to what Jesus is saying in Luke 10. We have looked at how to go out and find a person of peace. We have looked at how to share the Gospel, heal the sick, and so on. In this chapter, we are going to look at how we can help the people we have met grow up in Christ, and how to teach them to obey what Jesus has commanded us. Jesus (in the book of Matthew) says we should go out into the world, which is what I have been talking about in this book. After people have received the Word of God and repented, after they have been baptized in water to Christ, and after they have been baptized with the Holy

Spirit, there is still more. Yes, there is much more.

Matthew 28:18-20 states:

> *Then Jesus came to them and said, "All authority in heaven and on earth has been given to Me. Therefore go and make disciples of all nations, baptizing them in the name of the Father and of the Son and of the Holy Spirit, and teaching them to obey everything I have commanded you. And surely I am with you always, to the very end of the age."*

After people are baptized in water and with the Holy Spirit and receive a new life, we now need to teach them to obey everything Jesus has commanded. When people first come to Christ, they are, as the Bible says, newborn spiritual babies. We have been given the command to teach them to obey everything Jesus has commanded us. We are here to help them grow up and become strong in Christ.

As I have talked about in the last chapter, some of the people we reach are already in church. They love Jesus but have never fully understood the Gospel and what it means to obey Jesus. When these people hear and fully understand the Gospel, get born again, and get a new passion for God, everything changes. When they experience this new life, many of them already have a network of Christians around them. These people already have people they can continue to walk with.

There are also people you will meet who come from very religious, non-Spirit-filled churches, who, when they experience this new life, will need to leave their church because of opposition and because they now want more of Jesus and do not find that in the church they have been going to for many years. These people already know a lot about God and the Bible, but many things will be new to them. They will need a new fellowship and people to help them learn to walk as a disciple and to unlearn many of the things they thought were the truth.

We will also meet people who have not grown up in a Christian church who need milk and to start from the very beginning. They need a lot of help and people who will spend time with them to help them grow up and become strong in their new faith. New people need more help than those who have already been in church for years and already have an okay foundation.

Every person we meet is different. Every person is in a different place in their life and has different needs, but everyone needs fellowship. None of us are called to walk this life alone. We often say we are the body of Christ here on earth, and that is correct. But "we" is not me alone or you alone. "We" are *all of us together*. "We" alone is not the body of Christ. "We" alone is only one member of the body. "We" are one of many stones in the church that Jesus is building. You cannot live as a disciple *alone*, without like-minded people around you.

A person who comes to Christ, according to the Bible, is a new creation and is spiritually born again. They are now like a newborn baby and, like every newborn, are not created to be alone. They can be mature in age but still be babies in faith. And like babies need milk and a lot of care to physically grow and mature, people also need spiritual milk and a lot of care to spiritually grow and mature. The Bible talks about the different spiritual levels people can be on. There are those who are like little children, or babies, in faith, which is where we all start. The Bible also talks about young men and women in the faith, and fathers and mothers in the faith. It is important for us to understand these different stages of spiritual growth so we can know where we are in our lives, what our needs are, and what is expected of us. It is also important for the people around us, so we can know what we need to give them.

It is common sense that you should never serve a steak to a newborn baby, as babies cannot handle this. The baby would end up dying if the only thing we fed them was steak. A baby needs breast milk from their mother to grow up strong and healthy. But after a long time of drinking breast milk, the baby needs to start eating more solid food, and eventually, as the baby grows up and becomes mature, you can give them a big, juicy steak. In the same way that we would not give a steak to a newborn baby, it would also not make sense to give a young man or woman breast milk. Maybe they could live off of milk for a period of time, but they would never grow into the strong man or woman they are supposed to be. A young man or woman needs more than milk. They need a lot of solid food to grow up and become strong. So, we can see that people have different needs depending on where they are in their life. This is the same when it comes to their spiritual life and their walk with God. If a person who is now born again does not get what they need at that time to grow up spiritually in Christ, that person can die in their spiritual walk. At the very least, they will probably not grow up and become strong in their faith like they are supposed to do. The apostle John, in his first letter, wrote a greeting to people in three different stages. John gives his greeting to the children/babies, to the young men, and to the fathers in the faith.

1 John 2:12-14 states:

I am writing to you, dear children, because your sins have been forgiven on account of His name. I am writing to you, fathers, because you know Him who is from the beginning. I am writing to you, young men, because you have overcome the evil one. I write to you, dear children, because you know the Father. I write to you, fathers, because you know Him who is from the beginning. I write to you, young men, because you are strong, and the Word of God lives in you, and you have overcome the evil one.

As we read here, John wrote different things to these people in different stages, or levels of faith. He reminds the children/babies that they know God and that their sins have been forgiven. The reason John says this is because when people are new in their faith, they often doubt. They often experience attacks and fear, are unsure when it comes to their faith, question whether or not they are truly forgiven, or they fall into sin, and Satan tries to make them think they are now lost forever and can not be forgiven again. They really need someone around them. They need to be encouraged, like John does here in his letter. They need parents in the faith, someone who is like a father or mother to support them and help them grow spiritually strong. They need a lot of care and love.

To the young men, John says they have overcome the evil one and that the Word of God is in them. He tells them they have stood strong through the fights and battles they had in the beginning. They have grown up and are no longer children/babies. They are now young men and women who can eat the Word of God themselves. They do not need milk anymore because the Word of God is in them. They now need to be encouraged and challenged to take new steps in their walk with God so they can grow into mature spiritual parents.

John also wrote to the spiritual parents, those who have known God from the beginning, those who have been walking with God for a long time and truly know Him. They have experienced God and have seen the full picture when it comes to the Gospel and the Kingdom of God. These are some of the things John says.

If you look at what Paul wrote to the church in Corinth, it becomes even more clear that it is important we know there are different spiritual levels. In one of his letters, Paul expresses his disappointment with where the people were in their walk with God. He said they should have been grown-up by now, but instead they are still like babies who need milk. These people in Corinth were in need of milk because their actions showed they were still spiritual babies. Their actions of jealousy and quarreling showed they were still very immature when it came to their spiritual level, even after they had been Christians for a long time. We see here that sometimes people do not mature as fast as we would like them to.

1 Corinthians 3:1-3 states:

Brothers and sisters, I could not address you as people who live by the Spirit but as people who are still worldly—mere infants in Christ. I gave you milk, not solid food, for you were not yet ready for it. Indeed, you are still not ready. You are still worldly. For since there is jealousy and quarreling among you, are you not worldly? Are you not acting like mere humans?

Here, we see it is not always easy to help people grow up and mature. We see that it sometimes takes a long time. You can be a Christian for many years and still be very immature, but that is also what we sometimes see in the natural. There are people today in their mid-twenties who still cannot manage themselves and are very immature for their age. In 1 Corinthians, Paul wrote to those people who were still babies in their faith despite all the time they had to grow with Christ. They were still very fleshly in their actions. They still needed milk. Their actions showed they were without experience when it came to righteousness.

In the book of Hebrews, the author criticizes Christians who have

not come further in their spiritual walk. We read how they should have
been teachers by now, but instead they still needed someone else to teach
them. They actually still needed milk because they were without
experience when it came to righteousness and discerning good from evil.
Hebrews 5:11-14 states:

*We have much to say about this, but it is hard to make it clear to you
because you no longer try to understand. In fact, though by this time
you ought to be teachers, you need someone to teach you the
elementary truths of God's word all over again. You need milk, not
solid food! Anyone who lives on milk, being still an infant, is not
acquainted with the teaching about righteousness. But solid food is
for the mature, who by constant use have trained themselves to
distinguish good from evil.*

From these texts in the Bible, we can see that babies are people
without experience when it comes to discerning good from evil. But
full-grown, mature people are those who have been transformed in
their mind and thoughts and who know the will of God.
Romans 12:1-2 states:

*Therefore, I urge you, brothers and sisters, in view of God's mercy, to
offer your bodies as a living sacrifice, holy and pleasing to God—this
is your true and proper worship. Do not conform to the pattern of
this world, but be transformed by the renewing of your mind. Then
you will be able to test and approve what God's will is—His good,
pleasing and perfect will.*

So when it comes to our faith and being born again, we are all born
as babies in the faith, and in the beginning, we often face doubt and
confusion. As babies, we more often fall into sin and find it difficult to
discern between what is right and wrong. Our minds still need a lot of
renewing. We first need to learn to walk by the Spirit and not by the
flesh, and that can take time. But, as time passes, we should learn to
walk more and more by the Spirit instead of the flesh. We will eventually
become stronger in our faith and will not fall into sin as we did in the
beginning. In time we will know God and His will, and we will learn to

walk righteously before God and discern between right and wrong. We will start to grow closer to Him who is the Head of the church, and we will start to attain the whole measure of the fullness of Christ.

Ephesians 4:11-16 states:

So Christ Himself gave the apostles, the prophets, the evangelists, the pastors and teachers, to equip His people for works of service, so that the body of Christ may be built up until we all reach unity in the faith and in the knowledge of the Son of God and become mature, attaining to the whole measure of the fullness of Christ. Then we will no longer be infants, tossed back and forth by the waves, and blown here and there by every wind of teaching and by the cunning and craftiness of people in their deceitful scheming. Instead, speaking the truth in love, we will grow to become in every respect the mature body of Him who is the Head, that is, Christ. From Him the whole body, joined and held together by every supporting ligament, grows and builds itself up in love, as each part does its work.

Children/babies often fight, fall, become confused, and are easily deceived when it comes to wrong teaching. Therefore, it is so important for children/babies in the faith to have mature people around them who can help them, lead them, and guide them on the right path.

If we look at babies who have just learned to eat by themselves, no matter what you put in front of them, they will put it in their mouth without thinking very long about what it is. They do not question if what they put in their mouth is good or bad, or if it will help them grow up or kill them. They put everything they see in front of them into their mouth. Yes, even if a big, slimy worm would crawl in front of them, they would pick it up and put it in their mouth without questioning it because they are not yet able to discern what is good or bad to eat. God knew this. He came up with the amazing idea of a family. Babies should not grow up alone, but in what we call a family, with mature people around them to love them and help them grow because babies cannot manage by themselves. Yes, a baby needs adults around them to protect them and care for them so they can grow up into mature adults themselves and later have a family of their own. Just like a baby eats everything they can get their hands on, when a person is born again, they will eat "everything they hear." They cannot discern if the teaching they are hearing is good or bad. They cannot discern if the teaching is of sound doctrine or not. They need more mature disciples around them who can help them discern what is good to eat and what they should keep far away from.

> **It is the same in the natural and the spiritual. If people understood this, they would make many changes in the church today. Many changes would be made so people would become much more effective in making disciples.**

If we look at the natural life, I think most people dream about having their own kids. It is natural for people to want to reproduce and have their own children. There is nothing greater in this life than having a little boy or girl. I clearly remember taking our boy home from the hospital for the first time. I remember sitting there holding him in my arms for the first time. It was so special but also really scary because this was all new for us. It was special with all three of our kids. It is amazing to have a little baby. But as beautiful as they are, we do not want them to remain as babies forever. No, we want to see them grow up and, one day, even move away from home and have their own family.

As much as we love them, and as cute as they are, we still want those little ones to grow up, move away from home one day, and have their own family. The whole goal with our kids is for them to grow up, be independent, move away from home, and have their own family one day. Even though it may be hard in the beginning to see them go, that is truly what all good parents want for their kids.

It was such a joy for my wife and me to see our son get married to an amazing, beautiful girl. It made us so proud, and we felt like we had succeeded in our job of raising our son when he left home and got his own family. It was also hard to let go, but we knew this was how it should be. When our son and his wife later had their first boy and we became grandparents, we were even more proud. Wow, what a big blessing to be grandparents. We were so proud to see our son succeed like this and have an amazing wife and son. Later, they had one more son. Again, it made us so proud and honored as parents, parents-in-law, and grandparents.

No matter how much you love your children, no one wants to see their children single and living at home at forty years old. If you are forty years old and still living at home with your parents, there is something wrong. It is unnatural, and people will look at that and think that it is really time for you to grow up and leave home. In the same way that it is natural for babies to grow up, become independent, move away from home, and have their own family, it is also natural in people's spiritual walk with God to grow up, become independent, and have their own spiritual family.

When we get born again, we start off as spiritual babies, but we must not remain there. We must grow up and, in time, have our own spiritual children. When we grow up and have our own spiritual children, our job is to help them grow up and have their own spiritual children. The cycle should continue like that. When we talk about having spiritual children, we know, of course, that God is their Father, and it is He, not us, who gives birth to these babies. We are still somehow part of it. We are there, together with God, helping them to grow up into Him.

Just as it is beautiful to see our natural kids grow up, leave home and have their own family, it is the same with our spiritual children. It is truly amazing to see people growing up and starting to lead others to Christ. It makes me so proud when I see people I have led to Christ grow up, mature, stand on their own feet, and not depend on me anymore. It is amazing when I see them building a strong relationship with God, eating the Word of God by themselves, learning to listen to the Holy Spirit, and succeeding in the call Jesus has given them in leading people to Christ and building them up in Christ. This makes me so proud because this is what I am called to do. This is what we are all called to do.

I often meet Christians who are so proud to say that they have been in the same church for forty years, as this shows how faithful they are. When I hear that, I think, "Hmm ... What do you have to be so proud of? Should you not have grown up by now and learned to eat by yourself, instead of going to the same meetings and letting someone feed you Sunday after Sunday? Should you not have grown up by now, left home, and gotten your own spiritual family? Should you not be the one who is teaching other people, instead of letting other people teach you?" Yes, I know it may seem a little harsh to say it this way, but in general, we have lost something very important in the church. We have forgotten the different spiritual levels that people are on, and that people are there to grow up. We have forgotten that people should only be with us for a short period of time until they grow up and are ready to leave home and get their own spiritual family. That was how it was for the first church.

We all start as babies in the faith,
but we should not remain as babies.
We should grow up into spiritual disciples
who bear a lot of fruit for Christ.

A newborn baby is not ready to eat the Bible for themselves. You cannot give a Bible to a new believer and say, "Eat this." They need help from other people to digest the Bible, just like a mother digests food in order to produce breast milk to feed the baby. In the same way, spiritual babies need someone to digest the Word of God for them and explain it in a way that they are able to receive it.

Hebrews 6:1-2 states:

Therefore let us move beyond the elementary teachings about Christ and be taken forward to maturity, not laying again the foundation of repentance from acts that lead to death, and of faith in God, instruction about cleansing rites, the laying on of hands, the resurrection of the dead, and eternal judgment.

So when there are newborn babies around us, we should take the Word of God that we have eaten and explain it to them and start to lay down a foundation for them. We should, of course, teach them the

Bible and how to read the Bible for themselves. We should not just leave them the Bible and tell them, "Eat this." No, we should help them to rightly divide the Word of God. We should help them lay down a good foundation by teaching them repentance from dead works, about faith in God, about baptism in water and with the Holy Spirit, about teaching them to lay hands on people to pray for healing, about resurrection from the dead, and about eternal judgment. So in other words, we should give them the Gospel because this is our foundation. We should help them to understand this until they become mature enough and can start to eat the Word of God by themselves.

It is frightening today how many people have been sitting in church for years but who really do not understand true repentance, baptism in water, baptism with the Holy Spirit, or how they are called to share Christ and lay hands on the sick. Yes, there are many people in church who have heard sermons about the seven steps to a happy life or the ten steps to get rich but have gotten no real help to develop a good foundation in their life. People today need something other than what many churches are giving them. They need a spiritual family around them that loves them and is there to walk with them, who is there to help them set a good foundation in their life, and to help them understand the spiritual war they are in. They need to understand that they are not alone and that we will be there for them when they experience battles. We need to teach them to understand that it is normal to experience battles and to have doubt about their faith and salvation. We should remind them, like John did, who they are in Christ and how to continue walking in Christ.

We should help them to discern good and evil, and if they start to listen to wrong teachings, we should help them understand that they should be careful with those teachings. Satan hates it when people get born again, and he will do everything to hinder that from happening. Satan will also do everything he can to kill their spiritual life that has just started. We see that when Jesus was born, Herod tried to kill Him. But Jesus had an earthly father, Joseph, who was warned in a dream that Herod wanted to kill Jesus, so he and his wife Mary fled with Jesus.

Matthew 2:13-14 states:

When they had gone, an angel of the Lord appeared to Joseph in a dream. "Get up," he said, "Take the child and his mother and escape to Egypt. Stay there until I tell you, for Herod is going to search for the child to kill him." So he got up, took the child and his mother during the night and left for Egypt...

Here, we see how Joseph saved Jesus physically. We are also called to be there to save those spiritual newborn babies that God has entrusted us with when Satan tries to kill them spiritually. When Satan comes with doubt, persecution, resistance, and other things in an attempt to kill that spiritual newborn baby, we need to be there to save them. I have seen many people fall away from faith, especially in the beginning. When Satan comes with temptations and tries to get the new believers to fall into sin, we need to be there. When they want to draw back from fellowship and away from the church because of struggling with condemnation, we need to be there for them. They need the church. They need us to help them stay strong in God. They need our help to stand up again and continue in their walk with God. They need help to stand firm so that Satan will flee from them. They need fellowship. Spiritual newborn babies need you and me to help them.

I clearly remember how it was in the beginning when I came to faith. I remember all of the fights I had to go through. I remember when the doubt came and how I started to question everything, even my salvation, and wondered if this was the truth. I had so many questions, and I experienced really big attacks full of doubt and confusion. I remember in the beginning how I fell into sin and old habits and felt so condemned when I did. And when that happened, I remember how I wanted to give up and run away because I thought I would never overcome it. I remember in the beginning how I heard different teachings and started to get confused, not knowing what was or what was not the truth. I was often confused because the Word of God was not yet in me. Just as we read in the Bible, I was blown here and there by every wind of teaching and by people who did not know the truth. Ephesians 4:14 states:

Then we will no longer be infants, tossed back and forth by the waves, and blown here and there by every wind of teaching and by the cunning and craftiness of people in their deceitful scheming.

But God helped me. He did this by putting people in my life who were there to give me what I needed. He gave me some amazing spiritual parents who were there for me, and if I had not met them, I would not be where I am today. For this, I am eternally thankful to them. I remember so clearly how it was for me in the beginning. Sometimes, if I start to lose patience with the newborn believers around me, I just remember how I was in the beginning. And I remember how important it was for me that there were people who helped me and who were there for me.

When we forget how it was for us in the beginning, we can start to have unreasonable expectations for the newborn believers around us. As soon as we forget how it was with us, we start to become impatient, religious, and condemning toward new believers. We can be quick to think they do not need us anymore. This is what can happen when we start to forget how it was for us in our spiritual youth. So do not forget how it was for you and how God was patient with you through all of the mistakes you made. Remember how He forgave you over and over again and how patient He was with you.

I can also remember when I started to grow up, and how I was suddenly no longer a baby. I remember how I started to eat/read the Word of God by myself. I read the Word of God by myself and started to understand more and more what it was saying. I even started to teach/share with other people what I learned. Yes, I was no longer a baby. But, I was also not yet a full-grown adult, even though at times I felt like I was. At that time in my life, I often had difficulty listening to other people around me because I thought I was more wise and knew better. Sometimes, we become like rebellious teenagers who think we know everything and that we do not need our parents or to listen to those around us. But the truth is, I did not know everything. I was still very immature in some areas and sometimes even proud. When I failed in some way, I was very hard on myself, and I fell into a deep depression. As a young person in faith, you often go from one extreme to another. In one moment, you feel wise and proud, and in the next moment, you feel like you are a failure. You are often swayed from one idea to another, and you are often impatiently waiting to see things happen. Often, you want to see more things happen and for things to happen fast. You feel like you are ready to conquer the whole world, and you think you know exactly how to do it.

A young man or woman in the faith still needs a lot of love and patience. They also need freedom to make mistakes and to learn from them. They need to be challenged in their walk with God. I remember many unwise things I did, but I was so blessed to have people around me who would sometimes let me make mistakes and who did not control me too much so that I could learn from my mistakes. Through this, I could learn to take more responsibility for my own actions.

I remember when I believed God wanted my wife and me to buy a house. My father-in-law, who was one of my spiritual fathers at the time, did not say anything to me about it. But some years later, after I found out I had made a big mistake by buying a house, he told me, "Yes, I knew it was a bad idea." When he told me this, I was surprised and asked him, "What? You knew it was a bad idea? Why did you not tell me?" He said, "If I had told you that it was a bad idea, would you have listened to me?" When he said this, I realized the answer was no, I would not have listened to him. I would not have listened to him because I was convinced at that time that God wanted me to buy a house.

There were other times he and other people clearly told me what was right and wrong. It takes a lot of wisdom to raise young men and women in the faith. Of course, if someone wants to commit sin, we need to be very clear in telling them not to do it. But we need to find a balance and give them the freedom to make mistakes so they can grow up and be less dependent on us and more dependent on God and on the guidance of the Holy Spirit. We should not take this away from them by giving them all the answers because a young man or woman in the faith needs to be challenged. They need to have freedom to do things. They need to get their hands dirty by going on mission trips. They need to go out and pray for people. They need to teach the Word of God and do many other things.

I now look at myself as a mature adult in my walk with God, even though I know I still have a lot to learn. But, after twenty-five years of walking with God, at the time of this writing, and having experienced so many amazing things, I can now start to see the full picture and understand what it is Jesus is building here on earth. I understand His kingdom, how it is growing, and what we need to do to enter His kingdom and live in it. Yes, as a grown-up, I can stand more firm, and I am not challenged by the same things I was challenged by some years ago. It is not that I do not experience battles today. In fact, I experience even crazier and more difficult battles today than I ever have before, but the battles are different now.

Today, I do not struggle with doubts that God is real or doubts when it comes to biblical teachings. No, now I face persecution, lies, and many other crazy things. I experience things now that if I had experienced them as a new believer, I do not think I would have survived. I would not have been able to stand strong against the persecution or battles I face now. I think of that often. This just shows me that God is in control and that He does not give us more than we can handle. The more we grow in our spiritual walk with God, the battles will become stronger. But at that point, we will be stronger and ready to overcome the battles and stand over them in victory, keeping our hearts pure.

As a spiritually mature adult, you can begin to take responsibility when it comes to building the Kingdom of God, and you will also have many experiences to share with others. Today, this is how I see myself— a spiritually mature adult. I have been on quite a journey with God so far. I have personally been part of four church planting groups. I have been allowed by God to start this amazing movement called The Last Reformation. I have lived in over twenty different places. I have talked to millions of people. I have had many times of trials and testing. I have cried a lot. I have prayed a lot. I have fasted a lot. I have experienced so many amazing things with God. But even after all of this, I sometimes still see myself as a young man in the faith with so much to learn. Maybe twenty years from now, I will look back at my life right now and realize how I was still just a young man.

One thing I do know is that this life is a walk. It is a journey, and I have seen so many people begin their walk good but end up taking a wrong turn. Yes, I have seen people who start out walking in the Spirit but end up in the flesh. So we must remember that we need to keep holding onto Jesus and never let go of Him. We must be alert, as the Bible warns. I have also learned that we need each other. We need to help each other on this journey, and we must keep our first love of Christ. So, let's help each other and work together to see Jesus build His church here on earth! Let's build people up in Christ, who is the Head of the church. Let's see many people born again and help them grow up from babies into young men and women and into fathers and mothers in the faith, no matter where you are in your walk, whether you are a newborn baby in Christ, a young man or woman, or a full-grown adult who has been walking with God for many years.

We can all learn from each other, and we all need fellowship. We all need a family and people who love us and people we can walk with. The difficulty for many is to find families like this. This is much more than just attending a church a few hours every week. The good news is that the family is out there. Jesus is busy building his Church, and when you get hold of it, you will never let go. Much more about this later.

24

How To Grow Up

**When a person is truly born again,
you will see it in their life. There will be fruit in
their life that will show they are a new creation.
When there is fruit in a person's life,
they need milk so they can grow up and mature;
however, if the fruit is not there, that means
they are not born again, and they need
something much stronger than milk.**

I n the previous chapter, I talked about the different spiritual levels people are on and what they need to grow. In this chapter, I want to give you more practical tips on how to help people grow into mature disciples of Jesus. When we reflect on how the church is today, we need to admit we have not been very effective in raising people into strong, mature, independent disciples who bear fruit in their everyday life, who read the Word of God and listen to the Holy Spirit. I cannot say that every church is not very effective in raising strong, mature, and independent disciples. However, overall, the church has created a "seeker- friendly" mentality where people come Sunday after Sunday to listen to a sermon without maturing. Yes, people today go online to find a church that is the most comfortable and costs the least. Parents look for a church that has the best kid's worship and entertainment for their kids. It has become more about attending a church with good entertainment than good, biblical teaching. But, the truth is, it is not about finding a church with good entertainment or even about finding a church with good, biblical teaching. It is about following Jesus. We are on this earth to follow Jesus.

When I take a look at the churches today, I am sad to see how few really grow up and see good fruit in their everyday lives. Many people in the churches today continue to be spiritually immature for the rest of their lives. Yes, people can attend church and hear good, biblical teachings and still be spiritually immature. These people need someone to disciple them. They need someone to take them by the hand and show them how they can serve Jesus in their everyday lives. They need to understand that Jesus has called us into His ministry. The call of Jesus is for everyone, and it is for now! People need to understand this. They don't need to sit in the church and dream about one day being called to the platform to be used by God. People in the churches need to learn this today. Many people in the churches should be teaching others by now instead of needing someone else to teach them. So, let's be honest and admit to ourselves that we have done something wrong. We have not succeeded in raising strong, mature, independent disciples of Jesus Christ.

Another challenge in the church today is that many people are actually not yet born again. If we believe that everyone who confesses Jesus is born again, we are deceiving both them and ourselves. Maybe they confess Jesus and go to church every Sunday, but many of these people are still living in sin. Yes, many of them are still a slave to sin; therefore, they cannot live the life God has called them to. For some people reading this book, what I am saying right now is surprising, but believing in Jesus is not the same as making Him Lord and Savior over your life. Many people today have heard a very cheap version of the Gospel, a gospel without repentance, baptism in water, and baptism with the Holy Spirit, a gospel without denying yourself, taking up your cross, and following Jesus with your whole life. I have seen Christians, in their fellowship groups or in their churches, trying to give milk to people who are not yet born again. But they will not succeed in discipling them no matter how much time and energy they put into it if the person is not born again. There are clear signs as to whether or not someone is born again. We can see one of these signs in 1 John 3:6-10, which states:

> *No one who lives in Him keeps on sinning. No one who continues to sin has either seen Him or known Him. Dear children, do not let anyone lead you astray. The one who does what is right is righteous, just as He is righteous. The one who does what is sinful is of the devil, because the devil has been sinning from the beginning. The reason the Son of God appeared was to destroy the devil's work. No one who is born of God will continue to sin, because God's seed remains in them; they cannot go on sinning, because they have been born of God. This is how we know who the children of God are and who the children of the devil are: anyone who does not do what is right is not God's child, nor is anyone who does not love their brother and sister.*

Do not be led astray. From the signs mentioned in the Bible, we can see who is a child of God and who is not. We must not only confess Jesus as Lord and Savior, we must also hear the Word of God and obey it. We need to build on the Word of God, otherwise everything will fall apart.

Luke 6:47-49 states:

> *As for everyone who comes to me and hears my words and puts them into practice, I will show you what they are like. They are like a man building a house, who dug down deep and laid the foundation on rock. When a flood came, the torrent struck that house but could not shake it, because it was well built. But the one who hears my words and does not put them into practice is like a man who built a house on the ground without a foundation. The moment the torrent struck that house, it collapsed and its destruction was complete.*

As I have said before, I have seen many pastors and other people trying with all their strength to disciple the people around them without seeing much fruit. I have seen them trying to give milk to these people, but it seems like something is missing. These believers never mature.

Instead, they continue living in sin. They continue doing what they want instead of doing what Jesus has commanded them to do in His Word. They often lack the will, the desire, and the fire to do anything about the problems and the sin they have in their lives. They do not really change, and they do not really grow. If you see this happening with the people around you, there is a big chance that those people you are trying to disciple are not yet born again. If this is the case, instead of continuing to try to disciple them, you need to help them to get born again by sharing the Gospel with them. Go back to the foundation and lay that down for them again. Do not start trying to build on Christ if Christ is not yet in their life.

You cannot disciple someone to maturity who is not born again. You cannot give milk to someone who is dead. Milk will not bring them back to life. They need something stronger. They need blood. They need the blood of Jesus and the Holy Spirit to really understand the kingdom and to grow. A dead person needs something much stronger than milk. A dead person needs a new birth. They need the Gospel. They need to be brought to life by the power of God. Milk is something we give to people who are already born again, so a newborn believer needs milk. They need milk so they can grow up. A dead person (a person enslaved by sin and far away from God) needs the Gospel. They need to understand the Gospel so they can be born again and become alive in Christ. They need to understand what the Gospel is. They need to turn away from their sins and be baptized in water and with the Holy Spirit. Without the law being written on a new heart, without the old life being buried in water, and without the Holy Spirit and the power to live the new life, they will never be able to fully obey Jesus the way they are called to, no matter how much we try to help them. Religion cannot do it. Only Christ can.

I have met so many who have been attending or even serving in church for years, but then they experience the new birth and everything changes. The Word becomes alive to them, and they suddenly understand what they are reading. They have been preaching from the Bible for years, but now it is like getting a new Book. They understand it in a totally new way and are now able to obey it. Now there is also a hunger that was not there before, a hunger for more of God. It was like coming from religion into a totally new relationship.

When a baby is born, the baby will long for milk. The baby will scream until someone comes and gives it milk. You should not need to force feed the baby because the baby will naturally crave milk. If you need to force feed the baby, there is something wrong. This would mean the baby is sick. In the same way, when a person is born again, they long for the pure milk of the Word of God. They are hungry for the Word of God and are longing for more of God. Their spirit is crying out for that, and a forty-minute teaching in church every Sunday is not enough for the newborn believer. They want more. This is how it should be for our whole life, that we just cannot get enough of Christ.

I remember twenty-four years ago, when I came to Christ and got born again, I immediately had a longing for the Word of God. I have also seen this same longing in thousands of believers all over the world.

1 Peter 2:1-3 states:

Therefore, rid yourselves of all malice and all deceit, hypocrisy, envy, and slander of every kind. Like newborn babies, crave pure spiritual milk, so that by it you may grow up in your salvation, now that you have tasted that the Lord is good.

I had a longing for fellowship with God. I had a longing for the Word of God and a longing to be surrounded by brothers and sisters in Christ, which I still have today. These are longings every born-again believer has. You are longing for real fellowship, both with God and with the believers around you.

1 John 3:14 states:

We know that we have passed from death to life, because we love each other. Anyone who does not love remains in death.

I could not stop telling people about Jesus. I needed to tell people about my new, amazing life with Christ I had just received. It was so natural for me. No one needed to force me to do it.

Acts 4:18-20 states:

Then they called them in again and commanded them not to speak or teach at all in the name of Jesus. But Peter and John replied,

"Which is right in God's eyes: to listen to you, or to Him? You be the judges! As for us, we cannot help speaking about what we have seen and heard."

When I got born again, I could not continue living in sin. God had removed my stone heart and given me a new heart. He had written His law on my heart.

1 John 2:15-17 states:

Do not love the world or anything in the world. If anyone loves the world, love for the Father is not in them. For everything in the world —the lust of the flesh, the lust of the eyes, and the pride of life—comes not from the Father but from the world. The world and its desires pass away, but whoever does the will of God lives forever.

2 Timothy 1:9 states:

He has saved us and called us to a holy life—not because of anything we have done but because of His own purpose and grace. This grace was given us in Christ Jesus before the beginning of time ...

These things, along with other things, are the natural fruit of born-again believers. This is something we should look at when discipling people. If these things are missing, there is a big chance that person is not born again and needs the Gospel. If this is the case, they need to hear and understand the Gospel, repent from their heart, be baptized in water, and receive the Holy Spirit. You may also meet someone who is born again and has experienced this new life but who has lost their first love of Christ. If that is the case, then you need to help them get their first love of Christ back before God comes and removes their lampstand. We need to do this before we can see them truly grow.

Revelation 2:4-5 states:

Yet I hold this against you: you have forsaken the love you had at first. Consider how far you have fallen! Repent and do the things you did at first. If you do not repent, I will come to you and remove your lampstand from its place.

We need to be better at helping people get born again. We need to be better at helping people get back to Christ being their first love. This is where everything starts. After they are born again or return to Christ being their first love, we can continue to disciple them and see them grow.

It is fruitless to force-feed milk to people when they are not born again and do not have a longing for the Word of God. When people do not have a hunger in them to hear the Word of God and seek after God, you can pour into them, but they will not grow. For them to really grow, it needs to come from inside of them. This is the same when it comes to discipling people who do not have a desire to have fellowship with other Christians. We cannot force people to have fellowship with us. This desire also needs to come from inside of them. It is not something we can make them want. You can try to keep in contact with them and encourage them to live a holy life and to obey the Bible, but if they do not have this desire within them, you will not succeed.

If a tree (person) produces oranges, and you want the tree to produce apples instead, the solution is not to take all the oranges off the tree and tell the tree to produce apples. No, the tree will continue to produce oranges no matter what you say to it because it is an orange tree. The fruit is not the problem in this situation. The fruit just shows what kind of tree it is. This is the same when it comes to people. We cannot tell people to try hard to produce another kind of fruit. The solution is to try and help them understand the Gospel and help them to be born again, to become a new creation. They may need to repent, be baptized in water and with the Holy Spirit, or to make Christ their their first love again. If people do not have the longing to hear the Gospel and to repent, or they do not have the longing for Christ to be their first love, then shake the dust off your feet and move on. Yes, then it is time for you to move on and invest your time in other people who will bear lots of fruit. I know this can sound harsh, but I want to help both you and the people you meet so you do not spend a lot of time on people who will not bear good fruit, and so you will not give people a false belief that they are in Christ if they are not. It is important that you do not mislead people into thinking they are in Christ. It is better for people to see that they are deceived so they can repent and truly find God.

I was eighteen years old when I gave my life to Christ. I was the first one in my family to do this. Yes, my family and I were all baptized as babies in the Danish Lutheran Church and were later confirmed, but it was just tradition for us. None of us knew the Bible or understood the Gospel. None of us knew about baptism with full immersion, or baptism with the Holy Spirit. I did not even know there was an Old and New Testament or that there were any other churches than the Lutheran Church. When I started to seek God, I was longing after something greater than myself. Shortly after hearing the Gospel for the first time from a friend, I was ready to give my life to God. On April 5, 1995, I got baptized with the Holy Spirit, and it was an evening I will never forget. Later, I got baptized in water, but after this there was still some time that passed before I really experienced the freedom and fully understood what baptism in water meant. From the day I repented and gave my life to Christ, I had a longing for more. My life was changed. I was not completely free yet, but from that day on, I started a new, amazing journey with God's Spirit in me, longing for the pure milk of the Word of God. Not many days passed by before I bought myself my first Bible and started to read it. I was not a big reader. I had actually never properly learned how to read by the time I left school. At that time in my life, I do not think I had ever read an entire book before. But suddenly, I had a longing to read the Bible and get to know who God was. God helped me read, and I actually became better and better. Now, it is easy for me to read. I had such a longing to learn more about God that a forty minute teaching on Sunday was not enough for me. I needed more, and today, like many other born-again believers, I still have that same longing and hunger for God inside of me.

Since I was the first born again believer in my family, I felt quite lonely. I had such a longing to be around fellow brothers and sisters in Christ. I did not have anyone around me who believed what I believed, not even friends or work colleagues. They were all spiritually blind, so to them I sounded like a crazy guy who had just been brainwashed. They did not understand what had happened to me, and it was so difficult for me to share what I believed with them. Because of this, it became natural for me to spend more time with my new spiritually family, those who understood me and looked at the world the same way I did. I actually became closer with my spiritual family than with my biological family. God gave me some people in my life who became my spiritual parents. They meant a lot to me and were there for me in the beginning. These people were not pastors or leaders. They were not known or speakers in the church, but they were mature Christians who had a strong relationship with Jesus and who God used to help lay a foundation in my life.

One of them, whom I really consider a spiritual father, is my father-in-law, Eigil. When I met my wife, Lene, I began to develop a very close relationship with her parents. They became an enormous support in my life. My father-in-law was the person who gave me milk and helped me understand the Word of God. He was the one God used to lay a foundation in my life, a foundation I am still building upon today. Eigil never taught me in the way we might traditionally think of how to teach someone. We never once set up a meeting to share about a particular subject, while holding the Bible in one hand and a pen in the other. Although this is not wrong, it always happened in a much more natural way with us. When I visited Lene and her parents, we often ended up sitting on the sofa with our Bibles in our hands, with me asking hundreds of questions about what I had read in the Bible that week and about Eigil's experience with God. It was there on the sofa where I got milk. It was there on the sofa where a good foundation was laid down in my life. This actually continued for several years until I grew up and started to know the Scriptures almost as well as my father-in-law, Eigil. I reached a time where I was no longer a baby anymore but a mature disciple of Christ. I really believe teaching should come naturally, as it would in any family. Although I have been to meetings and conferences and have learned a lot from them, it was never the same as learning about God while sitting on the sofa with Eigil and his wife, Vera. With Eigil and Vera, I could ask the questions I had on my heart. With them, I could find the answers to the things

I was struggling with. We did not have any subjects that we needed to talk about, but we talked about what was happening in my life and about what the Holy Spirit was pointing at. This time with them was so much more personal, and it touched me so much deeper than anything I have ever experienced in a church.

When we look at the church today, it is clear that we really need a reformation. The church needs to look like a family and not like, as in many places, an institution. The church in many places (not all) has become an institution where there are a few leaders over a lot of people; whereas in a family, there are two parents over a few kids. Many people today have grown up without spiritual parents to help them, love them, and watch out for them. Today, there are many spiritually "paralyzed" children out there, and they need your help. I want to tell you that if you have grown up without good examples and without people who could give you what you needed, God is still enough. He can give you everything you need and change you in a way that you can now help and support others and give them what you never got.

When I think of my own walk with God, although I had good experiences, I also had some very bad experiences. Growing up was very hard for me. But, God has really given me everything I did not have. I am now able to be a good spiritual father to people around me and give them what I myself did not get. This is the same as with my physical walk. I have had some bad experiences there, too, but that does not need to influence my own family. God can change us in a way that we can give to the next generation what we never got ourselves. If you experienced a hard childhood, lacking a physical or spiritual family, that does not mean God cannot change your situation and use you to help other people.

The people around you who need help do not need theologians or big theological discussions. What they need are spiritual parents, people who love them and who have patience with them. They need someone who can spend time with them and who can open their home to them. They need people who can answer the questions they have and direct them and lead them through the everyday challenges they will face. They need people who can be a role model for them, not only in ministry but also when it comes to being a mother or a father and taking care of the house or keeping a job. They need a role model to show them how to live in this world and serve Jesus. So when you meet a spiritually newborn baby or someone spiritually immature, be there for them. You do not need to be a minister or a pastor. Just be there for them. Invite them over to your place and help them follow Jesus by sharing your life with them and what you have learned. Help them to read and understand the Word of God and how they can obey what they read. When you help other people grow, you will also experience growth yourself. When you are there for others, you will grow and feel that your life is making a difference. That is something that really brings joy and fulfillment. So, ask God who you should be there for and help. Ask Him to bring someone into your life to disciple.

My father-in-law and I did not come from the same church, but that was not a problem for us, nor was it a problem for God. It was so clear that God brought us together. Shortly after I got to know Lene and her parents, we went to a Christian meeting together. A man who was very prophetic spoke at the meeting. I would maybe even call him a prophet. During the meeting, he called my father-in-law, Eigil, up to the front to prophesy over him and said, "You have a son." Eigil answered, "No, I have three daughters." But the man continued with saying, "You have a son." But Eigil interrupted him and said, "No, I have three daughters." At this point, you would think the man would admit his mistake but instead he continued saying, "You have a son. He is a son for you. God will use your son, and your job is to just be there for him." Wow, what a strong word. I was standing in the back of the meeting and heard it all. When Eigil and I heard this, we knew who the "son" was. It was me. So Eigil nodded and said, "Yes, I have a son." And since then, Eigil has been there for me, and God has used his son like the prophecy said. So it was clear for us that God had given Eigil a spiritual son, me. Eigil was really like a father to me. People do not know Eigil, but in Heaven he will get his rewards. He has been faithful, being there for me and my family. He and his wife have been a big blessing to us.

I have met many leaders in my life, leaders who sadly enough have often wanted to use me to lift themselves up or to have success in their own ministry. I have met leaders who did not have a lot of time to be there for me. But a father is different than a leader. A father is not there for his own benefit. The only reason a father is there is to see his kids succeed. Paul was like a father for several people.

1 Corinthians 4:14-16 states:

> *I am writing this not to shame you but to warn you as my dear children. Even if you had ten thousand guardians in Christ, you do not have many fathers, for in Christ Jesus I became your father through the gospel. Therefore I urge you to imitate me.*

Fathers are also not afraid of their sons or daughters becoming bigger or more known than they are. A father does not see their children as a threat. However, I have often experienced that many leaders do. I have often seen leaders perceive people they have raised up as a threat because they have become more known than they were, and in the end, these leaders actually ended up fighting against them. This is what I call the "David and Saul syndrome." As soon as David got success, Saul changed his view of him, and it ended up that he tried to kill David. But Eigil was never like this. And today, I have been allowed to be there for many people in the same way Eigil was there for me. Of course, I cannot be there for every person I meet; therefore, it is good not to focus on too many people, but just on the ones God has placed on your heart. When you, like me, are a traveling minister, or have a big network and speak to hundreds or thousands of people all over the world, you cannot be responsible for the growth of every person you know or even for everyone you baptize or lead to Christ. That would be impossible. In the same way God brought me in contact with Eigil, I am sure He will also lead you to people.

We just need to understand how this works because currently, many of us have the wrong idea about this. Some of you think the people who disciple others must be in full-time ministry, but this is not true. We who are in full-time ministry (speaking about the general idea of full-time ministry because we are all full-time no matter if we work a normal job or not) cannot be there for everyone, but we can be there for a few. If we all help, then we can do this well. My father-in-law was a farmer. He was not an ordained pastor who traveled around the world to talk to thousands of people, but he had walked with God for many years and knew God by experience. He truly knew the Word of God. Eigil is not known throughout Denmark, and you will not read about him in Christian newspapers, but I am sure he is known in Heaven. I believe this because of the fruit I have seen through my ministry.

The weakest person around you can end up becoming the strongest evangelist or, in other ways, changing the world. Only God knows. Your job is to just be there for them.

If you are reading this book and are new in the faith, I want to encourage you not to wait for some "superhero" or a big, famous ministry to notice you and take care of you because there is a big chance that will not happen. Instead, you should look at the people who are already in your life. Maybe they are not known by others, but if they have been walking with God for years, they have a lot to offer you. So spend time with them, and let them help you lay a good foundation in your life. Although in time you may grow up and experience much more with God than they have, you still need their help right now. You do not need to be with the same person for your whole life. God has used different people in my life at different times to give and teach different things. So ask God to lead you to the person who will be a good support for you and who will help you lay down a good foundation in your life.

To you who are mature disciples, take care of those people God has put in your life, even if it is only for a short period of time. Always remember to allow the Holy Spirit to work in their lives and lead them. Be there for them, but do not take over the job of the Holy Spirit. And remember that their true Father is God who is in Heaven. Do not be quick to point out everything they need to change but, instead, help them by pointing them to Jesus. Help them to spend time with Him in prayer. Help them to fast. Help them to understand how the Holy Spirit speaks to us, and then let the Holy Spirit show them things in their life that need to be changed.

When I first came to God, there were many things in my life that needed to be changed, but the Holy Spirit dealt with one thing at a time. I remember when the Holy Spirit started speaking to me about the non-Christian music I listened to. I felt in my spirit that it was not good for me to listen to that music. So one night I took all my music, cracked all the CDs, and threw them all away. It was an amazing and freeing evening I will never forget. I am so thankful that I got rid of all of my music because the Holy Spirit spoke to me about it, not because others told me to do it. Sometimes, we can be too fast to try to play the part of the Holy Spirit, or are too religious and burdensome to people instead of giving time for the Holy Spirit to work in their lives and change their hearts.

I remember leading some people to Jesus in a city far away from where I lived. It was such a small city that there was no church, but there was a house church group that met in the city. The house church group belonged to a Pentecostal church that was located in a bigger city about thirty minutes from there. So I contacted this small house church group and tried to connect them to the people I had just led to Christ. We decided to meet all together, but when I arrived I thought to myself, "Oh, no, what do I do here?"

There were six Christians in the house church group, but when I met them I saw they were in three different places in their lives. It was like I could divide them into three different groups, each with two people. Two of them were lovely Christians who were on fire for Jesus. I could see they really loved Jesus, welcomed new believers right away, and wanted to take good care of them. Then there were two others who were neither good nor bad. They loved Jesus and could have given something to the new believers, but seemed to lack fire for God.

The last two people there, I saw as pure poison to the new believers. They were an old religious couple who were so condemning and showed no real life. At one point, the husband said, "I've been a Christian for forty-two years, and I've never missed one Sunday meeting. You can't be a Christian if you don't attend church every Sunday." From the way he said this, it was so clear that he was spiritually dead. He had no idea about how to take care of newborn believers. This couple would actually spiritually kill the newborn believers right away if they had fellowship with them. So what do you do in a situation like this? I wanted the new people to connect with two of them, but I really did not want them to meet the last two who were there.

Since then, I have learned that instead of just inviting people to church right away, I should try to find good, strong, mature, and loving people who are on fire for Jesus to connect them with. People do not need to come to a church where you never know who they will meet and who they will connect with. They need to be connected with the right people.

I have seen, time and time again, how God takes care of new believers and leads them to the right people at the right time, so pray for them and help them when you can. I do not believe there is only one model of this that works for everyone. I will not say that you should personally take care of those you lead to Christ because, in some cases, you will care for them, but in other cases, you will connect them with other people. For example, if a young man leads an older, more mature couple with three kids to Christ, it may be easier for the young man to connect them with other more mature people who can take over from there. But again, God is in control. Give people what you can give. Be responsible with what God has entrusted you with, listen to the Holy Spirit, and take care of the people you lead to Christ, or help them to connect with other people.

We can also say that the harvest is great but the workers are few in regards to spiritual parents. We really need more mature parents out there. We need fathers and mothers in faith who know God. We need mature people who can help the next generation grow. So let's start a new movement where we are there for each other. Be parents to those who are new in the faith. Invite them to your home and let them know you are there for them, but also remember that there comes a time when you need to let them go. Remember, they are not your kids but God's, so you need to let them go after some time. You need to let them grow up and learn to be less dependent on you and more dependent on God. The reason I am saying this is because people can misuse the role of spiritual parents where they try to control people. It is not meant to be like that.

Let's start a new movement. Let's help the next generation grow up, so that we, over time, can get more spiritual parents who can take care of the new generation of believers coming.

25

DEAR PASTORS AND LEADERS

**God wants to raise up a leaders
who can lead His people. He wants to raise up
leaders who can be examples to other believers.
He wants a leadership that will teach His believers
everything Jesus has commanded them.**

I would like to dedicate this entire chapter to the pastors and leaders in the church. If this is you, I want to tell you that we need you. We need you to help the body of Christ to step out and obey the call of Jesus. It is our responsibility as leaders in the church to teach the believers everything Jesus has commanded. We, as leaders, must not only teach the believers *some* things, but *everything* Jesus has commanded, just as He said in The Great Commission (Matthew 28:18-20). A true leader is someone who not only stands behind a pulpit telling others what to do but also obeys Jesus' commands and leads others by example.

I would like to remind you that as pastors and leaders in the church, the people in the church do not belong to us. They belong to our Lord and Master, Jesus Christ. We must always remember that we are not here to build our own church or our own movement. We are here as servants and disciples of Christ to build the Kingdom of God. The people whom God has entrusted us with will likely be with us only for a short period of time. Our job is to help them grow into mature disciples, to be less dependent on us and more dependent on God.

Eventually, the people we are teaching should mature and "leave" us to get a spiritual family of their own. It is important that we are not afraid to give them the freedom they need to grow and to make mistakes and to learn to be dependent on God. I am telling you this because, sadly, I have seen many leaders in the church with so much control that they have ended up ruining what God wanted to do. I have seen so many beautiful movements of God get destroyed because of pastors and leaders taking control. I have seen pastors and leaders pray for a revival and then when God answers their prayers and people start to live the life Jesus has called them to, they take control of the situation to stop it.

I know what I am sharing in this book is not easy for some of you to hear. I know what I am sharing goes against much of what some of you have heard all of your life. I also know it can be really hard to learn to give control over to God. Before God used me to start The Last Reformation, I was involved in church planting for twelve years in three different cities, so I know how difficult it is to start a new church. I know how difficult it is to be a pastor or leader in an older church with many traditions. I also know how easy it is to fall into the trap of control when things start to happen that are out of our control. I know about all the fears and insecurities that come with being a pastor or a leader, and I know how difficult it can be to hear what I am sharing in this book. You may ask yourself how the people in your church leadership will receive this message. You may ask yourself if many people will leave the church if you go this way and obey the call of Jesus that we have looked at. You may also ask yourself if it is possible to take some of what you have learned in this book but keep the church as it is. There are many things to consider. I also had many similar questions when I started this journey.

I remember fighting with these questions. I knew there was more to serving God and that this was the truth, but I was afraid because I did not know what would happen if I decided to truly follow the call of Jesus. While struggling with these questions, God sent a man from another country to visit me, and he asked me some questions that forever changed my life. The questions he asked made me think and helped me make the right decisions. He asked, "Torben, what do you want in life? Do you want a church with a thousand people, or do you want a thousand churches with ten people in each?" He then continued to ask me, "Torben, what do you want? Do you want a church with a thousand people or do you want to see a movement that will change the world?" These questions really made me think, and after some time, I made up my mind about what I wanted. I decided to pay the price, follow the call of Jesus, and see a movement that would change the world. This was the start of a new beginning for my family and me, where we stopped doing things our way and started doing them God's way. Since that time, we have said "Yes" to the call of Jesus, and it has been an amazing journey. Seven or eight years later, we have seen thousands of people's lives transformed and many new fellowships started. This is God's movement, not ours. It is His Kingdom that He is using us to build, not ours, and He is looking for people who are ready and willing to pay the price to follow Him. I do not know exactly how many people's lives have been changed through this, but I do know it is many, and that this is just the beginning.

Now, I would like to ask you the same questions that man asked me. What do you want in life? Do you want a church with a thousand people, or do you want a thousand churches with ten people in each? Do you want a church with a thousand people, or do you want to see a movement that will change the world? It is your decision. If you say "Yes" to the call of Jesus, and you pay the price for it, I guarantee it will not be easy, but it will be amazing, and you will see much fruit.

When I look back at my life, the only thing I can say I regret is that I did not decide to follow Jesus earlier. There is nothing more satisfying than doing what Jesus has called us to do and seeing Him build His church. It has not been easy, and it will not be easy for you. You will face opposition, and some people will probably leave your church. Or you may even end up getting fired. Not everyone in your church will want this. Many people are not ready to deny themselves and pay the price it costs to follow Jesus. Not all the people in your church will be willing to pay that price. Some of them only want to sit on the church pew Sunday after Sunday without lifting a finger. When you accept the call of Jesus and start to reform the church, this will become too much for some people and some of them will likely leave. But don't fear. God is still in control. He will take care of His Kingdom, as Acts 2:47 states, *"... And the Lord added to their number daily those who were being saved."* Your focus should be only on doing God's will, and you will see what God is able to do.

When you start making disciples and training those around you, you will be surprised at what God is able to do. You will see people come to Christ, and you will be surprised that people from your church would be so bold as to share Jesus with people everywhere. My hope for you, as pastors and leaders, is that you will decide to pay the price and follow Jesus' call, no matter what. And when people in your fellowship group or church see that you have made this decision, it will also help them receive the call of Jesus.

I want to tell you that we are here to help you. We have different tools available for you. We have teachings and so much more we can send you. You can read more about this at our website:

www.TheLastReformation.com

We also have free movies available at:

www.TLRmovie.com

These things are here to help you walk in the amazing life God has prepared for you and to help you minister to the people around you. Let's see the Kingdom of God grow, and let's lay down our own plans for something much bigger: to serve our Lord Jesus Christ and to do what He has called us to do.

Not long ago, I met with a small church of fifty people in Florida who were ready to follow Jesus' call. My family and I met with these people a few times and shared some of what I have been talking about in this book. We then took these people out on the streets to pray for people and show them how to pray for the sick and preach the Gospel. After this, we made a group on "Whatsapp" so the people from the church could share their testimonies and encourage one another.

We saw God do amazing things through these people once they stepped out on the Word of God. They shared testimony after testimony, and it was so amazing to see. The people from the church started to pray for the people they met in their workplace, school, and everyday life situations, and they saw so many people healed and set free. They met with their friends and family to share the Gospel with them, and they saw people come to faith. The whole church was transformed, and today, they are still living this life. Seven people left the church right away because they did not want this life, but within the next two months after these seven people left, the people who stayed had baptized over thirty new people who have now been added to the fellowship. And this was just the beginning.

Just a few weeks ago, my family and I baptized a man in America who got set free and received the Holy Spirit. This man then shared the testimony of what God did in his life with many people. Over the last two weeks, he and his friend have led over twelve people to Christ, twelve people who also got baptized and received the Holy Spirit. I could share so many stories like this from all around the world.

What I have been sharing with you in this book are the ideas that have also been behind some of the biggest church movements we have seen in third-world countries like the Middle East, Africa, and so on. These movements have often only been in poor and persecuted countries because when there is persecution, people cannot live the "normal" Christian life, so they must start to live the way Jesus called us to live.

People in the Western world are often too dependent on money, material things, and attending Bible schools. They do not recognize that we in the Western world are very poor when it comes to understanding what it means to follow Jesus and His call. But something new is starting to happen in the West. More and more people are hungry for a real life with God, and many of them are ready to pay the price it costs to get it. We are starting to see an explosion in the Western countries. Why? Is it because the harvest is suddenly starting to change in the Western world? No, that is not the reason. The reason is that God is starting to open the eyes of the people in the Western world when it comes to discipleship and Jesus' call. For many years, we in the western world have done it our way, and yes, we have seen some fruit, but it has been very little. If we stop doing it our own way and start to do it Jesus' way, we will see, like the people in those third-world countries, amazing fruit.

**Let's work together to help people understand
how to obey Jesus. God has given gifts to us,
the church, in order to equip us.
So let's use those gifts. Let's equip each other,
and together accept the call Jesus has given us.**

I encourage you, as a pastor or leader, to start with the people in your church. I know every church is different and that some churches are easier and some churches are harder to start new things in. Are you from a church where they, for example, do not believe in or practice the baptism of the Holy Spirit, or do not believe the gift of the Holy Spirit is for today? If so, then you have a long way to go. If so, you need to start by going back to the Bible to understand what it is really saying about these things before you start talking with the people in your church about what Jesus is saying in Luke 10.

It is really important that you start with the Gospel, and let the Gospel transform the people in your church. It is important that they are saved before you do anything else. As I have previously said, many people in churches today are not yet born again. When they are not born again, you will see that the fruit that follows a true born-again believer is missing. The Bible is clear about identifying born-again believers based on the fruit of the tree. In the last few years, we have seen many people in the churches get born again, and it is so beautiful. When this happens, these new born-again believers go from being only Sunday church-goers to disciples who follow Jesus in their everyday lives, and they bear much fruit. They go from living in sin to living and walking in freedom from sin, like Jesus has called us to do.

So, start with the Gospel and go against the lie that people get born again just by reciting a sinner's prayer. They also need to know what repentance is and that they need to be baptized to bury their old life and to receive the Holy Spirit. When the people in your church repent, get baptized in water, and receive the Holy Spirit, they are able to obey Jesus' words. Before this, they have not yet been set free and are therefore not able to obey Jesus and what I have been sharing with you in this book. But, when they do experience this new life and receive the power of the Holy Spirit, you will see that they are able to accept Jesus' call and obey it. When they repent and are baptized in water and receive the Holy Spirit, they will then need some discipleship, someone who will help them on the way.

My advice to you is that no matter how many people in your church receive you when you decide to obey the call of Jesus, do not compromise. You now know what the truth is, and you therefore have a responsibility. You need a lot of wisdom, but wisdom is not what many think it is. I have heard many say, "Yes, I know this is the truth, but we need to be wise," and they never do anything more. They are not wise. They are afraid, and they fear man more than they fear God. If you are in a church where they do not receive this, move on, as Jesus has called you to do. You cannot know if they will receive it if you never give it to them, so give them the whole Gospel. Explain what Jesus' call is and give them the chance to decide if they want to receive it or not. If they do receive it, amazing! If not, then I am sure God has amazing work for you to do in other places. I know this can sound harsh, but I am only saying what Jesus has already said for us to do. It is not easy to change an old church with years of tradition and wrong doctrine. Maybe you will soon experience that it is time to leave that church and its network and start over from the beginning. This is often much easier, but I know nothing is impossible for God. Some years ago, I also needed to leave a church I was working in, and it was not easy, but I knew I had a responsibility to react faithfully to what God had shown me.

Remember that as soon as you start to compromise, you will start to lose your first love and fire for Christ. I have seen so many people lose their first love and fire for Christ because they waited for a church to change that did not want to change. They thought it was wise to take it really slow and just wait for everyone in the church to be ready to change, but, in my opinion, this is not a good idea. I have seen so many people do this, and it always ended with the church not changing and with them losing their first love and fire for God. So be wise, and do not compromise.

If you are a pastor or leader in a church that already believes in the full Gospel of Christ, then I encourage you to still start with the Gospel. We often think those around us know the Gospel. However, just because a church has a good foundation does not mean everyone in the church or fellowship understands it and is born again. When you start with the Gospel, you will be surprised by how many people have not yet received it and are struggling with sin and other things. When they finally understand the Gospel and get born again and set free, their life will change forever.

We can look at people in the church today and think they are lukewarm and need to start to take their faith more seriously. But the problem for many people is not only that they are lukewarm and need to be more serious about their faith, but that they are not yet born again. The life and fire is not there in their life because they are still living in sin and need to understand the Gospel and get born again. So start with the Gospel, help people get born again, and do not compromise because you, as a pastor or leader, have a really big responsibility with this.

Paul, in Acts 20:26 said, *"Therefore, I declare to you today that I am innocent of the blood of any of you."* Paul said this because he knew he had a responsibility with those God had entrusted him with. Paul said he was innocent because he preached the whole truth of God and did not hold anything back. We see this in the next verse, Acts 20:27, which states, *"For I have not hesitated to proclaim to you the whole will of God."*

I am truly worried about many pastors and leaders I have met because many of them know the truth but are too afraid to say the truth out of fear of losing their job. Therefore, they compromise for the sake of peace. Do not be one of those people who fear man more than God. So what if you lose your job? God is in control, and He will take care of you. So be bold and speak the whole truth in love, even if it means you may lose your job. You are not the first one who has needed to pay the price to follow Jesus, and if that means some people will leave the church, then let them do so. It will not be the first time people have left the church. Just look at John 6. When Jesus spoke the truth, many left

Him. Sometimes it is better to have a few people leave the church so the rest of the people can come together to serve God the way He has called us to do.

Jesus is looking for people who are ready to build His church. He is looking for people who fear God and not man. He is looking for people who will speak the truth no matter what it costs.

Before I became a pastor and leader in a church, I was very busy serving Jesus and obeying Him. I was busy building the Kingdom of God and being a disciple of Christ. I did not care if people attended my church or another church, as long as they were truly following Christ. Before I became a pastor, I prayed and read the Bible so I could grow closer to God, and I was focused on how I, as a disciple of Christ, could obey Him. At that time, I saw a lot of fruit. But when I became a pastor and leader in the church, I suddenly started to change. I slowly went from focusing on building God's Kingdom to focusing on building the church as my own little kingdom. Everything in my life suddenly started to become about the "sheep" in my church and about getting more people to come. It suddenly became about "my" sheep, rather than about God's sheep, and every time I read the Bible, I thought about what message I should share with them. Everything became about "my" sheep and "my" church so that I forgot to obey Jesus myself. Suddenly, I was standing there behind the pulpit, telling people to follow me, but there was nothing to follow.

One day God gave me a strong dream, and in that dream, He showed me something very important that I have not forgotten to this day. In the dream, He showed me that it is not about building my church and that the sheep were not mine but His. He also showed me that I had forgotten I was also a disciple like the people in my church and that I also needed to follow Christ and obey Him. When I had this dream, I knew I needed to repent and return to God and do what I did before I became a pastor. So I stood in front of the people in my church and told them I was sorry and that I had done wrong. I told them I had been so focused on building "my" church and seeing them as "my" sheep that I had forgotten Jesus is the One who should build the church and that I was to be His disciple and obey Him. I changed a lot when God gave me that dream, and I started to seek God again and follow Him like I did before I became a pastor.

While Jesus walked here on earth, He said to follow Him. It was somehow easy to follow Him because Jesus was always on the move. If people wanted to follow Him, they knew what to do. They knew they would need to stand up, start to move, and follow after Jesus. Jesus did not just stand still behind a pulpit, telling people what they needed to do. No, He was a living example of how the people needed to live. God really spoke to me through that dream, and I saw that many things needed to change. I started to focus on my own life and on how I could follow Christ instead of how to get others to follow Jesus. I let go of control and started to understand it all belonged to Him. I understood it was God's church and not mine. When I realized all of this, I started to follow Jesus, and I started to experience many amazing things with God again. I started to have new testimonies every week about what God was doing in my life; whereas, when I was a pastor, the latest testimonies I had were two to three years in the past. Suddenly, I had new testimonies to share with the people I met, and I actually became an example that people could follow. They saw how I lived, and they could now follow me as I followed Christ. The people around me also started to change. They suddenly had an example to follow, and that was all they needed. They really did not need someone to stand behind a pulpit telling them what they needed to do and not doing it themselves. They needed someone who could show them what to do by example. Although some people left the church, many people in the church started to take responsibility for their own walk with God and started to truly follow Christ. Things started to grow like never before, and the freedom I experienced was so amazing. My responsibility shifted from needing to carry all the people in the church on my shoulders to simply following Christ.

I started to understand why so many pastors and leaders were burnt out and gave up after a short period of time. I realized this was because pastors and leaders have done many things their way instead of doing things Jesus' way. They have not really understood that they are also disciples just like those around them and that the church they are leading does not belong to them but to God. To you who are pastors and leaders, do not forget yourself. You, as a leader, also need to obey Jesus yourself. It is so easy to end up behind a pulpit, telling people what they need to do but not actually doing what you are telling them to do. It is so easy to take responsibility for the people in the church, but you have not been called to do this. Remember, everything belongs to God, and Jesus knows what He is doing. If you would like to know more about my journey and how God set me free, I recommend you read my book *The Last Reformation.*

As I have said many times, I am convinced that what Jesus says in Luke 10 is for us today. If you as a pastor or leader can bring this into the church, then I am sure you will see a change like never before. It is important you help people understand what Jesus says about the harvest being ready but the workers being few. Help them understand that it is not only about traveling to third-world countries to stand up on a platform to talk in front of thousands of people. It is about finding the person of peace in our everyday life and sharing the Gospel with them.

You should also show them how to share the Gospel with other people. Imagine how amazing it would be if you started to use the Sunday services to train people and make them ready to disciple others. Take the time to go through everything Jesus says with the people in "your" church. Maybe even let them read this book during the weekdays, and then use Sunday to talk about what they have read and to share testimonies about what God has done during the week. It is so important to encourage people to obey Jesus by taking a few steps at a time.

Find those people who are strong in evangelism, and use them to take the others out on the street to kickstart them. Kickstarting people is so important because it creates faith in people when they see God wants to use them. The love and fire for Jesus will grow in many, and for some, it will come back. If you decide to go this way and accept Jesus' call, you will see that the church will evolve more into a training center where people will come and get trained to go out and obey Jesus. And, in time, you will see many new fellowships starting. You may even end up meeting with all the new fellowships one or two times a month for a big celebration. You will see the Kingdom of God grow like a small mustard seed, which is what Jesus says in Matthew 13:31-33, which states:

> *The kingdom of heaven is like a grain of mustard seed, which a man took, and sowed in his field: which indeed is the least of all seeds: but when it is grown, it is the greatest among herbs, and becometh a tree, so that the birds of the air come and lodge in the branches thereof. Another parable spake He unto them; the kingdom of heaven is like unto leaven, which a woman took, and hid in three measures of meal, till the whole was leavened.* (KJV)

Let me ask you the same question that man asked me some years ago before God used me to start The Last Reformation. What do you want? Do you want a church with one thousand people or one thousand churches with ten people in each? What do you want? Do you want a church with one thousand people or a movement that will transform the world? Jesus, in John 14:15, states, *"If you love Me, you will keep My commandments."* If we love Jesus, then let's see His kingdom come and His will be done here on earth. Let's lay down our own ways and start to obey what He has commanded us to do. Let's stand together and see this happen. It is not about us, but it is all about Him and His kingdom.

26

LET THE NEW LIFE BEGIN

When one chapter ends, a new chapter begins.
This may be the end of the book,
but let this be the beginning
of a new and amazing journey, living
according to the call Jesus has given you.

I really hope and pray this will be the beginning of a new and exciting life with God, where you experience what Jesus has called you to do in Luke 10. Throughout this book, I have tried to point to Jesus and to the call He has given us. I really hope I have managed to quote and explain Jesus' words in a way that they have become real and alive to you. I know my own words cannot do this, but I know Jesus' words can transform a person from the inside out, especially when we take His words and act on them. I hope you will accept His call. I can pray for you, cheer you on, and remind you of Jesus' words, but in the end it is up to you and you alone. It is your responsibility to do something with what you have learned and to answer Jesus' call. It is up to you whether or not you choose to obey what Jesus is saying. I have said "Yes" to the call Jesus has given me, and I need to daily pick up my cross to follow Him. I am so thankful I have the opportunity to serve Him. There is nothing more satisfying than living for Jesus and seeing others repent and follow Him.

It is my hope that for the rest of my life, I will say "Yes" to the call of Jesus and follow Him for all of my days. I also hope many others will do the same. It is not easy to follow Christ, and it is hard when people persecute you, but this is what Jesus promised we would experience. He promised us persecution. It is hard to die to your flesh, and it is not always easy to listen to the Holy Spirit. I often think of the four grounds I shared with you in the beginning of this book and how I need to remind myself that I will not become ground two and compromise, and I will not become ground three and let the deceitfulness of riches, worries, and longing for other things take over so that I do not bear fruit. I want to be the good ground. Being the good ground is a decision I need to make again and again. There are many things that like to come in and steal our focus, and it is not always fun and easy to follow Jesus. It is not always easy to fast, and your flesh does not always want to pray, but you know this is necessary if you want to bear good fruit. For example, when you fast, you can experience that your stomach growls and all you want to do is eat. But there is nothing we will go through on earth that can compare to the joy there is in finding Jesus and doing His will. There is nothing like being used by God.

As I write this text, it is just day three since I visited a home where the people in the home had gathered many people. It was such an amazing evening. We got there and started eating and having fellowship. Then we gathered everyone, and I took a good amount of time sharing the Gospel of the Kingdom, how Jesus is our King, how we need to be born again to be able to see and enter His Kingdom, and what it is to actually follow Him. After sharing about this and many other things, we started to pray for everyone there. The first one I prayed for was a woman who loves Jesus but had not yet received the Holy Spirit. She had been baptized in water, but that was many years ago, many years before she had come to personal faith and true repentance. I prayed for her, and the Holy Spirit came over her in a very strong way. She got baptized in the Holy Spirit and started to speak in tongues for the first time. Right after that, we went in and baptized her in the bathtub. Her husband had a problem in his ears, and he got healed. We saw several others get healed, set free, and receive the Holy

Spirit that night, and it was just amazing. One person met God in the kitchen. At one point, a few of us were standing and talking in the kitchen. I prayed for a woman, and God came to her very strong. She fell down right there in the middle of the kitchen and was crying loudly and deeply. A lot of deep pain left her, the Holy Spirit came over her in a strong way, and she spoke very loudly in tongues. It was an amazing evening and something all of us will never forget. I just love serving Jesus like this and seeing the Kingdom of God grow. I love seeing lives change and become like lives we read about in the Bible. Sharing Jesus and seeing God come, like we read about in Luke 10 or in the book of Acts, is something you can never get enough of.

There is a price we need to pay to follow Jesus, but that is nothing compared to the fruit you will see and the joy of serving Him. This world truly has nothing to give us compared to what a life with Jesus gives us. Living with Jesus is amazing! He is so incredible, and when you step out on His Word, you will see He has so much more for you. You will experience how He truly becomes your life.

Paul, in Philippians 1:21, states, "...*To live is Christ* ..." When you look at Paul and the way he talked about life on earth, you can see he is divided in two. Paul longs to break away from this world so he can be with Christ because he knows that is best, but he also knows he needs to be here on earth so he can reach the people around him with the Gospel.

Philippians 1:21-24 states:

For to me, to live is Christ and to die is gain. If I am to go on living in the body, this will mean fruitful labor for me. Yet what shall I choose? I do not know! I am torn between the two: I desire to depart and be with Christ, which is better by far; but it is more necessary for you that I remain in the body.

Paul, in these verses, says he longs to be with Christ because he knows that is best. He does not say, "Jesus, please don't come back right now because I love my life here on earth so much. I want to travel and buy a big house. So please, Jesus, don't come back because there's so much I want to do." No, Paul was finished with this world and with what this world had to offer him. He was focused only on Jesus and on being with Him. He was longing to see Him in His resurrected body but until that time came, Paul knew his mission was to spread the Gospel on earth so the other people around him could repent and receive eternal life. He was here to see the Kingdom of God grow. This should be the same for you and for me. Our life is not about having a big car or a big house. It is not about what this life can offer us. It is about Christ and Christ alone. We should long to be with Him, but we should also know there is a lot of work to be done here on earth. As long as we are here on earth, let us work for God.

Now, I would like to remind you what we have been looking at in this book and about the call Jesus has given you. First, I need to ask you some questions. Have you repented, turned away from your sin, experienced freedom through baptism in water, and experienced a new life with the Holy Spirit? Are you free from sin, or are you still living in it? If you are not yet born again and walking in the freedom Christ paid for, then you need to start there. You must repent, turn away from your sins, turn to God, and call on Jesus to come set you free. Find someone close to you who can take the time to share the whole Gospel with you and help you to be born again. Find someone who can baptize you in water and with the Holy Spirit. If you do not know anyone around you who can help you, you are welcome to go to our map at www.TLRmap.com. There you can find someone near you who can help. It is so important for you to be born again, to receive freedom from your sins, to wash away your old life through baptism in water, and to receive the power of the Holy Spirit to start this new life. This is where we all should start. So before you do anything else, make sure you have repented and are truly born again, as we have been looking at. If you are already born again, then this new life of obeying Jesus' call starts today. Yes, start to obey Jesus' words today!

Let us show Jesus we truly love Him by keeping His commandments, and let us show the people out there we love them by sharing the Good News of the Kingdom of God.

Let's take another look at some of the things Jesus says, and then I will give some practical tips. In Luke 10:2, Jesus states, *"The harvest is plentiful ..."* Start praying that God will open your eyes to truly understand that the harvest is plentiful. Remind yourself that what Jesus says about the harvest is also true in your city and that we should not say there is still three months until the harvest because the harvest is ready now. Meditate on these words by speaking them out loud. Say to yourself that the harvest is ripe and plentiful and that it is just waiting for you. Pray for God to remove the veil from your eyes, that Satan's lies would be revealed, and that the lie that has created so much fear when it comes to reaching out to people and seeing them set free, would disappear. Let's stop blaming the harvest for our lack of fruit and begin believing that it is plentiful and ready as Jesus says. The harvest is ready and plentiful even in your city, no matter what you have experienced before. Our experience does not change the Word of God. We should never change the Word of God in order to fit our experience. We should change our experience to fit the Word of God.

Jesus also says in Luke 10:2, *"The workers are few. Ask the Lord of the harvest, therefore, to send out workers into His harvest field."*

Let's start to obey Jesus by praying God would send out His workers. Let's stop praying for a revival like it is something that comes by itself without us stepping out in obedience to God. Instead, let's start to pray that God will send out workers into the harvest. Take God's Word and pray in faith and confidence that He will answer your prayer. Pray and beg Him to send out workers to reach the people in your workplace or school, in your city and in your country. Pray daily that He will send out workers to those close to you who do not know God yet or who are religious and are missing this life I have been talking about throughout this book. Pray to the Lord of the harvest to send out workers from your church and from the other churches in your area. You can pray this in confidence, knowing God hears you and that He will give you what you ask for.

1 John 5:14-15 states:

This is the confidence we have in approaching God: that if we ask anything according to His will, He hears us. And if we know that He hears us— whatever we ask—we know that we have what we asked of Him.

God will hear you, and He will start to send people out into the harvest. He will also answer your prayer by sending you. Set your alarm to 10:02 (Luke 10, verse 2) in the morning and in the evening every day as a reminder to pray for God to send workers into the harvest. Yes, let's pray this and also go out and obey Jesus. Go out, and Jesus will be with you. Remember, not only does Jesus send us out like lambs among wolves, but He also tells us He will be with us until the very end. Let's not be afraid of the wolves out there. They cannot really hurt us. People will persecute us and mock us, and some may even end up physically beating us or killing us. But so what? Even if some of them would kill us, we should not fear because Jesus, in Luke 12:4-7, says:

> I tell you, My friends, do not be afraid of those who kill the body and after that can do no more. But I will show you whom you should fear: fear Him who, after your body has been killed, has authority to throw you into hell. Yes, I tell you, fear Him. Are not five sparrows sold for two pennies? Yet not one of them is forgotten by God. Indeed, the very hairs of your head are all numbered. Don't be afraid; you are worth more than many sparrows.

We have nothing to fear. Instead, we should rejoice when people do this to us because we will have a big reward waiting for us in Heaven. Matthew 5:10-12 states:

> Blessed are those who are persecuted because of righteousness, for theirs is the kingdom of heaven. Blessed are you when people insult you, persecute you and falsely say all kinds of evil against you because of Me. Rejoice and be glad, because great is your reward in heaven, for in the same way they persecuted the prophets who were before you.

You will often feel like a little lamb that is being surrounded by big, scary wolves. The fear is real, and it is not always easy, but remember, the wolves will always be there. Jesus has never promised to remove the wolves, but He has promised something much better. He has promised to go with us. The first step is always the hardest, but as you go, you will experience how Jesus is truly there, and the fear will become less and less. So step out and share Jesus with those people around you, and learn to be rejected with a smile. It is very important to learn to be rejected without letting it bring you down. Rejection is part of the call, so do not let it influence you negatively.

Let's learn to trust Jesus. In Luke 10:4, He states, *"Do not take a purse or bag or sandals; and do not greet anyone on the road."* Do not be afraid when you find yourself in a place where you do not have your daily needs. God knows what you need. Our job is to seek first His Kingdom and to do His will, and all these things will be given to us (Matthew 6:36). We need to stop worrying about tomorrow, for tomorrow will worry about itself. Instead, we need to learn to seek God and do His will.

Matthew 6:26 states:

Look at the birds of the air; they do not sow or reap or store away in barns, and yet your heavenly Father feeds them. Are you not much more valuable than they?

Yes, we can trust Him. Let's also remember to not be distracted. There is so much in this world that can distract us and steal our focus away from Jesus and His call. It can even be teaching or other things that may seem good but, in the end, can end up distracting us from Jesus' call. By teaching, I mean that some people go from teaching to teaching, without ever obeying. They end up with a big head and a lot of knowledge but no obedience. This is especially a problem here in the Western world. You do not need to learn Greek and Hebrew before you start to obey Jesus. Just start today, and learn while you are obeying. Our focus should not only be on getting more knowledge but on being more obedient. Yes, knowledge is important, but let's keep it simple. Let's not end up like the Pharisees who studied themselves blind. They were proud of all their "knowledge," and they went so wrong. The knowledge blinded them in a way that they rejected Jesus and His Word. So let's keep reminding each other why we are here on earth and what our call is all about.

Let's find the person of peace out there. If we keep seeking, we will find them. If we keep asking God to lead us to the person of peace, He will do it. Luke 10:5-6 states, *"When you enter a house, first say, 'Peace to this house.' If someone who promotes peace is there, your peace will rest on them; if not, it will return to you."* So when we find that person of peace and enter their house, let's pray God's peace will rest on that place, so it can be a house like Cornelius' in Acts 10, where the whole household came to faith. Luke 10:7-8 states, *"Stay there, eating and drinking whatever they give you, for the worker deserves his wages. Do not move around from house to house. When you enter a town and are welcomed, eat what is offered to you."* So when we find that person of peace, sit down with them and eat and drink what they serve. Let's not be too quick to move on from person to person or from house to house. When we find that person of peace, let's stay with them and try to also reach the whole household. Let's share the Gospel with them, and when they receive it, let's build them up in Christ so they can become strong and mature disciples. Remember, we are not called to preach to as many people as possible. We are called to make disciples and teach them to obey everything Jesus has commanded us.

Let's also obey Jesus in healing the sick, casting out demons, and preaching the Gospel. Luke 10:9 states, *"Heal the sick who are there and tell them, 'The kingdom of God has come near to you.'"* Jesus paid a high price for every person we meet out there, so let's be bold and pray for those we meet. Let's take every opportunity to share the Good News of the Kingdom of God. You do not need a special gift of healing to obey this. All you need to do is take a step in faith and start to lay hands on people and pray for them. If you need someone to kickstart you, I am sure there are people near you who are ready to help you. There are people out there who can take you out on the street to kickstart you. If you do not know anyone, then check out the map at:

www.TLRmap.com

You can find a person near you. If you cannot find anyone near you, try to join one of the kickstart weekends happening all over the world.

Let's not be ashamed of the Gospel, for it is the power of salvation to everyone who believes. There is truly salvation in the Gospel of Christ, and we cannot compromise the Gospel. Help people understand that they have sinned and broken God's law. Help them understand that Jesus has paid the price for them. Tell them about Romans 3:23, which talks about how we have all sinned and fallen short of the glory of God and that we can be freely justified by His grace to the redemption that is in Jesus Christ. Tell them about Ephesians 2:8-9, which makes it clear that we are saved by faith and not by works, by stating, *"For it is by grace you have been saved, through faith—and this is not from yourselves, it is the gift of God—not by works, so that no one can boast."* Share with them how, according to 1 Corinthians 15:3-4, Jesus rose up again on the third day and that He is the only One who can take away our sins. Tell them, as it is written in John 3, that they can be born again of water and the Spirit. Help them to understand, as Jesus says in Mark 16:17, that they need to believe and be baptized. Explain what true repentance is and that as Romans 6 informs us, baptism in water is where we bury the old life. Inform them that baptism, according to the Bible, is not just a symbol, but it is a totally new beginning, where you truly wash away your sins and put on Christ (Galatians 3:36). Work with them so they understand the whole Gospel, and help them to get born again, receive the Holy Spirit, and speak in tongues like we see in the Bible. Preach like the Bible has commanded us to, not what our traditions say.

Let's preach like Peter in Acts 2:38, which states, *Peter replied, "Repent and be baptized, every one of you, in the name of Jesus Christ for the forgiveness of your sins. And you will receive the gift of the Holy Spirit."*

There is nothing more beautiful than seeing a person being born again. It is so amazing to see a person come out of the water as a new creation, then receive the Holy Spirit and speak in new tongues.

When it comes to getting started with finding the person of peace, most people already know one or two people in their network who are very open. You should start by meeting and sharing the Gospel with them. When the first person receives the Gospel, then try to meet with their friends and family and those they know who may be open to God. Try to set up a meeting with the new people who have just gotten born again, where you can focus on reaching those around them. It can be in a home, or in a café, or another place that is easy for everyone. When you meet with their friends or family, let the new disciple share with them what has just happened to them, and how they have gotten born again. There is nothing like a testimony like that. That will prepare their hearts for you to share the Gospel and what it means to follow Christ, afterwards. This way they not only hear the Gospel, but they see the power in the Gospel and that itis the truth, by the transformation they see in their friends. When we do it this way, the Gospel really becomes alive, and you will see many give their lives to Jesus. If you do this, you will not only have led one person to Christ, but two, three, and it just grows from person to person, and from network to network. This is often how we reach the whole household, by reaching them one by one.

It may also happen that right away you can start by gathering many people in the home of the person of peace. Maybe the one you lead to Christ or helped to get free, baptized, and so on, is ready to open their home and invite a bigger group of friends and family over. Then you may be sitting in a house with ten or twenty people all around you while you share the Gospel and tell them about life with Christ. As more people give their lives to Christ, you can start to do the same in their homes also. Then you will be in several homes with many people. When this happens, it is really good to invite other mature Christians along to help you follow up with people so you do not have to do it all alone. Remember to be led by the Holy Spirit in all of this, even when it comes to who you should invite with you to help you because we want this to continue the way Jesus leads it and not control it ourselves.

You may also lead someone to Christ who does not have anyone around them, so you could invite them to your church, or to join a fellowship group, and they can grow there. It will be different from person to person. With some, it goes really fast, and with others not. Our job is just to start doing it and let Jesus build His church by putting together all of His living stones. Let it spread the way God wants it to spread, from person to person, from house to house, from network to network.

Matthew 13:31-33 states:

> He told them another parable: "The kingdom of heaven is like a mustard seed, which a man took and planted in his field. Though it is the smallest of all seeds, yet when it grows, it is the largest of garden plants and becomes a tree, so that the birds come and perch in its branches." He told them still another parable: "The kingdom of heaven is like yeast that a woman took and mixed into about sixty pounds of flour until it worked all through the dough."

When you start to do it this way, you will really see that this is how the Kingdom of God is growing, like a small mustard seed or like a little yeast. Everything starts small, but by doing this, it will end up really big. When we talk about finding the person of peace and doing it this way, we also need to remember to move on when people do not receive our message.

Luke 10:10-12 states:

But when you enter a town and are not welcomed, go into its streets and say, "Even the dust of your town we wipe from our feet as a warning to you. Yet be sure of this: the kingdom of God has come near." I tell you, it will be more bearable on that day for Sodom than for that town.

This is very important to remember because we will meet those people who do not want it, and they can easily slow down or even destroy what has been started. When you meet people who will not receive your message, then shake the dust off your feet and move on. Do not spend too much time discussing it with them. Move on and keep looking for the people God is calling.

As I have said several times in this book, it is important that we do not try and control the growth of the Kingdom of God, but to let Jesus build His church the way He wants. He knows much better than we do, and He really knows what He is doing when we let go and let Him build. Then, when you start to see the fellowships grow, you will also see how God will send other people with other giftings to help you. Remember, God has also given us people who are apostles, prophets, evangelists, shepherds, and teachers in order to equip the body of Christ to do ministry. Maybe God will send people to help you from other fellowship groups, or perhaps the people who will help you will be the people you have previously led to Christ, who have grown into mature disciples. You will see those people who were once babies quickly grow up and leave home to find their own spiritual family. And as time passes, you will end up sitting back, looking at the first, second, third, and fourth generation of disciples.

People often ask me what to do when house groups/fellowships grow, and how they should do things when they meet. To answer that, we have many resources on our website, but the simple answer is to keep it simple and remember the call Jesus has given us. When you grow, new things come up that you will need to talk about and address.

You can do this while still keeping it simple and focused on the call Jesus has given. The problem is that, as things grow, you often get away from the simplicity and call of Jesus that you may have had in the beginning, and then it starts to die.

A simple tool you can use is "in, up, and out" ("in to each other, "up" to God, and "out" to those we need to reach for the Kingdom of God). I do not see a certain model displayed in the Bible that we should use every time we meet. Everyone's home is different and there can be different people coming from time to time. What you will do one evening will not work the next. For example, if you have a gathering, and two people come in, do not just follow the program. Share with the new ones, and get them soundly saved. I think a fellowship should always have a focus on "in, up, and out." We need to have a focus on "in" to each other—to get to know each other and become a family, "up" to God—as it is because of Him that we are here, and together we want to serve Him, and "out" to others—because there is also a mission out there, and Jesus has given us His call to "go."

When you meet, you could start by talking about the past week and what God has been doing since the last time you met. You could talk about what God is doing in your life and what you are struggling with. Pray for each other and spend time with each other and become a family. It is not only about spending time with each other but also about spending time with God together. You then may want to start with communion and seek God through prayer and worship. Read the Word of God together and take the time to let the Word speak to you. You may then take Jesus' words and talk about what they mean, how to obey them in your everyday life, and also how to help others obey them. You may end the fellowship meeting by talking about how to reach others with this. Who do we know who is a person of peace, and how can we reach out to them? Try to also set a time during the week when you can meet to reach out to people who need the Gospel. It can be people you already know or people you do not know. This "in, up, and out" is a simple tool you can use when you start to meet with people for fellowship. On our website, you can access many free resources that can help you obey the call of Jesus and help you see fellowships grow and multiply. You can read more about this and about the new TLR Jesus family we are starting all over the world, on our website at:

www.TheLastReformation.com.

Do you want to be a part of this and see the Kingdom of God grow? Are you ready to say "Yes" to the call of Jesus? If so, it is going to cost you. As I have previously said, there will be opposition and persecution. It will be hard, and there will be many problems. There will always be problems when you work with people. That is just how it is. There will also be spiritual attacks because our enemy, Satan, wants us to keep sitting in our church pews, doing nothing for the Kingdom of God. He wants us to be lukewarm. The minute we start to be on fire for Jesus and start doing what Jesus has commanded us to do, we become a threat to Satan's kingdom, and he will try to stop us. Yes, when we start to heal the sick, cast out demons, and lead people to Christ, we are a threat, and Satan will fight us and send every kind of attack. There will be spiritual attacks full of thoughts of doubt, fear, and other things. You will experience opposition from your family and other people who are close to you. You will experience persecution from the religious people around you. These religious people will be challenged by the life you are living and will try to bring you down and make you compromise. Persecution will come, and it will be hard, but do not give up.

Discipling new believers is a lot of work, and it can sometimes feel similar to raising a newborn baby. The process of discipling a new believer will not always go as fast as you want it to go, but remember that those who are new to the faith need time to grow and make mistakes. Keep going, and keep working with them. Seek God to find strength and wisdom to continue. Remember to love your enemies and to love those who persecute you. Matthew 5:44 states, *"But I tell you, love your enemies and pray for those who persecute you ..."* Ask God to give you love for everyone around you and to keep your heart pure. Nothing from the outside can hinder God's plan for you as long as you keep your heart pure. If we allow bitterness and disappointment to enter our hearts, everything will fall apart. We need to accept and expect opposition. Hard work is part of following Christ. When you start to live this life, read the book of Acts again because now you will start to see yourself in the book of Acts. You will not only be reading about something that happened many years ago, but you will see that much of what the disciples experienced in the book of Acts is happening in your life today. You will see that the book of Acts is the only book in the Bible that never has an end. Jesus is the same yesterday, today, and forever, and His call to us will forever be the same.

Jesus came to give us life and to give it in abundance, but an abundant life is not gained by owning two cars, a big house, and everything this world has to offer. An abundant life is a life full of meaning. It is a life where you serve Jesus and where you see the kingdom of God grow. It is also a life where you bear fruit in your everyday life. Decide that you will be like Matthew, who was willing to follow Jesus' calling no matter the cost. Decide you will not be like the rich young ruler who walked away from Jesus feeling sad because he loved this world and his riches more than he loved God. Remember, you are not alone in this. God is with you, and we and others are here to help you if you need help. Do not be scared. Use the videos and other tools we have to help you share the Gospel and pray for people. I recommend that you go online and watch our free Pioneer School. The online Pioneer School is twenty-nine lessons that will set you free to live this life. In the lessons, I take you through how we should live as disciples, what the Gospel is, and how to share it. I talk about how to pray for people and so much more. You can find these videos on www.thelastreformation.com or on YouTube. We also have three free movies that can help you live this life, too.

Maybe consider joining our Pioneer Training School, or one of our Luke 10 schools, located all over the world. You will also find information about the schools on our website. And maybe this is a good book to read again. If you read it again, I believe you will pick up new things that you did not see the first time because you are now hopefully starting to see the bigger picture of the Kingdom of God and the call of Jesus. Maybe come together and read this book as a group. You can take a few chapters at a time and talk about each chapter, what it says, and how you as a group and as an individual can obey it in your everyday life.

Take one step at a time. When you are faithful in the small things, God will put you over more. If you do this, in a very short time you will experience what I have been describing throughout this book. Together, let's serve our Lord and Savior, Jesus Christ, and obey the call He has given us!

God bless you,

Torben Søndergaard
A disciple of Christ

The Last Reformation

Back to the New Testament Model of Discipleship

Much of what we see expressed in the church today is built on more than just the New Testament. It is built, instead, mostly on the Old Testament, Church culture, and Paganism. It is therefore imperative that we as God's people dare to stop and take a closer look at the Church today and compare it to the first Church we read about in the Bible. If we are to succeed in making disciples of all nations then we must go back to the "template" we find in the Bible.

Let the reformation begin!

Most of us as Christians have inherited a way of being church and being disciples. Torben challenges us to question this by using examples from the Bible and from Church history. This book is challenging and sharp, but we all want to see more people believing in Jesus, disciples trained, and churches growing stronger and multiplying. This is why we believe **The Last Reformation** *is important for our thinking about how we want to be and do church in our times.*

*From the Foreword

This book may be purchased in paperback from
www.TheLastReformation.com,
www.TheLaurusCompany.com, Amazon.com,
and other retailers around the world.

Also available in eBook formats for electronic readers
from their respective stores.
Available in Spring Arbor for Retailers.

Outside the USA: Amazon.ca, .co.uk, .de, .at, .fr, .it, .es
and other retailers around the world.

Sound Doctrine

Teaching that leads to true fear of the Lord

Sound Doctrine is both different and prophetic. It was written out of a call from God Who gave the author the message one chapter at a time each day over a two-week period following 40 days of fasting and seeking God. It is a testimony of how the true Word of God changed the author's life and how it can also change the lives of others.

After the 40-day fast, Søndergaard was filled with new revelations from God. He felt he had to express some of the things God had given him, so he began to write. Each day over the next two weeks, God gave him another chapter. The book you are holding is the fruit of that time.

There is much misunderstanding about the "fear of the Lord." Some call it a reverent awe. Others call it a deep respect. Some believe God is just waiting for the opportunity to punish them. Some do not even consider it at all. But what is it really? What is true fear of the Lord? Torben Søndergaard's teaching on "sound doctrine" answers that question in a way that will cause Christians to honestly desire to live a more holy and pure life free from sin.

This book may be purchased in paperback from
www.TheLastReformation.com,
www.TheLaurusCompany.com, Amazon.com,
and other retailers around the world.

Also available in eBook formats for electronic readers
from their respective stores.
Available in Spring Arbor for Retailers.

Outside the USA: Amazon.ca, .co.uk, .de, .at, .fr, .it, .es
and other retailers around the world.

Christian, Disciple, or Slave?

What is a Christian? The answer to this essential question today unfortunately depends on who you ask. In this book, you get the biblical answer to what a Christian really is, and how you can become a Christian. You will also be taken on a journey through the Bible as we look at various words people use for those who follow Jesus, words such as "Christian," "disciple," and "slave."

Many of us have heard the expression: "I am a Christian, but in my own way," or "I am a Christian, but am not so much into it." Is it even possible to be a Christian in one's own personal way? The author argues that, according to the Bible, the answer is no, just as it is not possible to be a disciple or a slave in one's own personal way.

The book is written for both Christian and non-Christian. A radical book, it takes a hard look at what Jesus Himself said about being a Christian. Jesus' words are extremely radical, but it is the place where we get the true answer to the question: "What is a real Christian?"

This book may be purchased in paperback from
www.TheLastReformation.com,
www.TheLaurusCompany.com, Amazon.com,
and other retailers around the world.

Also available in eBook formats for electronic readers
from their respective stores.
Available in Spring Arbor for Retailers.

Outside the USA: Amazon.ca, .co.uk, .de, .at, .fr, .it, .es
and other retailers around the world.

DVD Movies
and Other Resources

***The Last Reformation: The Beginning* DVD Movie**

***The Last Reformation: The Life* DVD Movie**

***7 Days Adventure with God* DVD Movie**

***The Last Reformation* Audio Book**

Torben Søndergaard's books can also be found
in other translations on the website below.

These resources can be found on the author's website at:

www.TheLastReformation.com

ABOUT THE AUTHOR

Torben Søndergaard

Torben Søndergaard is founder of The Last Reformation, a movement that has spread all around the world the last few years.

This movement is helping the Church come back to the life we read about in the book of Acts. They are training and discipling thousands of believers to spread the gospel and see people healed, delivered, and born again. They are doing that through their many training schools across the world and the 3-day kickstart weekends, along with the free online Pioneer School.

Torben has written several other books and booklets and produced three movies that are available on DVD or on their YouTube channel. The YouTube channel has over 100,000 subscribers and has been seen by millions.

Torben and his wife, Lene, have three children and two precious grandchildren.

See more on their websites:
TheLastReformation.com • TLRmovie.com
TLRmap.com • YouTube.com/TheLastReformation

CPSIA information can be obtained
at www.ICGtesting.com
Printed in the USA
BVHW042110020420
576760BV00016B/654